Surrealism

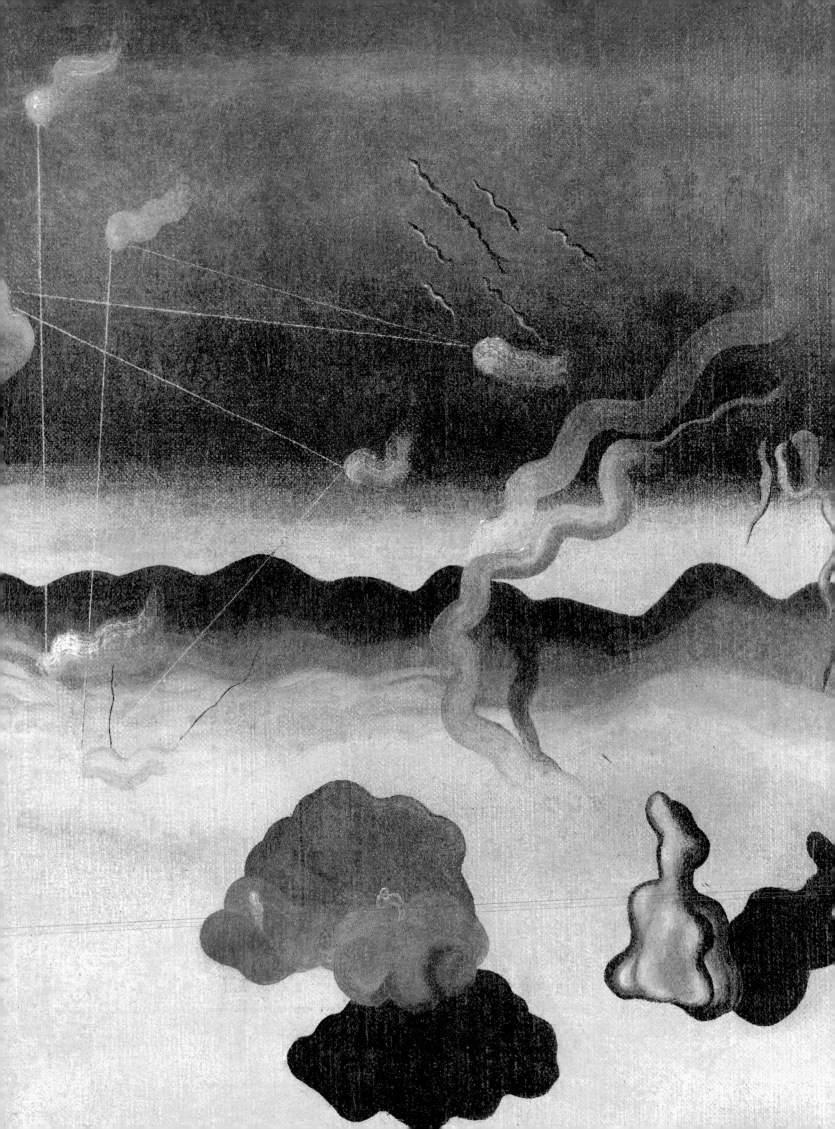

RENÉ PASSERON

Surrealism

·TERRAIL·

Cover illustration
Victor Brauner
CONSPIRATION
1934, oil on canvas
Centre Pompidou-MNAM-CCI, Paris.

Page 1
Surrealist review
ARSENAL, SURREALIST SUBVERSION
Private Collection

Page 2
Yves Tanguy
UNTITLED
1927.
Private Collection, Paris.

Editor : Soline Massot and Anne Zweibaum
Layout : Marthe Lauffray
Translation : Joan Koenig and Jack Liesveld
Iconography : Maryse Hubert
Copy editor : Christophe Gallier
Lythography : Grafiche Zanini

© FINEST S. A./ÉDITIONS PIERRE TERRAIL, PARIS 2001
25, rue Ginoux, 75015 Paris

Publication number : 283
ISBN : 2-87939-229-2
Printed in Italy

Salvador Dali
DREAM CAUSED BY THE FLIGHT OF A BEE AROUND A GRENADE, A SECOND BEFORE WAKING
Thyssen-Bornemisza Collection, Madrid

Pages 6 and 7
Joan Miró
PLOWED LAND
1923, oil on canvas.
Solomon R. Guggenheim Museum, New York

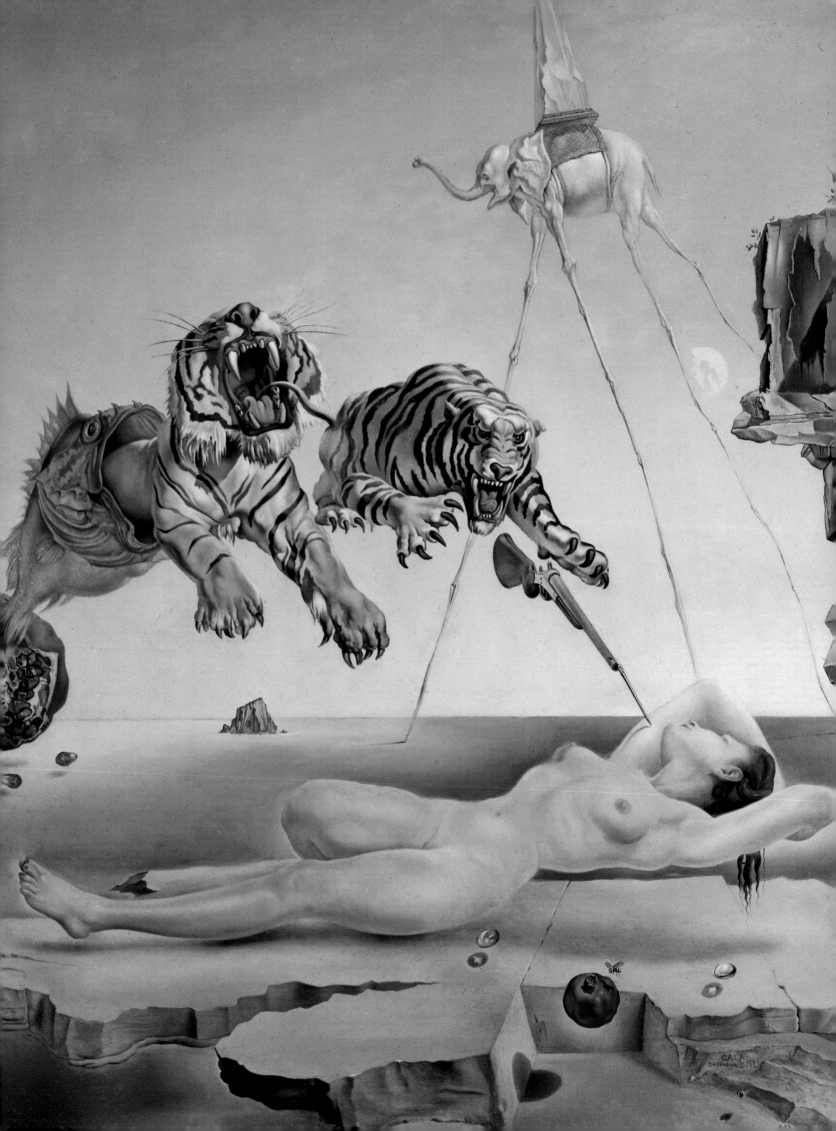

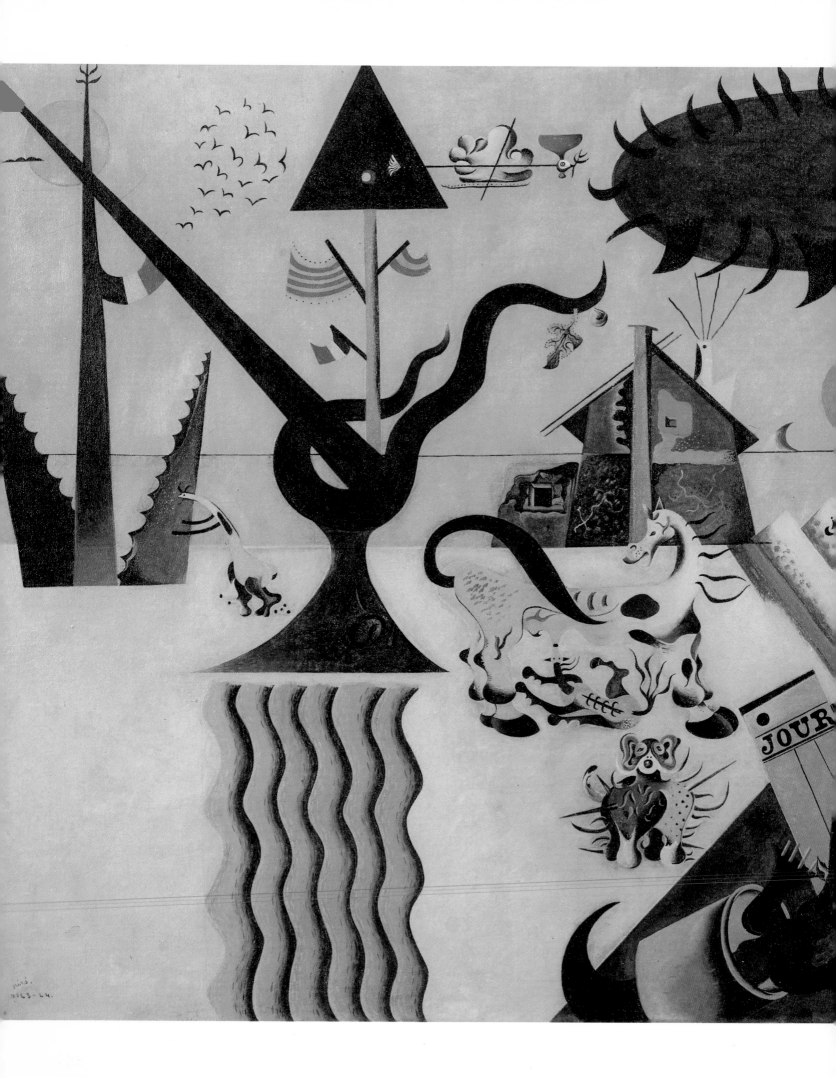

Contents

Introduction   9

I. 1916-1924: The Ascension   11
Psychosis and Poetry
The Dada Storm
"Drop Everything"
The First Manifesto

II. 1924-1930: Plenitude   47
Surrealism Takes Hold
Love, the Tragic and the Sexual
Painting, Photography and Cinema
The Second Manifesto of Surrealism

III. 1930-1940: Expansion   87
Back to Mental Pathology
The Conquest of Objects
Political Problems
Around the World

IV. 1949-1947: Dispersion   129
Exile
"We Are Here to Stay"
The Return of Breton

V. 1948-1966: Persistence   169
Friction and Polemics
Influence and Creation
Eros and Thanatos

Conclusion: "The Final Split"   193

Bibliography   202

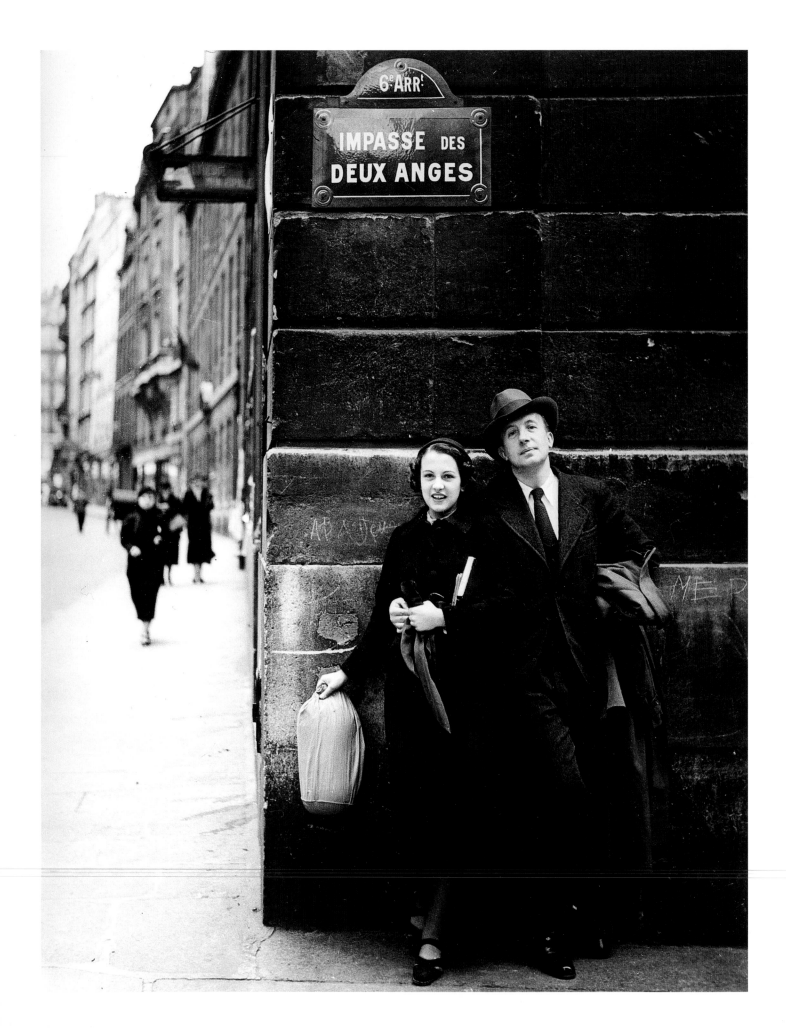

Introduction

The name "historical Surrealism" is sometimes given to a phenomenon of civilization that, between 1920 and 1940, drastically changed artistic creation in France, and later, throughout the world. The upheaval concerned mainly poetry and painting, but also personnel and private values. It is therefore possible to write its history. But the story would be superficial and anecdotal if the events were not accompanied by an evocation of the hidden side even more secret than what Walter Benjamin called "the last snapshot of European conscience."

Carrying the spirit of Romanticism and Symbolism into the 20th century, Surrealism was born in the aftermath of the profound shock of the First World War. Their experimental spirit and need for political commitment led the movement's poets toward an ethic of revolt, the consolidation of Freud and Marx. Then, after the Second World War, this desire to "change life" became progressively more pessimistic and libertarian, and was finally reduced to l'amour fou (wild love), tied up with the freedom of Eros. This is all to say that Surrealism, with its stylistic diversity is not an artistic "school," like Cubism. Its greatest originality was the integration of artistic creativity with philosophy. It only provided some of the major works of the 20th century by making art a means of protest against morals and a means of knowledge of mankind. The persistence of this aim, more or less avowed, is still stirring today.

Man Ray
NUSCH AND PAUL ÉLUARD
(IMPASSE DES DEUX-ANGES)
About 1934, gelatin silver print.
Centre Pompidou-MNAM-CCI, Paris

1916-1924
The ascension

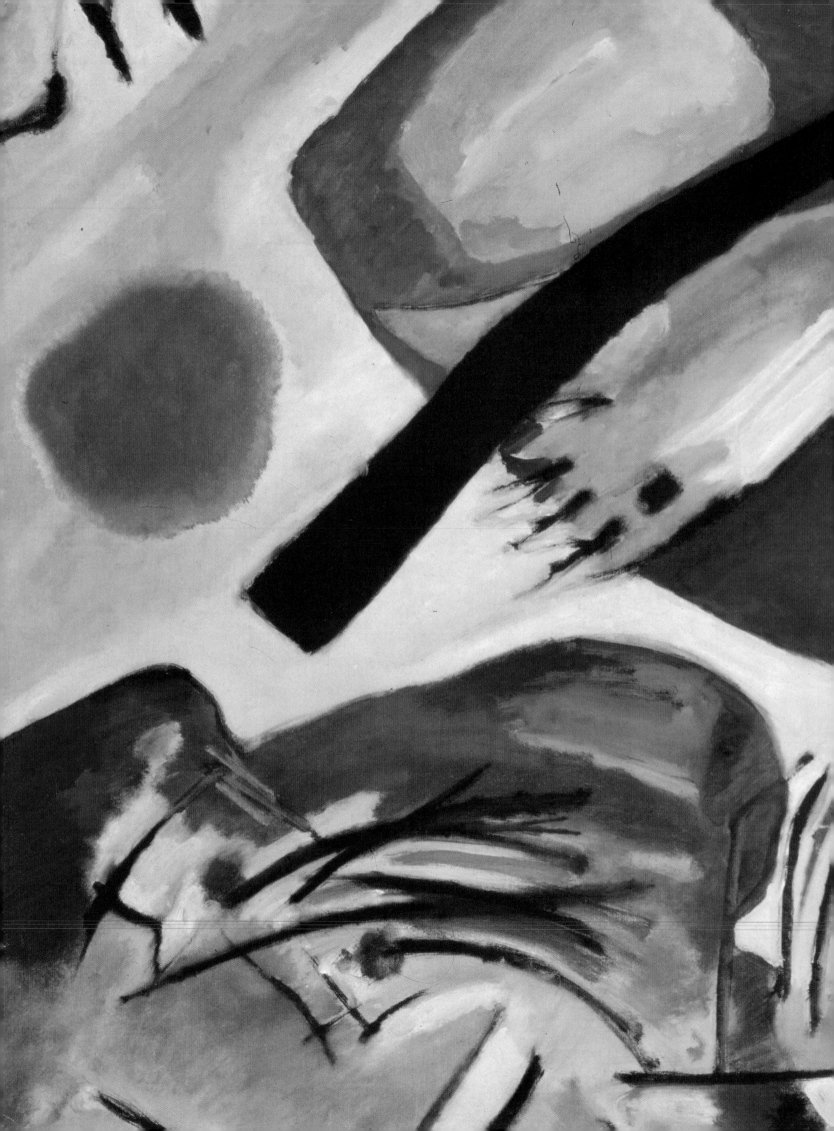

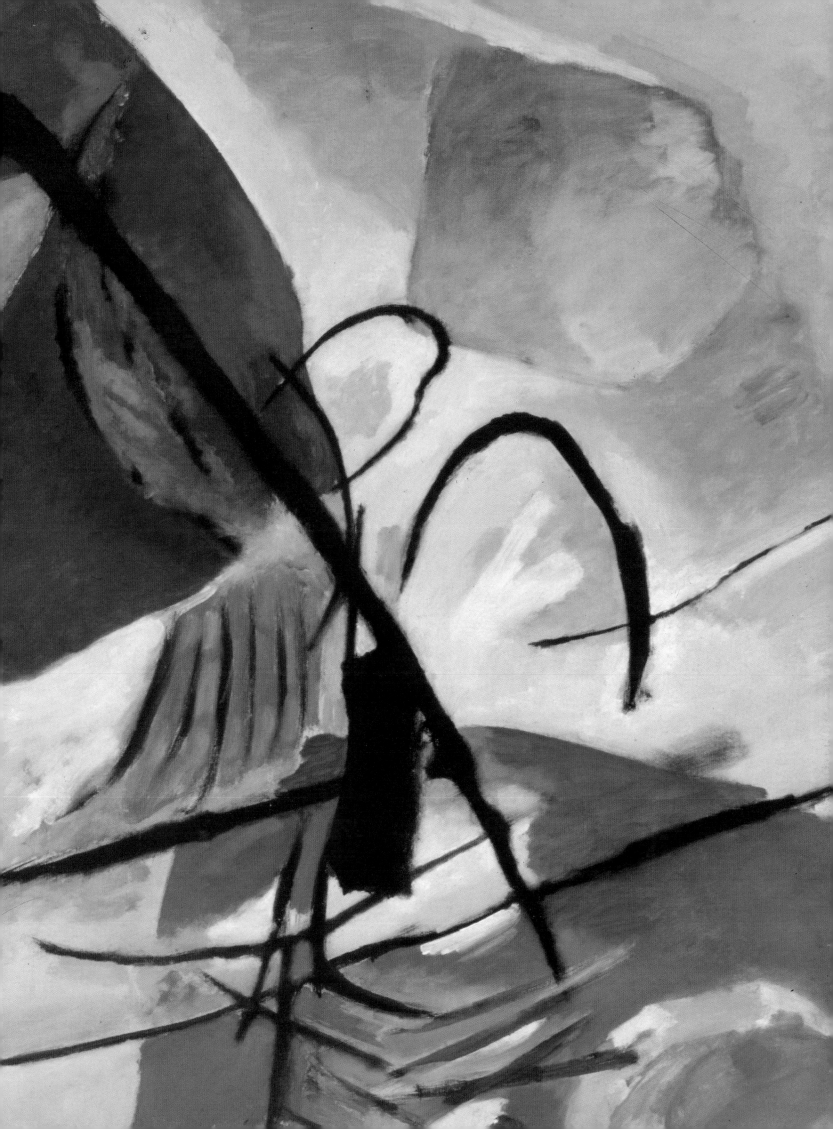

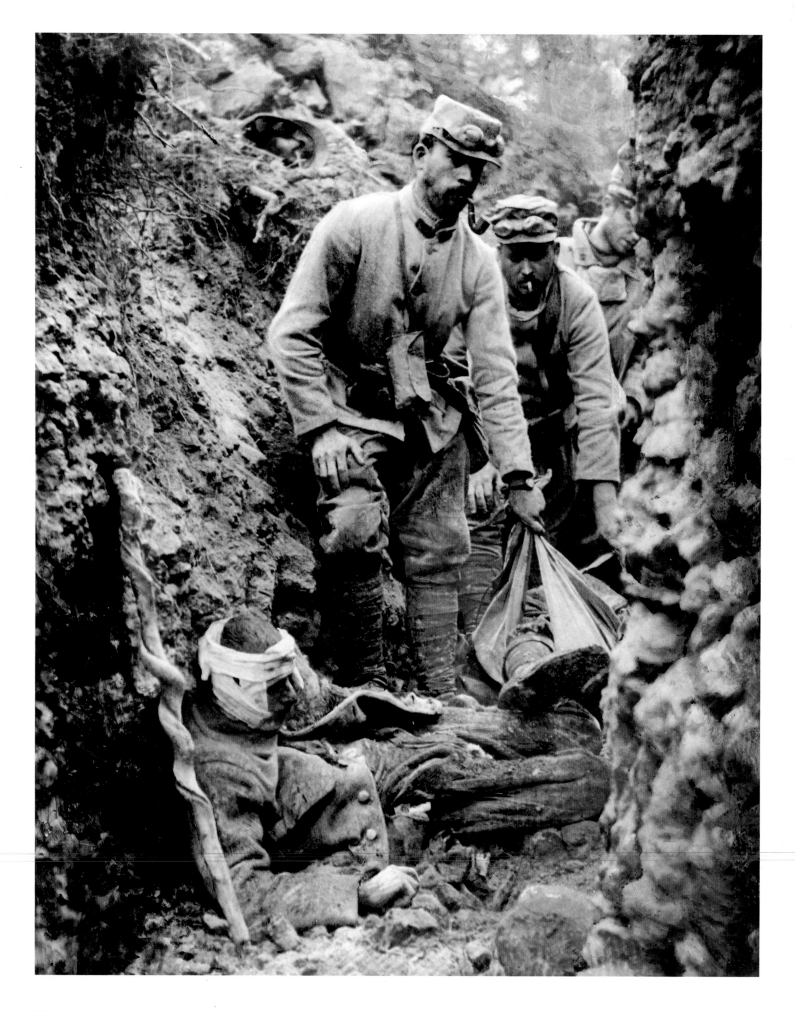

Pages 12 and 13
Vassily Kandinsky
PAINTING WITH BLACK ARCH
Detail, 1912, oil on canvas.
Centre Pompidou-MNAM-CCI, Paris.

1914-1918 WAR

The First World War ravaged the continent. 1916. In the Bay of the Somme in northern France, the English army wallowed in the mud. In Verdun, the incessant firing on both sides pulverized anonymous bodies in the name of some horrible notion of glory. "Raise the dead!" Le Chemin des Dames leads only to death. In April, 1917, the miserable failure of the almost month-long Nivelle offensive aroused public indignation. Revolt began among the soldiers reclaiming equal rights in the face of death. In the Chambre des Députés, the Socialist deputy Brizon openly denounced the massacre. Fifteen thousand women went on strike. Mutiny was to be severely punished. The previously censured "Chanson de Craonne" was adopted as a revolutionary anthem. Health services were unable to cope with more than one hundred thousand wounded, without counting those who'd gone crazy.

The only glimmer of civilization in the midst of this symphony of pain and hatred came from *care*. Stretcher-bearers, doctors, nurses, volunteers in the Red Cross and in the overcrowded hospitals – *there,* a tremulous remnant of the human spirit remained. Is it a coincidence that the future Surrealists, having understood throughout the war the degree of protest necessary, indeed even anarchist revolt... Is it a coincidence that André Breton and Louis Aragon, both young interns mobilized to care for the wounded, and Breton, fascinated by the fate of the mentally ill – were all to be swept up in a sort of generalized neurosis?

Psychosis and Poetry

In July 1916, Breton, a medical auxiliary in Nantes, was transferred at his own request to a psychiatric hospital in Saint Dizier. The hospital regrouped soldiers driven mad by the war, as well as prisoners awaiting trial. This is where the notion of Surrealism was born. Breton states in *Entretiens* (Interviews, Gallimard, 1952, p.29): "The time spent in this place, and the attention with which I studied what was happening have counted immensely in my life and have undoubtedly had a decisive influence on my manner of thinking" His letters dating from August of 1916 to Paul Valery, Guillaume Appolinaire and Theodore Fraenkel (also a medical student in Nantes) showed to what extent Breton, already a poet, was intrigued by the stranger functions of the mind. The reading materials that his senior advisor, Dr. Leroy provided him with, led to his request for transfer to the care unit of Babinski, the noted neuropsychiatrist at the Salpétrière Hospital in Paris. He arrived in 1917. Breton would keep Babinski's works in his library throughout his life. Babinski maintained that hysteria is a purely mental phenomenon, with no neurological basis. This is a notion that would be taken up by Surrealism, when Breton was to compare it to the poetic power of delirium in his *Eloge de l'Hystérie* (In Praise of Hysteria, 1928) or in *The Immaculate Conception,*"an essay of pathological simulations. It is with a poet's eyes that Breton first read Freud and Kraepelin (the author of several definitive books on paranoia) – "Precocious dementia, paranoia, twilight states, Ah, German poetry, Oh Freud and Kraepelin!" Breton wrote in a letter to Fraenkel, September, 1916.

Poetry, German or not, was close to Breton's heart. And if he then tried to go against his heart, his taste for scientific knowledge couldn't hold him back, for all that, from pursuing medicine. He would attempt, rather, to make poetry itself a means of knowledge. There, we find the legacy of a certain European Romanticism and Symbolism – the essential path for the Surrealistic adventure in the future.

In November 1916 Breton was assigned to a unit of stretcher bearers (along with Fraenkel) and plunged into the "vertigo" of the atrocities of the front. A poem describes this state: "Soldat," sent to Appollinaire 20 December 1916 – poetry offering an apology for delirium as a means of escape from the unbearable reality, a way of spiritually surpassing the "vie sordide" (sordid life). The experience of the mentally ill brings an absolutely new dimension to modern poetry, as seen already in 1916 in the Surrealist movement in the making. The "Derealisation Surrealist" (**Surrealist Derealization**, *Philosophie du Surréalisme*, Alquié, 1955) which Breton was to clearly affirm in his "Discours sur le Peu de Realite" (**Discourse on the Lack of Reality**, 1924), would make poetry the "compensation for the misery we have to bear."

Breton's stay in Paris in 1917 provided many important encounters. He frequented Apollinaire, who introduced him to the poet Louis Soupault, a fellow admirer of Rimbaud. In late September at a party in a barrack-room in the Val de Grace (military) Hospital, Breton met Arragon. What followed was the kind of endless conversation filled with wonder, the kind that can only take place between two twenty-year-old poets. "*Sur ce boulevard sans cesse remonté, redescendu*" (On this street, endlessly walked up, walked down)…

Louis Aragon was the illegitimate child of a police official, Louis Andrieux, and a woman so young that for some time, she would pass herself off as being Aragon's sister. His father never acknowledged him, and from early childhood he displayed an extreme sensitivity. From this first meeting with Breton, a friendship was born. Breton's prolific readings of Aragon were to open up new perspectives of poetry which followed that of Rimbaud, Stéphane Malarmé, Pierre Reverdy, and were often marked by the memory of Jacques Vaché, whom he'd met in Nantes. It was Vaché, with his peculiar form of nihilistic dandyism in his dazzling *Lettres de Guerre* (War Letters, published in 1919), that would revive a latent pessimism in Breton – his childhood had not been a happy one, an unloving mother, sometimes prone to violence were a somber backdrop to Breton's solitary nature – which, as a poet and a theoretician, he never managed to fully hide.

During the years between 1917 and 1920, destiny seemed to lead the future Surrealists'paths one towards the other. Eugene Grindel was treated for tuberculosis in a sanatorium in Davos. During those years, free from his family, Grindel read Whitman, Nerval, Baudelaire, Rimbaud, Apollinaire's *Les Soirées de Paris*, Marx and Lautréamont. Released on the eve of the war, sent direct-

ly to the front, he would remain there for the entire war. Gassed, suffering from pulmonary gangrene, he was discharged in 1916. That same year, he adopted the pen name Eluard, his grandmother's name, and published his first collection of poems, *Le Devoir* (**Duty***)*. In Davos, he met Helena Dmitriovnia Diakonova, whom he called Gala. He married her in 1917. Gala would be his muse until 1930 when she married Dali. She was to remain a mastermind behind the Surrealist movement for many years. *Le Devoir et l'Inquietude* (Duty and Anxiety) was published in 1917 and Eluard joined the group of the *Revue Littéraire* **review** *Littérature* in 1920. He was to become one of the most important poets of the 20th century.

The artilleryman Max Ernst could have showered with shells the infantryman Paul Eluard in the Somme during the war years, but destiny would have it otherwise. They met in Paris later, becoming close friends.

As for Benjamin Péret, he enlisted at the age of 16. Fleeing his family, he fought the entire war, first in a Calvary regiment, then in a unit specializing in sound detection. Due to the French occupation of the Rhineland, he was discharged only in 1920.

The painter André Masson was one of the most affected by the war. Mobilized in 1915, he was seriously wounded in April 1917 in the Chemin des Dames battle. Dragged from hospital to hospital, including the Maison Blanche Psychiatric Hospital, he would only be discharged in 1918. He wrote in his memoirs, *La Mémoire du Monde* (World Memoirs, 1974), that his sense of self "had been forever damaged…" In his painting we find recurring themes such as the wounded bird, tearing apart, viscosity – all disturbing gore. But we'll come back to this.

Giorgio De Chirico
**PREMONITORY PORTRAIT
OF GUILLAUME APOLLINAIRE**
1914, oil on canvas
Centre Pompidou-MNAM-CCI, Paris.

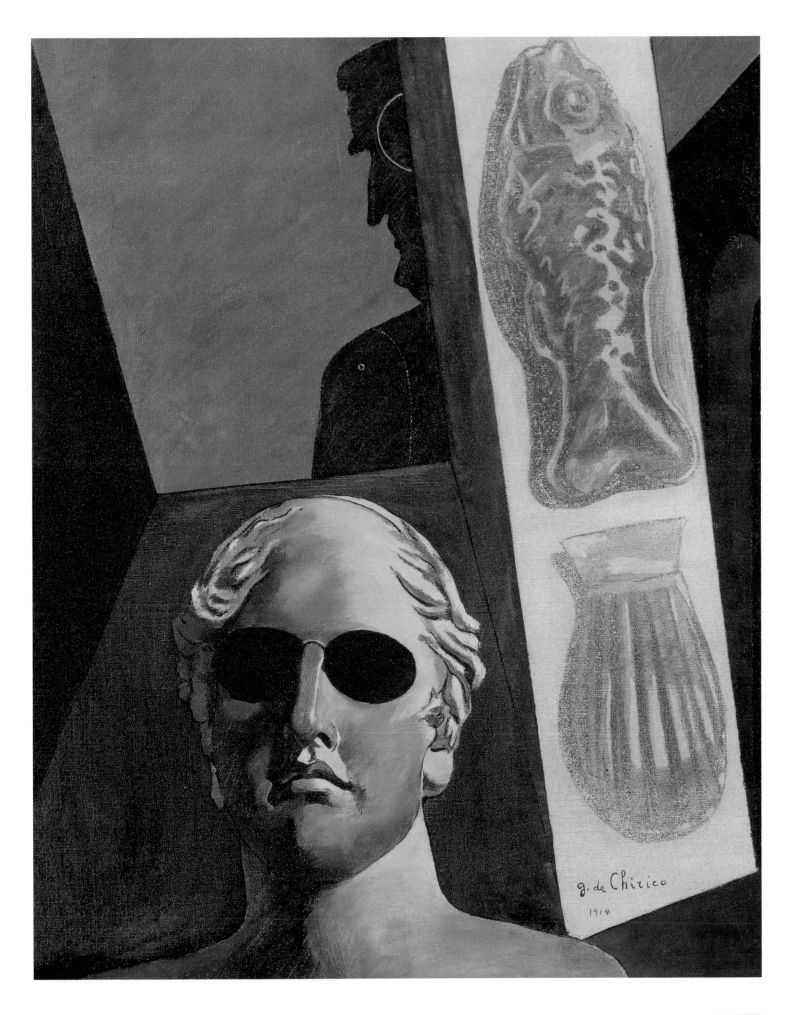

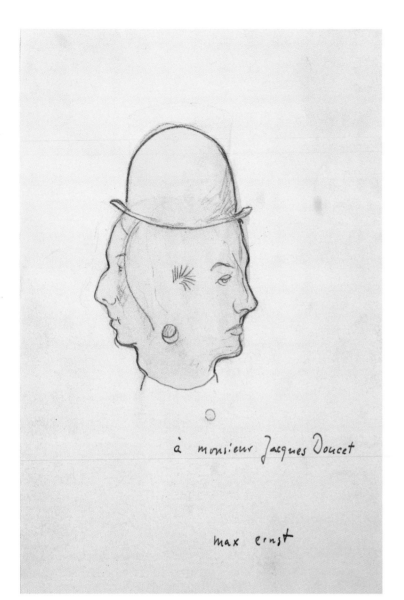

Max Ernst
**DOUBLE PORTRAIT DE PAUL
ÉLUARD AND MAX ERNST**
1925, drawing on paper
Bibliothèque littéraire Jacques Doucet, Paris

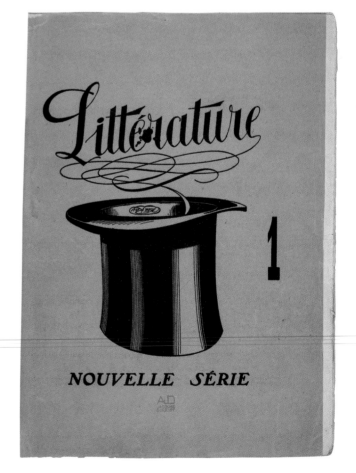

COVER OF LITTÉRATURE N°1
1919.
Bibliothèque littéraire Jacques Doucet, Paris

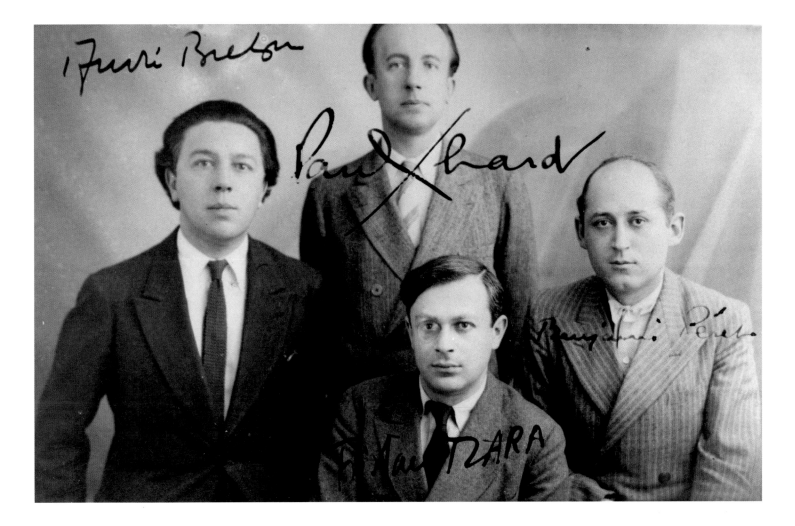

André Breton, Paul Éluard, Tristan
Tzara and Benjamin Péret, 1932.

LITTÉRATURE N°5
1st October 1922
Bibliothèque littéraire Jacques Doucet, Paris

While the aforementioned were on the battlefield, the young poets in Apollinaire's circle were discussing psycho-pathological research. Seeking a new form of poetry, beyond Reverdy's Symbolism and Malarmé's verbal asceticism, they tossed about ideas that would take form some time later. Breton's liveliest repartees took place with Reverdy. For Reverdy, poetry, as all works of art carry with them a new form of reality with no direct relationship with life. Thus, art should be a *presentation* of art itself, and not a *representation* of a reality lived elsewhere. Breton compared this idea to the concept of poetry rather emanating from the darker side of life, where Eros would sustain the unpredictability of a poem. Already, the *phrases de demi-sommeil* – all that the spontaneity of the dream state suggests in everyday life, in desire, in love, indicate the emergence of a new path that would lead towards "*automatisme,*" **the automatic writing** of the *Manifesto* of 1924. Breton's lessons of desire are pertinent to the case. Poetry will be the reality of the soul, not of things. A reality of language and its movements, of plastic shapes radiated by inner fantasies. Only allowing oneself to give into that which springs from a preconscious state will allow poetic energy to exist... In her monumental study, *Andre Breton, Naissance de l'Aventure Surréaliste* (André Breton, Birth of the Surrealist Adventure, Jose Corti, 1975, p. 136), Marguerite Bonnet notes that Breton's poems from 1918 refrain from charming, but rather seek to displease by breaking language forms, to stifle the song while it's still in the throat (*mettre le pied sur la gorge de sa propre chanson*) according to Aragon's expression. This refusal of rhythm, or musicality in poetry – from Giorgio de Chirico to Eluard, by way of Marcel Duchamp – would be a constant in Surrealist expression. It would grow into a global refusal of any form of feeling, in any domain, even love, in favor of an interior clairvoyance and of a moral protest – a feeling that the Symbolist Odilon Redon found "*bas de plafond*" (without much up there – a loose screw), and that Duchamp condemned in impressionist painting as too "retina oriented" that same feeling that the Cubists had already surpassed, according to Apollinaire, by creating a new form of painting based not upon appearance but on structure.

Breton and his friends still hesitated, not knowing which way to turn. The end of the war was a time of strange developments, and people seemed almost surprised by the return of peace. Shouldn't we start all over again? Many artists and poets settled down. André Derain became classical and Vlaminck, the most violent of the Fauves, turned to painting the commonplace. Picasso went beyond Cubism toward his "*période duchesse*" the sketches of his young wife were worthy of Ingres. Apollinaire let himself be carried away by admiration for the Futurists, to extolling the war. He would

die of Spanish flu at the time of the armistice. (People in the streets were shouting, "Down with William," referring to William II, German Emperor, while he lay dying.) Rumor had it around 1916 that there was a certain Cabaret Voltaire in Zurich, where something was being set up around Tristan Tzara. Feelers went out. The echo of Dada's effervescence had reached Paris.

In 1918 Breton and the future Surrealists were reading Lautréamont. They found in *Les Chants de Maldoror* a formidable expression of lyrical nihilism, excluding any resignation to void. "I made a deal with prostitution, in order to destabilize family life." (Chant I). Lautréamont's Dionysian immoderation and the force of his oratory style appealed to Breton's lyrical temperament. He soon left behind the punchy concision of Rimbaud, like that of Dada, favoring long phrases in the style of Chateaubriand. It is also noteworthy that Tzara too was a poet of inspiration – the Gongorism or declamatory style of Dada poetry and pamphlets, as Duchamp's play on words, would remain foreign to him. Often the same was to be the case for Surrealist poetry. Starting with *Les Champs Magnétiques* (Magnetic Fields), an example of "automatic writing" published in 1919 by Breton and Soupault, Surrealism had achieved its first major work of poetry. The practice of "psychic-automatism" owes as much to Lautréamont as it does to the flow of words of certain mentally ill, previously mentioned. *There* is the new way. Is this a sign? The book ends with a dedication to Jacques Vaché...

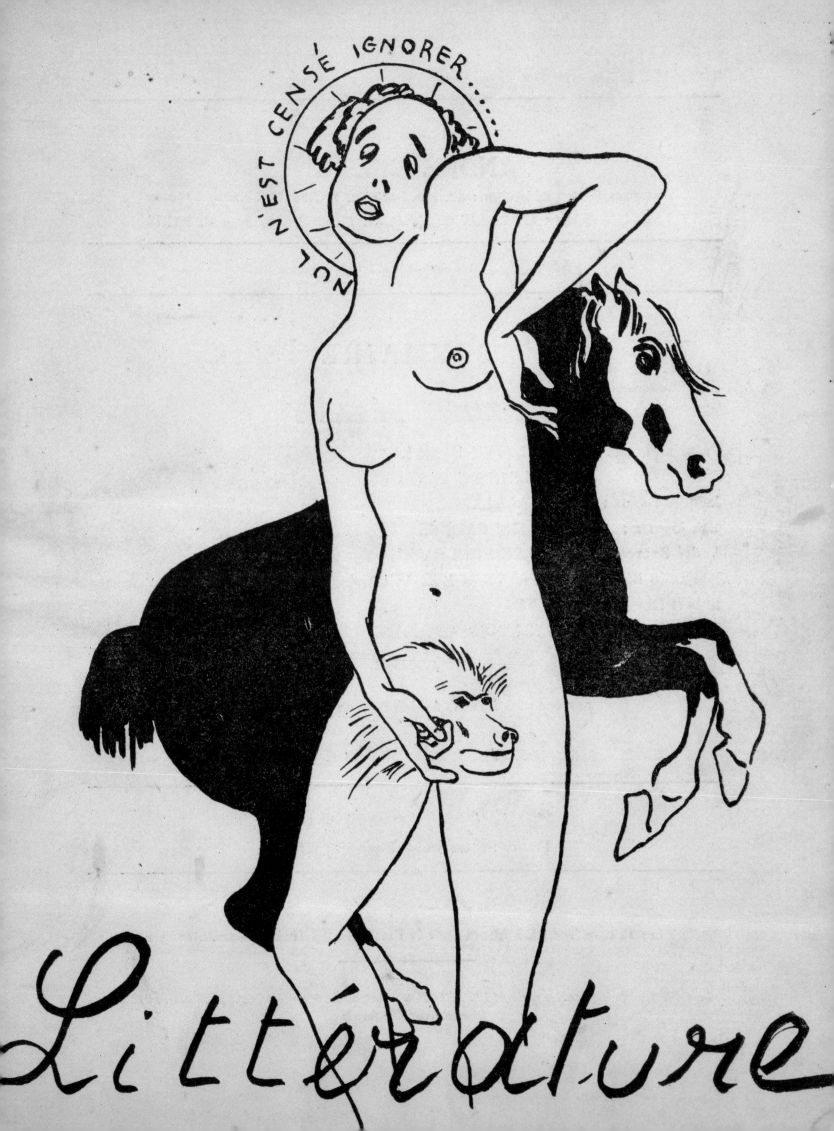

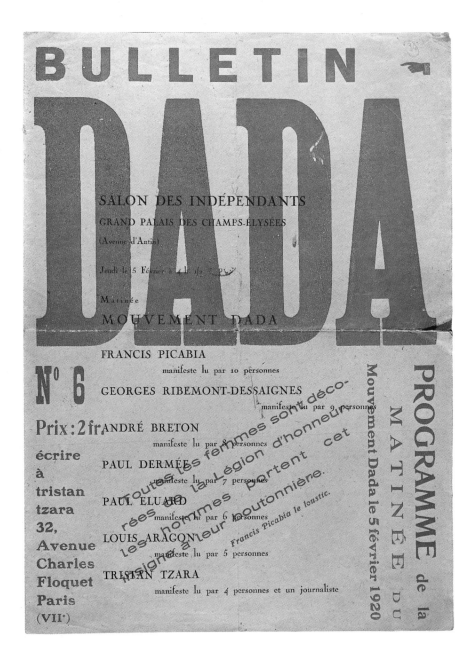

BULLETIN DADA N°6
1920.
Private Collection.

Tristan Tzara
A NIGHT OF CHESS
Dummy for the review 391 n° 6.
Bibliothèque littéraire Jacques Doucet, Paris.

The Dada Storm

The Dada movement was founded in Zurich, 6 February 1916, by Hugo Ball, and given this ridiculous name completely by chance. Meetings were held at the Cabaret Voltaire, in an atmosphere charged with unrest – all violently anti-establishment. Present were those not in the War, who were politically aggressive and desperate in the face of what the supposedly civilized Christian western world was becoming. At first excited by the notion of a renewal of art, "which is right now the only thing in itself accomplished" (Tzara, *Dada 1*, July 1917) Dada was to become more radical, more anti-art in Tzara's *Manifesto* (*Dada 3*, December 1918). This work overwhelmed Breton, he felt he had found in Tzara the reincarnation of Vaché.

'Didn't Dada's nihilism, denouncing the 'blue-horizon'society (World War I veterans, who wore blue) of the times, add a politically anarchistic dimension to the new poetry, thereby becoming "the development of a pro-

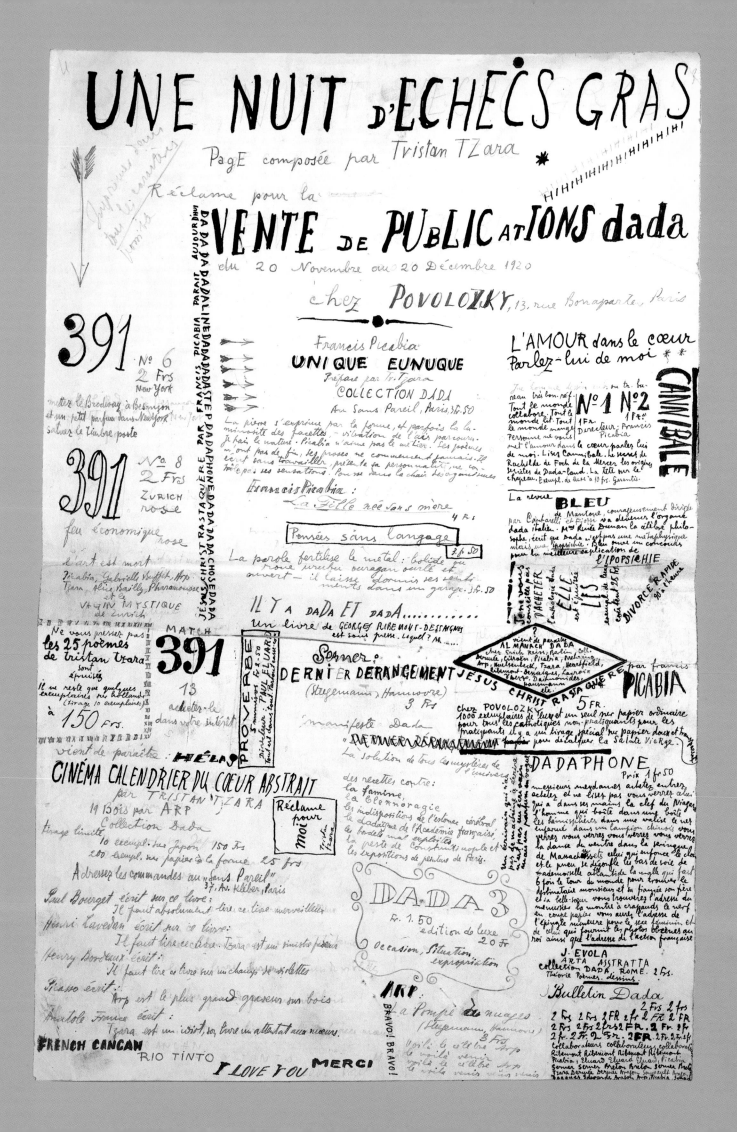

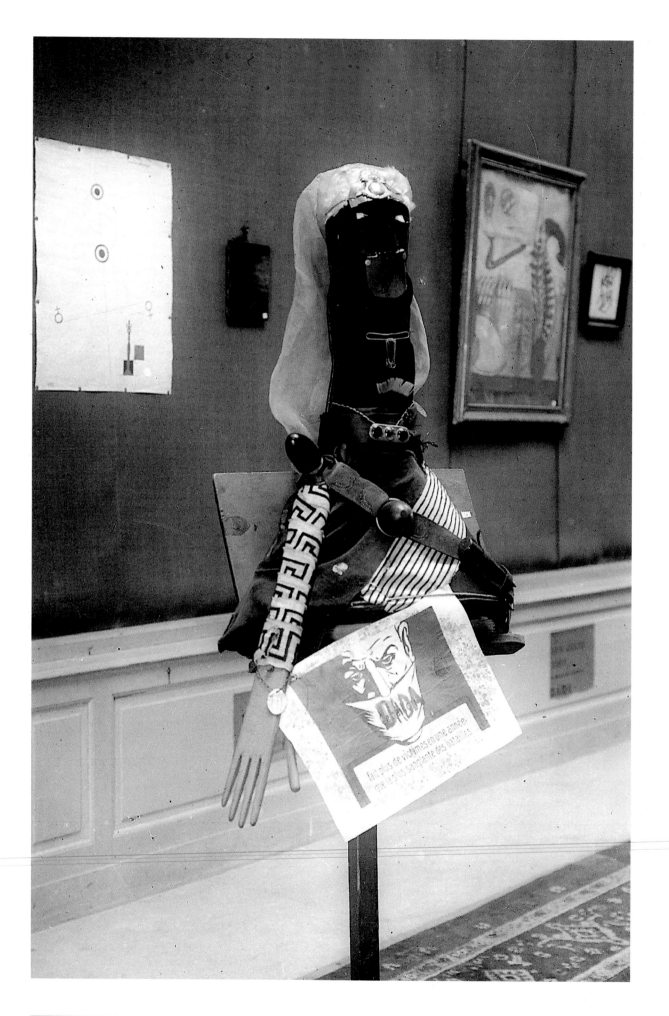

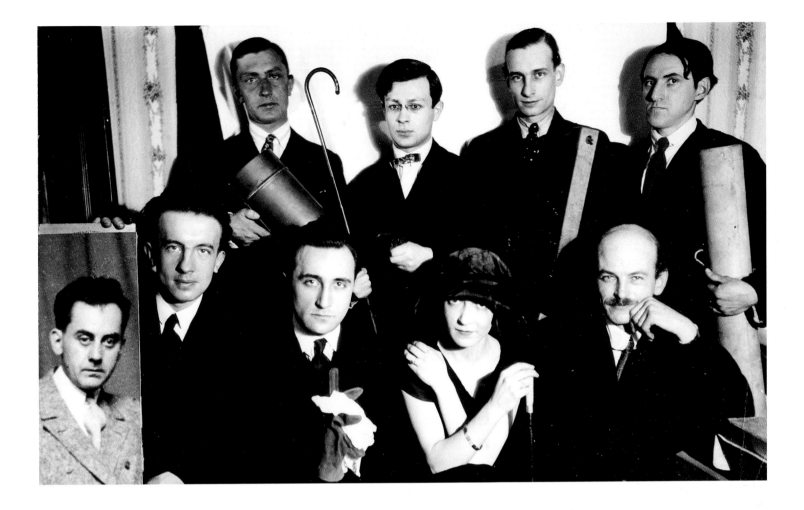

Dada Exhibition at The
Montaigne Gallery.
Paris, 1921.

Man Ray
THE DADA GROUP.
Standing, left to right :
P. Chadourne, T. Tzara,
Ph. Soupault, S. Chadourne ;
seated, left to right :
P. Éluard with the photo of Man
Ray, J. Rigaut, Mme Soupault,
G. Ribemont-Dessaignes.
about 1922, collage of two
gelatin silver prints.
Centre Pompidou-MNAM-CCI, Paris

test?" Would Surrealism simply become a kind or war-
med over Dada? Along with Marguerite Bonnet and
Maurice Nadeau, among others, I find it impossible to
adhere to Michel Sanouillet's affirmation in *Dada à
Paris* (Pauvert, 1965), that "Surrealism is Dada without
the humor" (p. 432), or indeed, that it was to be "the
French version of Dada" (p. 420). First of all, because
Dada is not funny, it has nothing to do with the ambient
humor of the day. Secondly, the movement that would
soon be called Surrealist, tying an experimental spirit
with the need for contest, not only was born long before
the explosion of Dada in Paris – in an historical context
that had absolutely nothing to do with Zurich – but still
completely ridiculed the France's "national genius" to
which Michel Sanouillet referred (p. 425)… Breton the
stretcher-bearer was profoundly moved by the paranoid
delirium of a wounded soldier, the memory of which
would remain with him throughout life. His only means
of coming to terms with the barbarous aspect of war,
would be in a spirit of experimentation and of care, the
spirit Freud, (whom Breton would meet in 1921 in

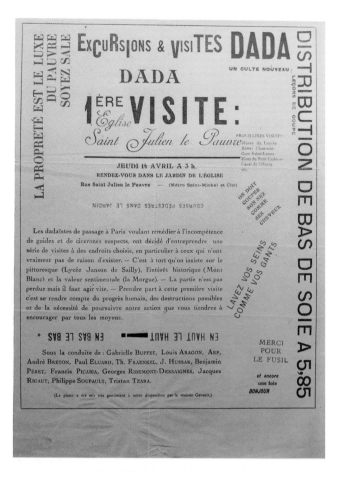

Notice for the Visit to Saint-
Julien-le-Pauvre, 1920.
Private Collection.

Vienna – encounter for that matter barely successful), a medical spirit foreign to Dada (Tzara had always hated the Freudian school). There was no question of Breton conferring a quasi-mystical dimension to the revolt, nor sharing in Tzara's motto: "Severe necessity without discipline or morality, and let's spit upon humanity." (Preface to *La Première Aventure Céleste de M. Antipyrine* [The First Celestial Adventure of Monsieur Antipyrine], the beginning of the "Dada Collection," 1916). Breton had been dizzied by the haughty despair of Jacques Vaché – who committed suicide in 1919 by an overdose of opium – and this shared despair couldn't bring Breton to allow a public fuss preventing concentrated listening to an inner message. "Without discipline, nor morality?" No doubt. This was to be Surrealism's message, and

around 1912-13 Breton was reading anarchist newspapers. But the poet himself was to maintain a very strict personnel discipline in order to proceed from fabricated poetry to "automatic writing." As for "spitting upon humanity" Tzara himself, a future Surrealist before later adhering to the Communist Party, might have simply seen this as a rather empty metaphor.

The din of the Dada meetings in Paris had, as a major effect, the attraction of young artists and poets in search of an identity to the rising Surrealist avant-garde. Benjamin Péret for example, joined the Dadaists immediately upon being discharged. Max Ernst arrived, Paul Eluard was there… Terrific pranks were imagined, for example: the public was invited to a Bach concert, a hullabaloo greeted them. "On stage, we beat on the keys, on boxes to make music, until the audience protested, went crazy." (Georges Hugnet, "L'esprit Dada dans la Peinture," *Cahiers d'Art*, 1932-1934.) Sarcastic and incongruous behavior such as getting undressed on stage or speaking all at once, they bet they could empty out a hall in less than twenty minutes, and they did. The first "Lundi" (Monday) organized by la revue *Littérature* (a review founded in 1920, where one found the names of André Gide, Paul Valery, Léon-Paul Fargue, Eluard, Aragon, Breton, etc…) – just as Stéphane Mallarmé held his "Mardis" (Tuesdays) among friends – was a major event, a sort of publicity; the Dadaists proposed the replacement of art, by "slogans." And Dada was launched in Paris.

Was it really all that funny? It was seriously a question of ridiculing art. In Germany, the Weimar Republic was shaky, and the death of Karl Liebknecht and Rosa Luxemburg marked the end of the Spartakist movement (1919) – during an art exhibition in Berlin in 1920, had been proclaimed, "Art is dead," and "Dada is political." Richard Huelsenbeck and Raoul Haussmann, the organizers of this manifestation which had drawn crowds, soon settled down and joined the German Communist Party. Baargheld, a banker's son, founded the review *Die Schammade* in 1919 in Cologne. Then the review *Ventilator*, with Max Ernst, Hans Arp and the members of *Littérature*, plus Tristan Tzara and Francis Picabia, organized an exposition *à scandale* in 1920. (One entered through the toilets, where a young communicant read licentious poems while Saint Theresa showed her black stockings…) The Surrealists applauded these novelties, but in fact, anti-clericalism, or religious protest were a French tradition, going back at least to the Symbolists Mossa and Odilon Redon at the end of the nineteenth century. Clovis Trouille, discovered by Breton at the Salon des Surindépendants in 1936, painted his first canvases such as *Le Palais des Merveilles* in 1907. The works to come – *La Saint Vierge*, by Picabia, a spirt of ink; films by Dali and Buñuel, notably; poems by Péret, surely the most obsessionally anti-clerical of the Surrealist poets; and Breton's famous formula, "God is a Pig" (in *Le Surréalism et la Peinture*, Gallimard, 1965, p. 10) – all demonstrate that the Surrealists' anti-Christian attitude owed more to Lautréamont's visionary, rhapsodic prose, or to Sade's eroticism (they were to be the only ones to defend him in France in the thirties), than to funny but ultimately vacuous performances. Agitation isn't enough. One has to get down to an act. Does anyone remember that Rimbaud scribbled "Death to God" on a church? It's only his work that remains, and that continues to have an effect.

To the anti-clerical tradition was added that of hatred for the bourgeois, strong since Baudelaire. Surrealism wouldn't have needed Dada to take up the flame. They furthered the debate by denouncing any expression of a sense of belonging to a place or cultural entity. During the "Barrès Trial" (May 1921), they attacked the reasoning of the do-gooders – this was the pamphlet incriminating Anatole France *Un Cadavre* (a corpse), handed out at his funeral in 1924. Then there was the temptation of joining the political struggle of the proletariat… The Surrealists were, in fact, all members of the bourgeoisie, having "betrayed their class" on purpose.

Surréalist Group at Saint-Julien-le-Pauvre in 1920.
Left to right : Crotti, d'Esparliès,
Breton, Rigaud, Éluard, Ribemont, Dessaignes, Péret,
Fraenckel, Aragon, Tzara and Soupault
Bibliothèque littéraire Jacques Doucet, Paris

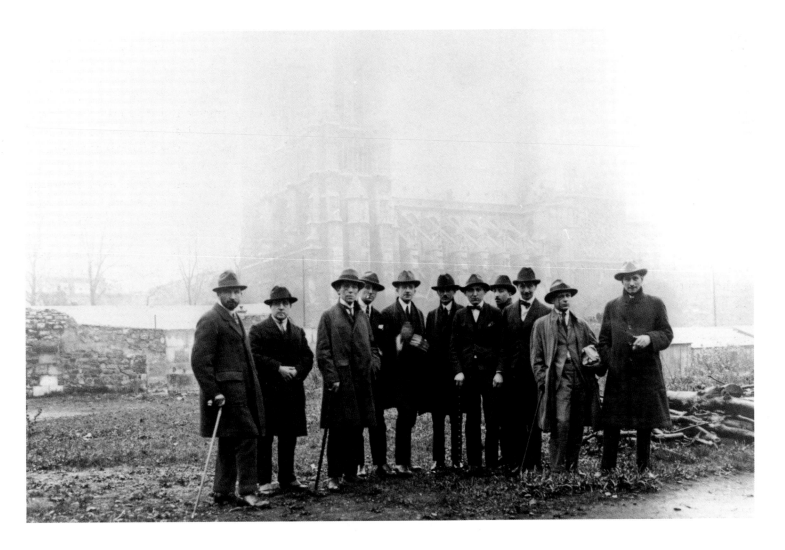

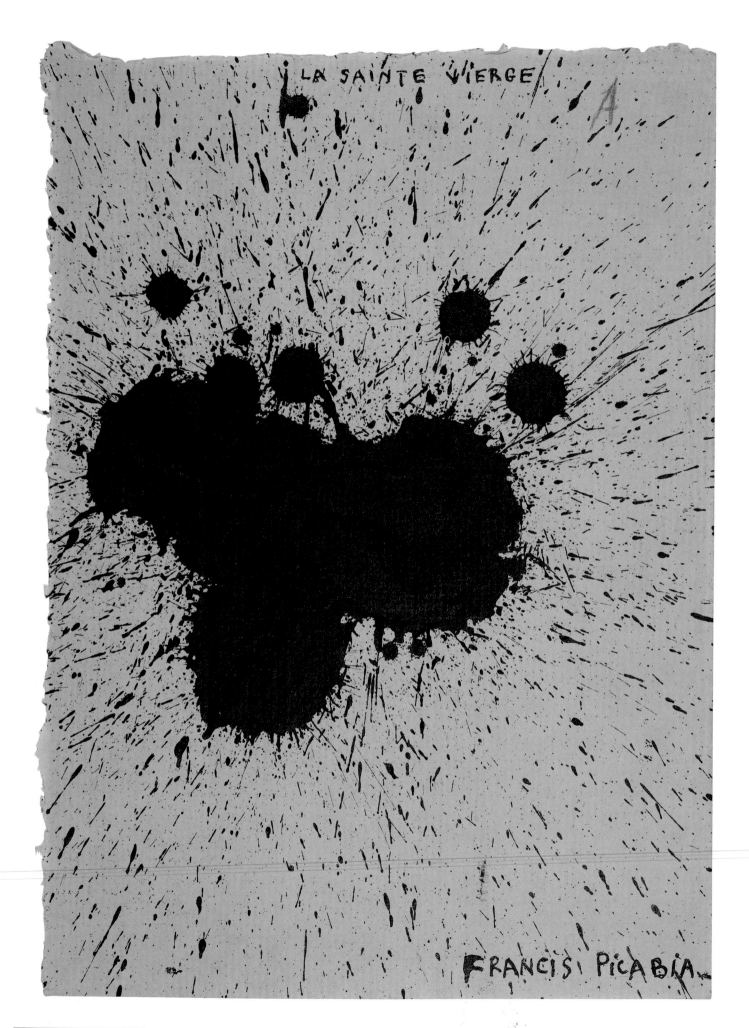

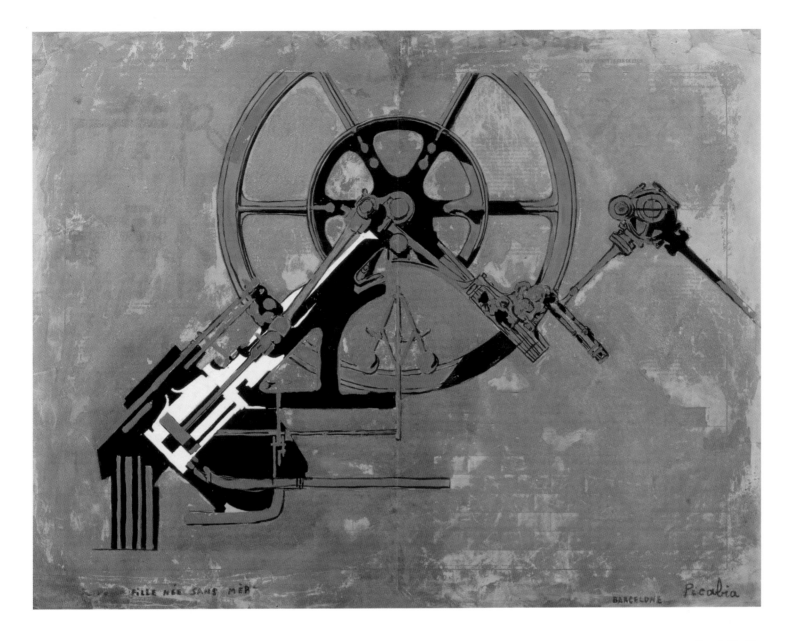

Francis Picabia
GIRL BORN MOTHERLESS
1916-1917, Gouache on paper
Scottish National Gallery of Modern Art.
Edimburg.

Francis Picabia
THE HOLY VIRGIN
1920, Inch on paper.
Bibliothèque littéraire Jacques Doucet, Paris.

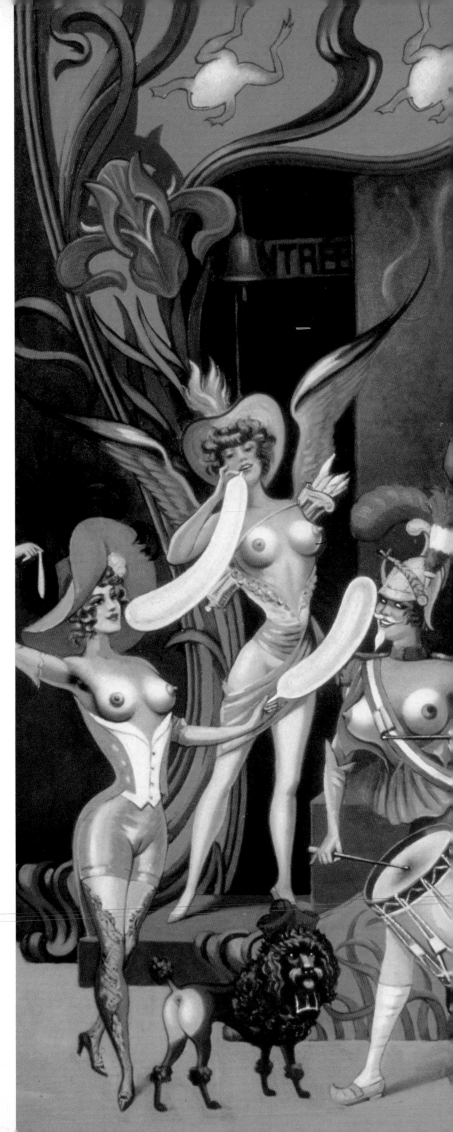

Clovis Trouille
THE PALACE OF WONDERS
1907/1927/1960, oil on canvas.
Private Collection.

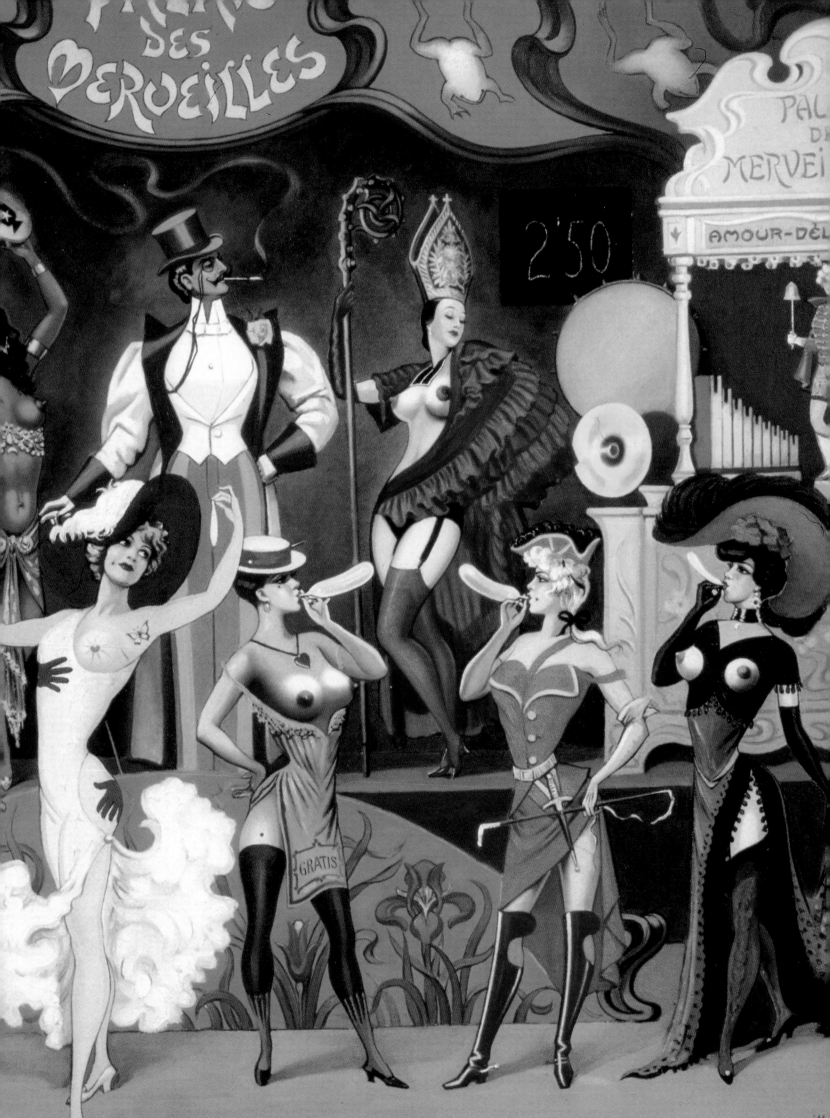

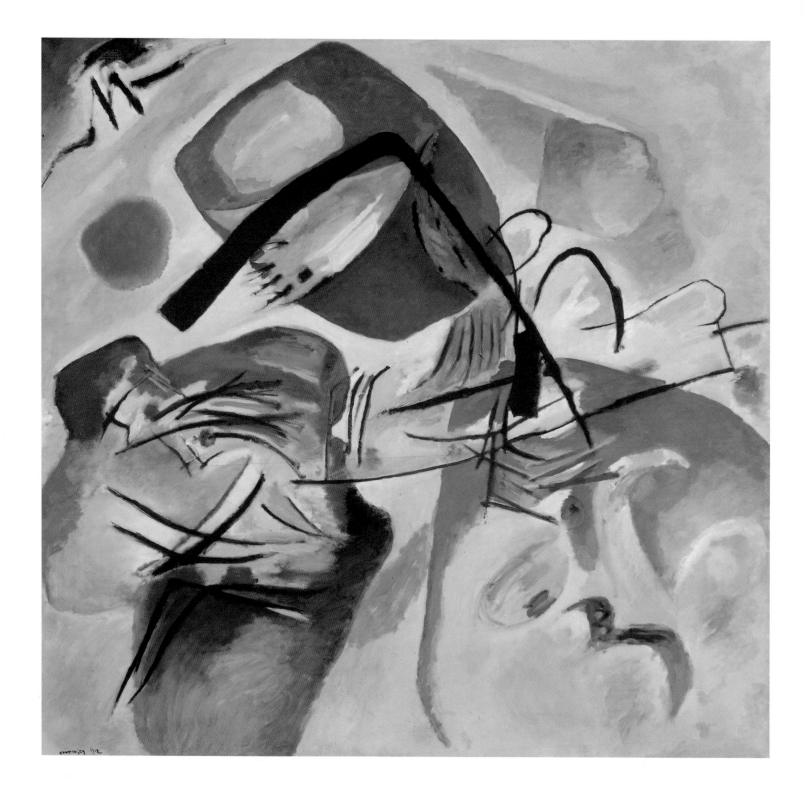

"Drop Everything"

It was in regard to Picasso's decor for *Les Mamelles de Tirésias* (The Breasts of Tiresias), a "Surrealist drama" by Guillaume Apollinaire (1917), that the word *Surréalisme* first appeared publicly. The poet had created it a short time before to describe the stage curtain Picasso had made for the review *Parade*, by Jean Cocteau and Eric Satie. By adopting the word, Breton was paying homage to Guillaume Apollinaire, about whom he would write, "To have known him was a blessing." Another blessing: the example of Marcel Duchamp. The Surrealists had certainly seen examples of breaking-away and artistic freedom since ruptures at the end of the 19th century – precursors such as Gustav Klimt, Wassily Kandinsky, Pablo Picasso, Paul Klee, Marc Chagall or Giorgio De Chirico. But Duchamp went beyond painting with his *readymades*, such as the famous porcelain urinal, presented upside down, entitled *Fountain*. He seduced the Surrealists not only by putting a mustache on the Mona Lisa, which was subtitled *L.H.O.O.Q.* (*"elle a chaud au cul"*/"she has a hot ass"), but by leaving his *Grand Verre, La Mariée Mise à Nu par Ses Célibitaires, même* (The Large Glass, the Bride Stripped Bare by Her Bachelors, Even) unfinished in 1922. Example to follow?

During the course of a secret party, decisive for their future, Breton and Soupault swore never to make a career out of literature. Since their discharges in 1919, Breton and Aragon had ardently pursued the non-pursuit of a career, to the dismay of their families who hoped they would enter the medical profession. They didn't do anti-art, but developed creative life as a new *art de vivre*, in total contrast with the fatuity of the "*pohètes.*"

In fact, it was at the time of the "Procès Barrès" (Barrès Trial) that Breton and Tzara angrily went their separate ways. There was a level of philosophical seriousness around the Barrès trial about which Dada cared little. As early as 1922, " It's with a certain relief that Breton and his friends distanced themselves from Dadaism," (Maurice Nadeau, *Histoire du Surréalisme*, p. 54). Breton realized that a break was necessary, even with professionals at breaking-up! He proclaimed: "Drop everything. Drop Dada. Drop your wife. Drop your mistress. Drop your hopes and your fears. Conceive your children by the side of the road. Drop the prey for obscurity. Drop your need for a comfortable life, that which is offered for a secure future. Get on the road." (In *Les Pas Perdus.*)

Should one associate the surprising disappearance of Eluard in 1924 with the doctrine "Drop everything"? He left, telling no one, and it was from Singapore that he telephoned Gala and Ernst (who were at the time having an affair, accepted so it seems, by Eluard) to come and

Vassily Kandinsky
PAINTING WITH BLACK ARCH
1912, oil on canvas.
Centre Pompidou-MNAM-CCI, Paris.

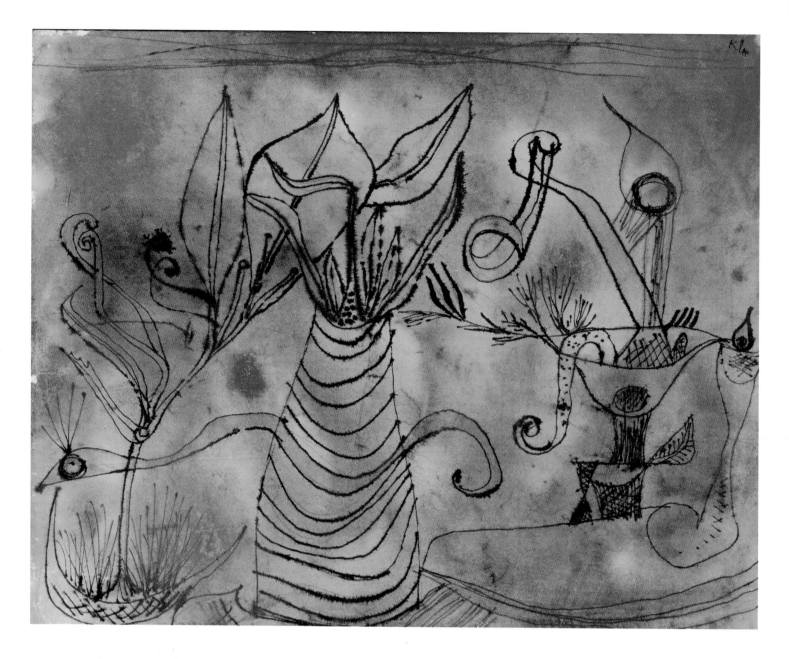

Paul Klee
STILL-LIFE WITH SERPENT
1924, ink and
gouache on paper
Galleria Internazionale d'Arte Moderna,
Venise

get him. They followed as quickly as possible; Gala brought back Paul and Ernst returned on his own. The friendship between Ernst and Eluard was always to remain steadfast.

These young people hadn't a cent. However they weren't alone. While Aragon had been the cultural advisor (1922-26) to a rich fashion designer, Jacques Doucet, also a collector of manuscripts, Breton had, thanks to Paul Valery, found a job as a corrector at the *N. R. F. (Nouvelle Revue Française)*. He would read Proust's prose out loud, (so close to his own). Is this when he became

thoroughly disgusted with the novel once and for all? The review *Littérature* survived the Dada storm, and continued from March 1922 until June 1924. It remained eclectic and confused; Breton was "bored there."

During this time, chance meetings continued to be fortuitous. On Rue Blomet, not far from the Bal Nègre, André Masson rented a studio in 1922 and found himself living next door to Joan Miró. Antonin Artaud, Louis Aragon, Michel Leiris and Georges Limbour were regulars at the atelier, as well as André Masson. Breton bought Masson's *Les quatre Eléments* (1923), and he in

Marc Chagall
DOUBLE PORTRAIT
OF A GLASS OF WINE
1917, pencil and watercolor on the
back of a page printed in cyrillic.
Centre Pompidou-MNAM-CCI, Paris

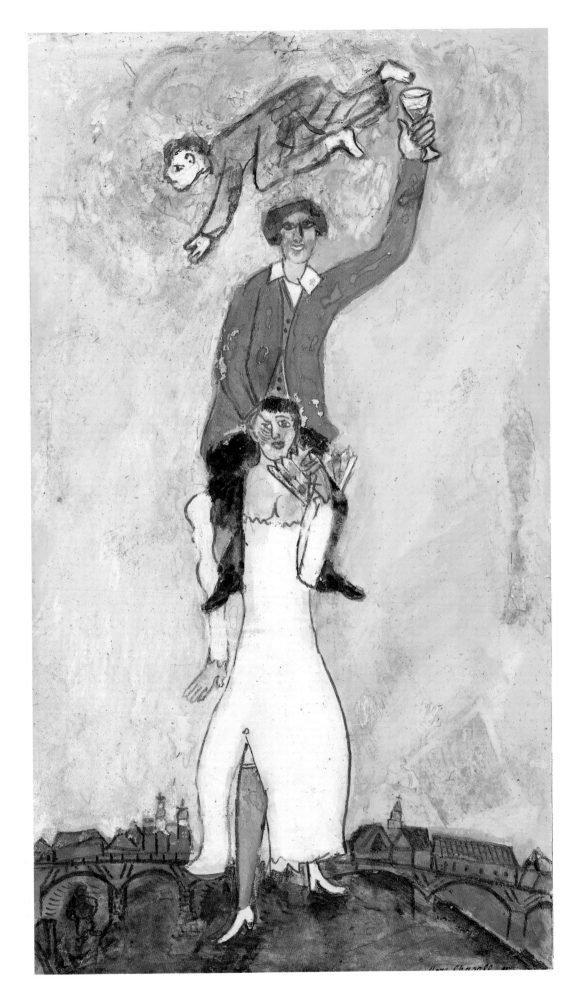

Page 36
Giorgio De Chirico
MELANCOLIA
1912, oil on canvas.
Estorick Foundation, London.

Page 37
Giorgio De Chirico
SPRING IN TURIN
1914, oil on canvas.
Private Collection.

Page 38
REVIEW 391 N°8
February1919, in which is
reproduced a painting by Marcel
Duchamp, Mona Lisa L.H.O.O.Q.
Bibliothèque littéraire Jacques Doucet,
Paris.

Page 39
Marcel Duchamp
FOUNTAIN
1917/1960 copy of the original
made in New York in 1917,
porcelain.
Centre Pompidou-MNAM-CCI, Paris.

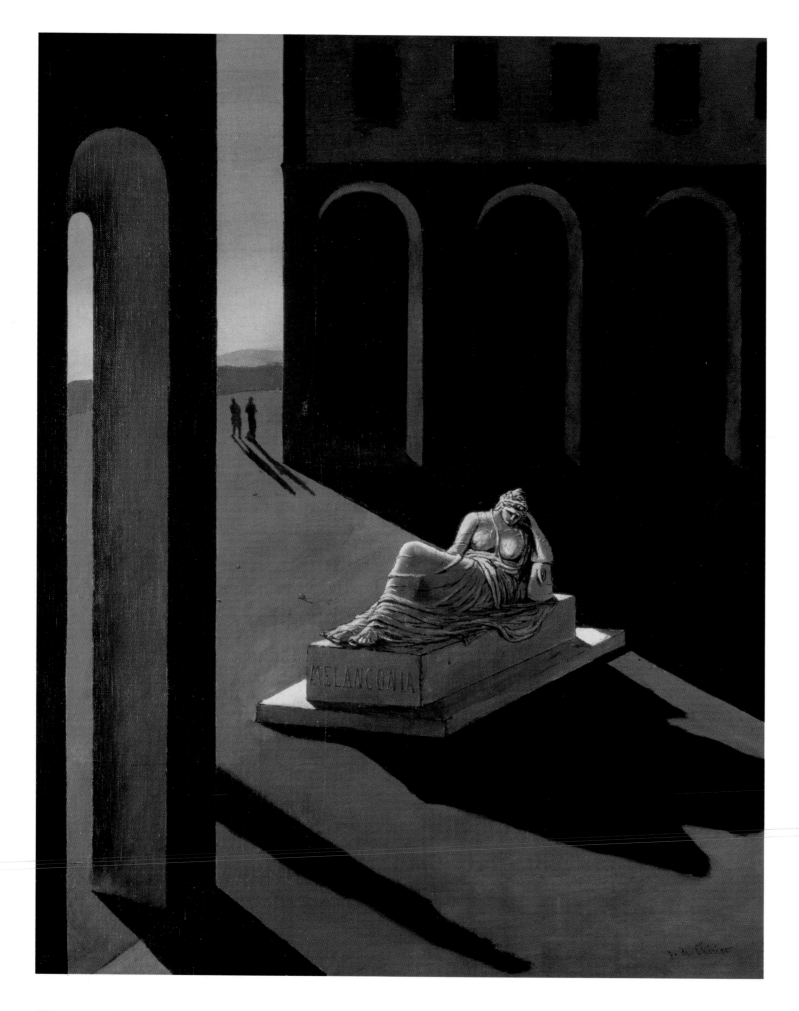

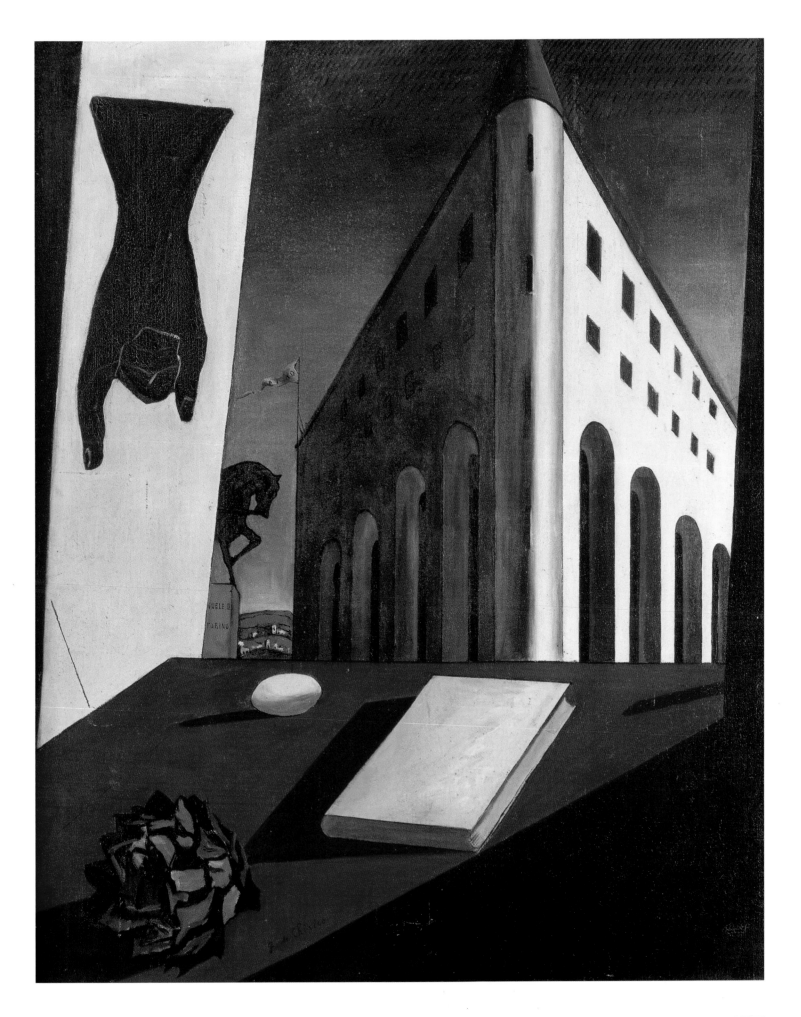

391

Au pluriel

"*Une définition n'a jamais été qu'un mot pour un autre — et le commun des mortels l'appelle erreur*".

De plus en plus, de moins en moins. Trois cent quatre vingt onze est un oiseau à poils, la Vierge satisfaite le tient dans ses bras, la pluie des grands jours, un biceps bien tendre, une ombre à plusieurs, les paupières comme des ongles ou les ongles comme des heures ou.

Petit, petit trois cent quatre vingt onze est de ma mère et des liqueurs de dessert, de plus en plus, de moins en moins, une lumière derrière un coup de poing, un coup de poing sur une lumière.

Je suis comme les autres, je vais au café. Aussitôt, j'entends : " Garçon un 391 des dimanches." Je suis discret, je ne répète jamais ce que j'écoute dans les water-closets.

Un aimable désordre simili or n'étant qu'un effet de l'art, j'ai pu enfanter deux ou trois fois dans ma vie une belle religieuse aux cornes d'ivoire, une belle, très belle.

Le livre sur lequel j'écris est ouvert à la page 202.

En le lisant, les Cubistes ont bien pleuré.

PAUL ELUARD.

Eh bien oui, la lettre signée Paul Eluard n'était pas de Reverdy ! Je m'amusais infiniment auprès de celui-ci, d'une réponse qui ne peut s'adresser à lui mais bien au véritable auteur de la lettre. Ce dernier s'amusait qu'à votre deux fois, ce serai par dans " Picabia ", ne remplaçant le nom de sympathique Reverdy par le sien, il s'est frappé de voir combien cette note lui est facilement applicable !

FRANCIS PICABIA.

TABLEAU DADA par MARCEL DUCHAMP

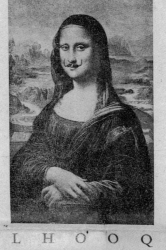

L H O O Q

Manifeste DADA

Les cubistes veulent couvrir Dada de neige ; ça vous étonne mais c'est ainsi, ils veulent vider la neige de leur pipe pour recouvrir Dada.

Tu en es sûr ?

Parfaitement, les faits sont révélés par des bouches grotesques.

Ils pensent que Dada peut les empêcher de pratiquer ce commerce odieux : Vendre de l'art très cher.

L'art vaut plus cher que le saucisson, plus cher que les femmes, plus cher que tout.

L'art est visible comme Dieu ! (voir Saint-Sulpice).

L'art est un produit pharmaceutique pour imbéciles.

Les tables tournent grâce à l'esprit ; les tableaux et autres œuvres d'art sont comme les tables coffres-forts, l'esprit est dedans et devient de plus en plus génial suivant les prix de salles de ventes.

Comédie, comédie, comédie, comédie, comédie, mes chers amis.

Les marchands n'aiment pas la peinture, ils connaissent le mystère de l'esprit...........

Achetez les reproductions des autographes.

Ne soyez donc pas snobs, vous ne serez pas moins intelligents parce que le voisin possèdera une chose semblable à la vôtre.

Plus de chiures de mouches sur les murs.

Il y en aura tout de même, c'est évident, mais un peu moins.

Dada bien certainement va être de plus en plus détesté, son coupe-file lui permettant de couper les processions en chantant " Viens Poupoule ", quel sacrilège ! ! !

Le cubisme représente la disette des idées.

Ils ont cubé les tableaux des primitifs, cubé les sculptures nègres, cubé les violons, cubé les guitares, cubé les journaux illustrés, cubé la merde et les profils de jeunes filles, maintenant il faut cuber de l'argent ! ! !

Dada, lui, ne veut rien, rien, rien, il fait quelque chose pour que le public dise : "nous ne comprenons rien, rien, rien".

" Les Dadaïstes ne sont rien, rien, rien, bien certainement ils n'arriveront à rien, rien, rien ".

Francis PICABIA

qui ne sait rien, rien, rien.

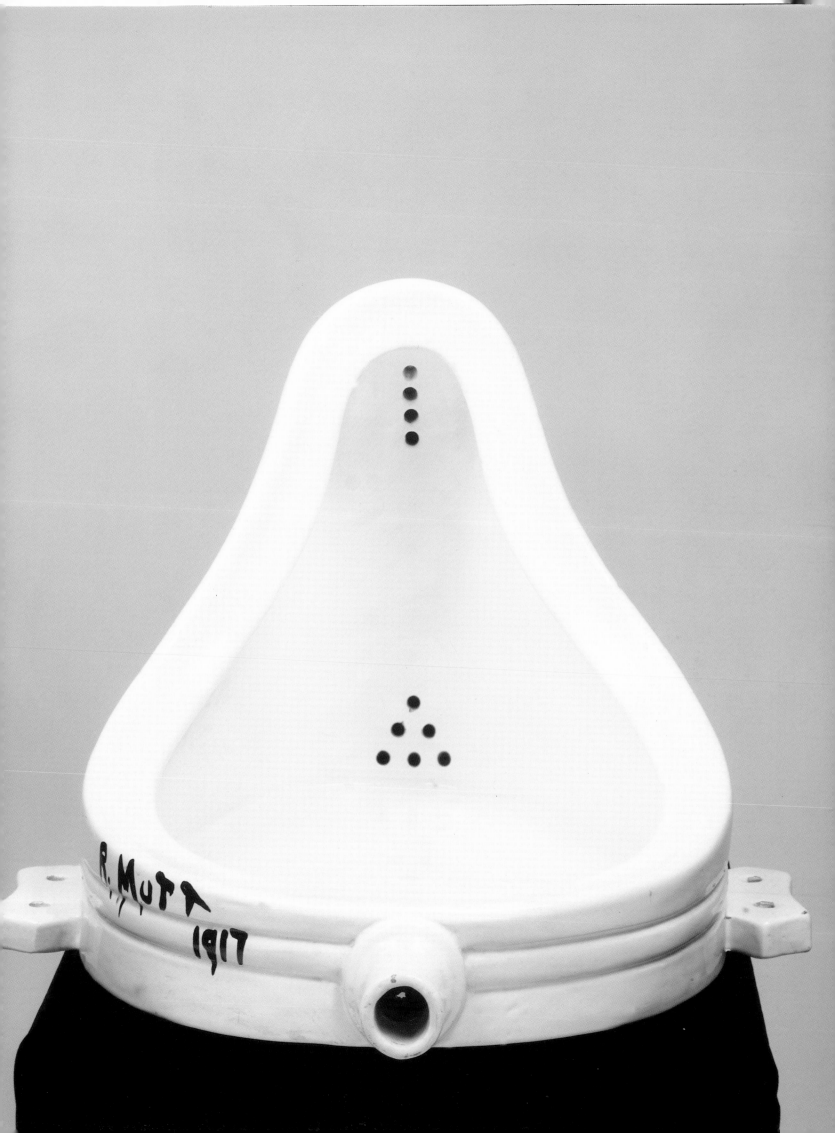

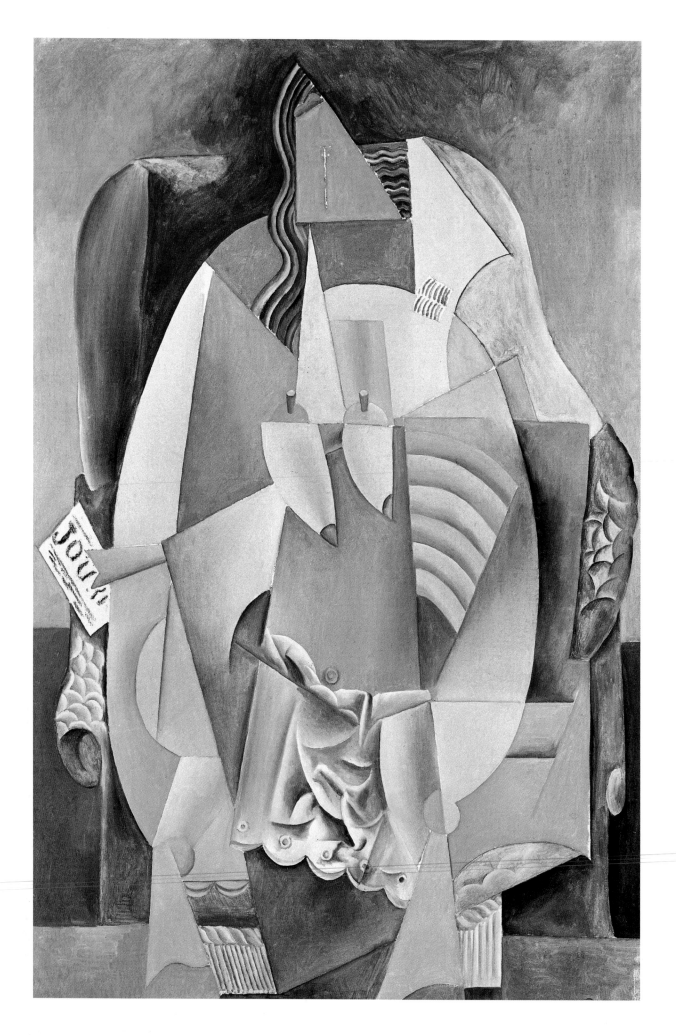

Pablo Picasso
WOMAN IN A BLOUSE IN ARMCHAIR
1913, oil on canvas.
Collection Ingeborg Pudelko, Florence.

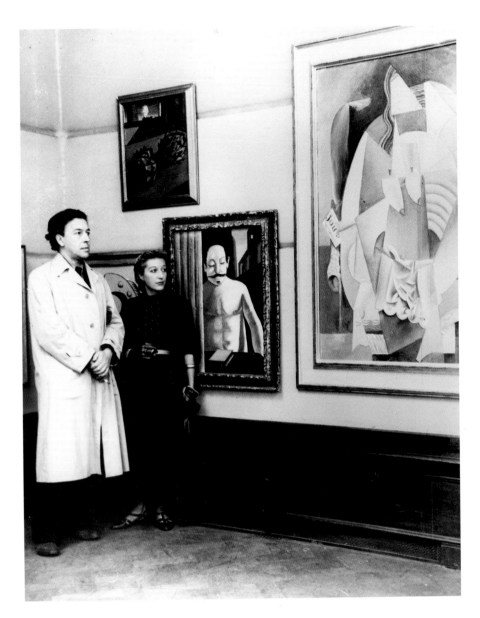

André Breton and Jacqueline Lamba
at the Surrealist Exhibition in London
in 1936.

Bibliothèque littéraire Jacques Doucet, Paris.

turn introduced the Catalan Joan Miró to Breton. In 1923, Yves Tanguy and Jacques Prévert, having met at a party in Lunéville, lived at 52 Rue du Chateau, in a locale that Marcel Duhamel rented for them.

New arrivals swarmed around Breton – the actor, Antonin Artaud, Maxime Alexandre, Georges Limbour and Andre Masson (who passed directly from his Cubist painting to "automatic drawing," skipping Dada completely) Joseph Delteil, J. A. Boiffard, Jean Carrive, Francis Gérard, Pierre Naville, (who's future lay in sociology and Trotskyism), Marcel Noll, Georges Malkine, etc. These "friends" met in cafés, which would remain, throughout the movement, as privileged places of discussion and debate. Breton was going on 30? Handsome, somewhat well-padded, rather solemn, speaking rarely, never laughing, but warm, some would

say solar. Jacques Prévert would write that Breton's disciples "loved him like a woman…" This, however, had nothing to do with the latent homosexuality found in certain military or ecclesiastic gurus. Breton, loved by women, always idolized them. The Surrealists openly berated Paul Claudel and later Ehrenbourg, who had dared to label their activity as "*pédérastique…*"

It has been said that Surrealism was not particularly feminist. For them, certainly women were not the bellicose amazons depicted by the Futurists, but rather, according to Baudelaire's formula, beings that projected on life "the most shadow and the most light." Or beings such as the magician elicited by Breton in *Arcane 17* (1946), those of Gustave Moreau, Symbolist painter whose pictures had enchanted the adolescence of the same André Breton. This in itself was a considerable

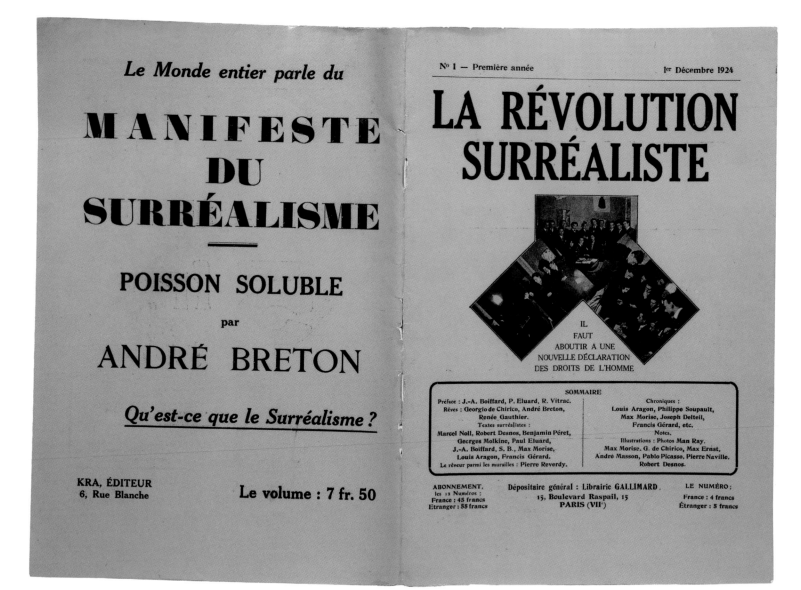

achievement considering the macho attitudes, not only of Dada, but also of Freud and even of the revolutionary parties, not to mention the Catholic church. Frequently quoting Rimbaud, "When woman's infinite servitude will be broken… when she will finally live by and for herself, man – up until now abominable – having given her dismissal, she will be a poet, she also." (Letter to Paul Demeny, 5 May 1871). The Surrealists stated along with Breton that "In Surrealism, woman will have been loved and celebrated like the great promise, one that remains, after having been kept." (*Surrealism dans Ses Œuvres Vives*, Surrealism in Its Vivid Works, 1962.) There were many prominent women artists and poets at the time – Maria Toyen, Léonora Carrington, Dorothea Tanning or Joyce Mansour… In fact, for years, through disputes and reconciliation's, the Surrealists were linked by a sort of passionate friendship, guided by a shared artistic mission.

The important thing was in the "interventions," the investigations and what must rightly be called creation. The break with Dada had been definitive after the failure of the "*Congrès pour l'Etablissement et les Directives de l'Esprit Moderne*" (Congress for the Establishment and the Directives of the Modern Spirit, 1922) This pompous title, certainly indicative of a "revolutionary" seriousness, was to qualify the group for years. The *Bureau de Recherches Surréalistes* (Office for Surrealist Experimentation) was created, and the review *La Révolution Surréaliste,* in which the first number dated 1st December 1924 contained dreams and "Surrealist texts" by Louis Aragon, Jacques Baron, Marcel Noll, Robert Desnos, Benjamin Péret, Georges Malkine, Paul Eluard and Philippe Soupault, etc. The cohesion of the group was being reinforced. The publishing house Kra published the *Manifesto of Surrealism*. The movement was well underway.

André Masson
THE FOUR ELEMENTS
1923/1924, oil on canvas.
Centre Pompidou-MNAM-CCI, Paris

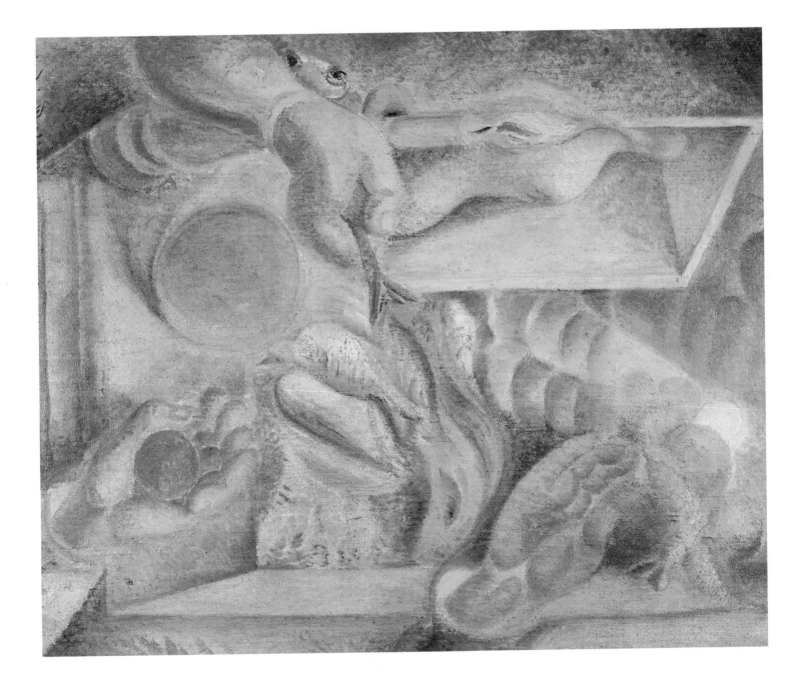

The First Manifesto

Let's summarize the main ideas proclaimed in this first manifesto:

1. Reality, as presented in the novel, is *"sans envergure"* (insignificant), but the imagination, so often put in quarantine, "ne pardonne pas" (is ruthless).

2. The experience of delirium is cited in order to justify the exclusive reliance on an inner source in establishing a world view. Dreams, as in Freudian analysis, depend upon this source.

3. The interior dream world requires the abandon of anything that could hinder the "automatic" spontaneous nature of thought. Hence, this definition of Surrealism:
SURREALISM, n. Psychic automatism in its pure state, by which one proposes to express – be it verbally, by means of the written word, or in any other manner – the actual functioning of thought. Dictated by thought, in the absence of any control exercised by reason, exempt from any aesthetic or moral concern.

4, This automatism, justified by previous psychiatric experience, where "phrases from a state of half-sleep" played an important role, implies a leap of faith: "I believe in the future resolution of these two apparently contradictory states. The synthesis of dream and reality, will form a new absolute reality, a super-reality, if you will."

5. What is poetry? "Man proposes and disposes. He and he alone can determine whether he is completely master of himself, that is, whether he maintains the body of his desires, daily more formidable, in a state of anarchy. Poetry teaches him to. It bears within itself the perfect compensation for the miseries we endure."

6. Art, daily life and love become poetry when they tend toward a "fusion of the imaginary and the real." We find examples in the writings of Dante, Shakespeare, Nerval, and Lautréamont... Breton enumerates those who have more or less committed "acts of Surrealism" Jonathan Swift, the Marquis de Sade, René de Chateaubriand, Benjamin Constant, Victor Hugo, Edgar Allen Poe, Charles Baudelaire, Athur Rimbaud, Stéphane Mallarmé, Alfred Jarry, etc. One notices in passing, this affirmation: "Vaché is Surreally in me."

7. Evoked next are present friends, who claim to be talentless: "We, who have allowed no filtering of our thoughts, have been only the deaf receptacles of so many echoes, modest tape recorders, who barely see the lines we draw, we serve perhaps an even nobler cause... We have no talent." This affirmation applied to Philippe Soupault, Roger Vitrac, Paul Eluard, Max Morise, Joseph Delteil, Louis Aragon, and Robert Desnos, whose extreme dream activity would assure the future of the movement.

8. Then came the guidelines, how to experience the "magic art of Surrealism" through the practice of automatic writing: After you have settled yourself in a place as favorable as possible to the concentration of your mind upon itself, have writing materials brought to you. Put yourself in as passive or receptive, a state of mind as you can. Forget about your genius, your talents, and the talents of everyone else. Keep reminding yourself that literature is one of the saddest roads that leads to everything. Write quickly, without any preconceived subject, fast enough so that you will not remember what you're writing and be tempted to reread what you have written. The first sentence will come spontaneously, so compelling is the truth that with every passing second there is a sentence unknown to our consciousness which is only crying out to be heard…"

9. Surrealism acts therefore as a drug, (*stupefiant* in French) the "anti-image drug:" It is "the somewhat fortuitous juxtaposition of two terms that shed a particular light, the *light of the image* to which we are infinitely sensitive." To cite some examples where the image "the strongest is the one that shows the highest level of arbitrariness."

10. In passing, certain key words were mentioned such as *Freedom:* "The mere word *freedom* is the only one that still excites me."
Madness: "It is not the fear of madness that will force us to leave the flag of imagination at half mast."
Childhood: "The spirit that plunges into Surrealism will joyfully relive the best part of his childhood."
Death and memory: "Surrealism will introduce you to death, our secret society. It will glove your hand *(main)* swallowing the deep M with which the word memory begins."
Language: "Language was given to man in order that he makes use of it in a Surrealist manner.
Supernatural: "Decidedly: the supernatural is always beautiful, anything supernatural is beautiful, in fact only the supernatural is beautiful."
The work, with an homage to distraction, ends with these Rimbaud-sounding words: "It is living and ceasing to live that are imaginary solutions. Existence is elsewhere."
One could interpret this in a mystical way, a call for the transcendental or the Divine. Let us confirm that the "new style of mysticism" that Aragon called for in a work dating from 1925, remains anchored in earthly life. In *Le Surréalisme et la Peinture,* Breton adds: "Everything that I love, everything that I think and feel, lead me towards a philosophy of immanence, in which Surrealism would be contained in reality, neither superior nor inferior."
So, Surrealism relies on the powers of the imagination, exacerbated by love, desire and revolt, in order to reach the supernatural level of poetry in all areas of life. We will now see how historical circumstances would modify its actions, both in terms of artistic creation and political commitment.

1924-1930
Plenitude

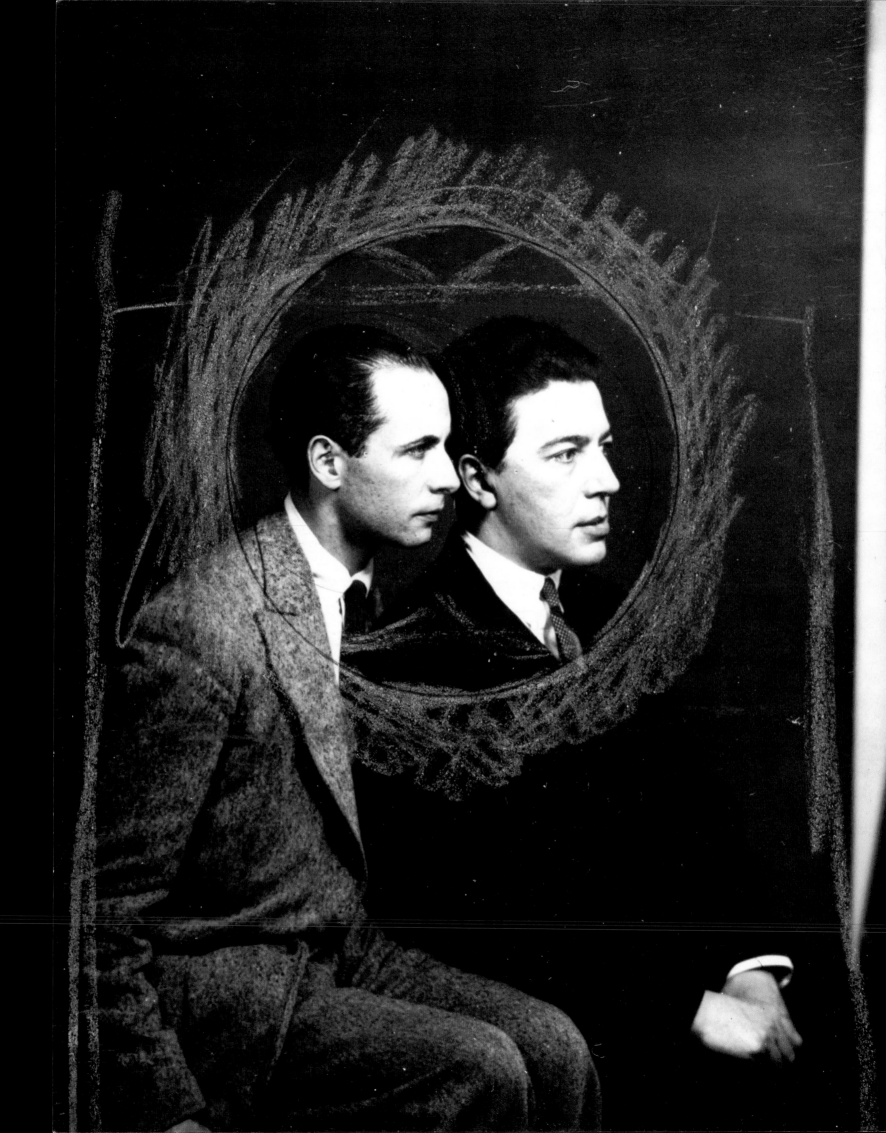

Pages 48-49
Max Ernst
FOREST
About 1928, oil on canvas.
Scottish National Gallery of Modern Art,
Edimburg

Man Ray
LOUIS ARAGON AND ANDRÉ BRETON
about 1925, gelatin silver print.

The pamphlet calling Anatole France "a cadaver" unleashed verbal violence among the Surrealists. Aragon had said, "Some days, I wish I had an eraser to erase the vileness of humanity." But he also would say in passing, "I somehow like the fact that the man of letters salutes both the tapir Morras and Moscow gone senile…" This insult was to create a rift between the Surrealists and Jean Bernier, director of the Communist review *Clarté*.

Surrealism Takes Hold

It was simply that the Surrealists conceived of the revolution only in terms of ideas. Aragon – who one day would become a member of the French Communist Party – responded to Bernier's article, notably, that the October 1917 Revolution "on an ideological level, is at the most a vague ministerial crisis." A declaration 25 June 1925 stated, "Surrealism…is a cry from the mind that turns upon itself, determined to desperately crush all obstacles… And if need be, with real hammers." One could have imagined in this last phrase some indication of social commitment, but for the moment the Surrealist revolution remained in the mind as a source of inspiration. Another document cited by Maurice Nadeau stated: "The idea of any sort of Surrealist revolution…aims to create a new form of mysticism." These atheists certainly had religious souls. In fact, discussion moved along at a good pace within the group. Their nihilism put the Surrealists before the choice of living or not, facing the tragedy of existence. In the first issue of *La Révolution Surréaliste*, along with accounts of dreams, there was a column where all recent suicide cases were tallied, along the starting-up of a survey, "Is suicide a solution?" The shade of Vaché continued to hover over Surrealist feelings, but the young people were too vigorous and too alive, to answer affirmatively to the survey. In fact, there were very few suicides among the Surrealists about this time – in spite of the repercussions among them over Mayakovski's suicide. (This would not be the case after the Second World War.) Only René Crevel – who had written in *Détours* (Gallimard, 1924): "A cup of herbal tea on the gas stove, the window tightly shut, I turn on the gas; I forget to light the match…" was found dead, one morning in 1935, next to his stove with the gas on…

The creativity of the Surrealist poets and painters was intense. Coming out: Pierre Naville's "automatic" text, *Les Reines de la Main Gauche, L'Ombilic des Limbes,* by Antonin Artaud, *Deuil pour Deuil,* by Robert Desnos, *Simulacres* by Michel Leiris and André Masson, *Proverbes Mis au Goût du Jour,* by Paul Eluard and Benjamin Péret, *Mourir de ne pas Mourir,* by Eluard, *Les Mystères de l'Amour,* by Roger Vitrac and *Le Libertinage,* by Louis Aragon.

In Germany Max Ernst had made his first collages in which old engravings became a sort of visual poem, very different from Picasso's *papiers collés* or Dada's *photomontages.* This was one of Surrealism's better inventions. To be convinced, one only needs to look at such a selection published as *Une Semaine de Bonté ou les Sept Elements Capitaux* (A Week of Happiness or the Seven Capital Elements, Jeanne Bucher, 1934). Ernst had met Breton in the Tyrol and allowed himself to be drawn into Surrealism, after having flirted with Dada. In 1925, he invented *frottages* (rubbings), soon to be assembled in the album *Histoire Naturelle* (Jeanne Bucher, 1926). He recounted his discovery in an key text:
Beginning with a childhood memory in which a mahogany panel across from my bed had created an optical illusion in my half-sleep, and finding myself one rainy day in an inn at the seashore, I was struck by the way in which the wooden floor, worn to the grain by a thou-

sand washings, became an obsession of my distorted view. I decided then to try to find the meaning of this obsession, and in order to aid my meditative and hallucinatory faculties, I made a series of drawings from the planks by posing on them, randomly, sheets of paper which I then undertook to rub with a lead pencil.

All we find in this text is worthy of the guidelines of the *First Manifesto of Surrealism* – visions in a state of half-sleep, obsession, hallucinatory faculties, the work of chance, and technical invention.

Other references to suggestive chance took place over the years in this group where "Surrealist games" were played. For example, the game of "*petits papiers,*" in which each person writes or draws something before hiding what has been written, so that the following person continues by chance. The game produced: "the exquisite corpse will drink the new wine," hence the name, *Jeu du Cadavre Exquis*. In the game "Questions and Answers," one would say, "I have a question;" the other, "I have an answer:" then both would announce what they had to say. This produced some interesting results: "What is suicide? – Several deafening rings." Or, "What is physical love? –It is half of pleasure." In the review *Variété* (Surrealist issue, 1929) one finds the game, "If/When," which is played around a table, each person writing a sentence beginning with "if" and one beginning with "when." An typical outcome: "If there were no guillotines… – wasps would take off their corsets." In spite of the mental stimulation provided by these "games" and

the abundance of works produced, there were tensions within the group at this time, 1924-1925. Pierre Naville, a keen politician, questioned the very existence of Surrealist painting and wondered if the association of the word revolutionary with the Surrealist movement was anything other than an embellishment. What could this "mysticism" mean other than a revival of old superstitions? ÒIn N° 2 of *La Révolution Surréaliste* there is an attempt to overcome these questions by a cry of a moral nature: "Open the prisons. Dismiss the army. There are no common law crimes." This text, while strongly utopian, ends with these words which are still relevant: "We learned without surprise that in America at Christmas, several executions had been suspended because *the prisoners had nice voices.*" And now that they've sung, they might as well die, to carry out the exercise. In these cubicles, on the electric chairs, the dying wait – Would you let them be killed?"

One should not be surprised by this libertarian outcry. It was to be just one of the trademarks of all the Surrealist protests – which in no way contradicts the notion of spiritual revolt. Mysticism rejoins violence in two *Addresses* (N° 3), one directed to the Pope, the other to the Dalai Lama. To the brutality of "Beware! Pope, dog," on one side, the other answers, "We are your very faithful servants, oh great Lama…Oh acceptable Pope, Oh Pope of the true spirit!" Logic and reason, so-called Western, are also denounced in a *Lettre aux Ecoles du Bouddha (Letter to the Schools of Buddha)*, in which one suspects Artaud's

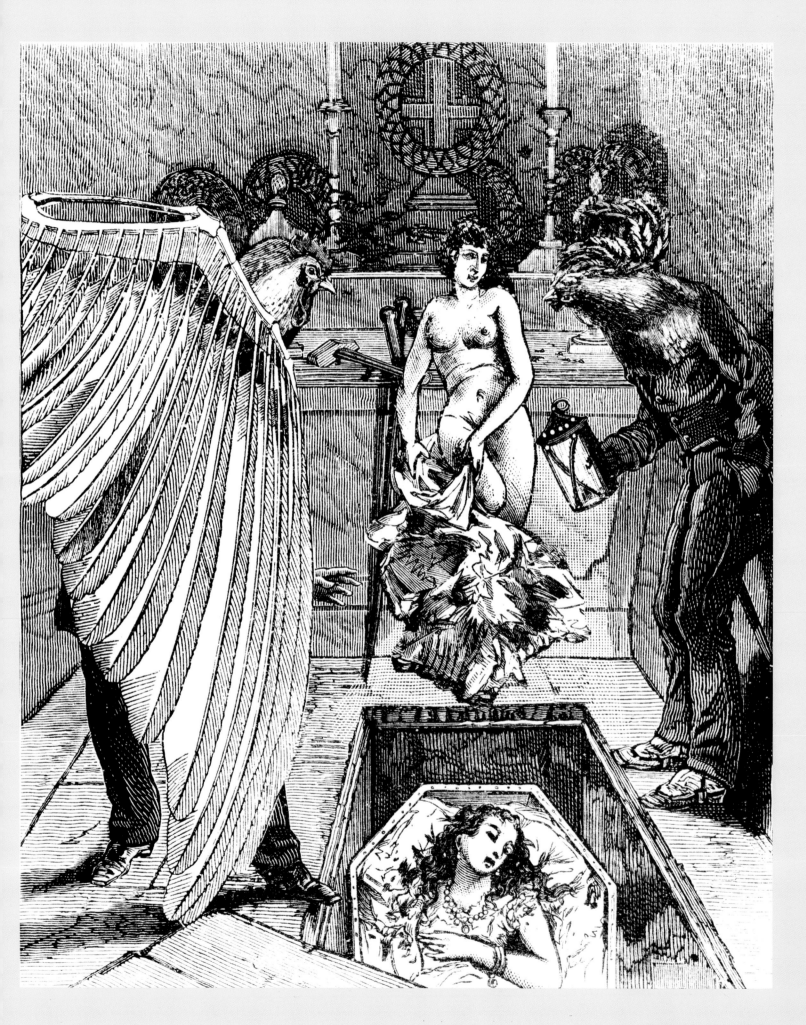

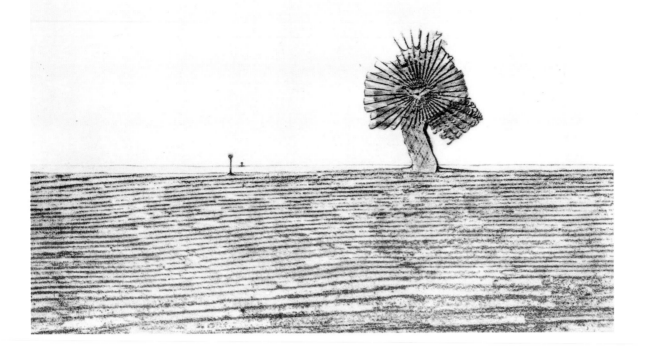

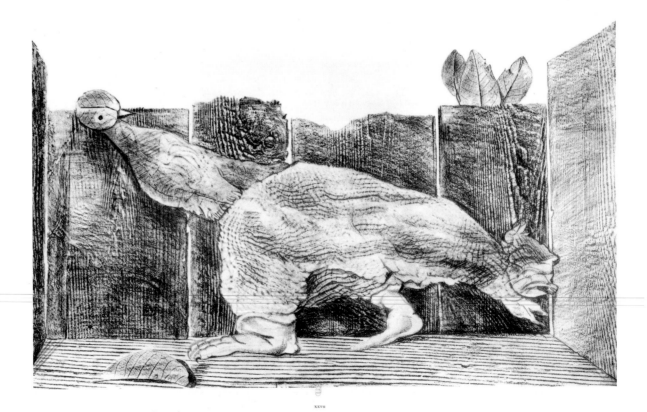

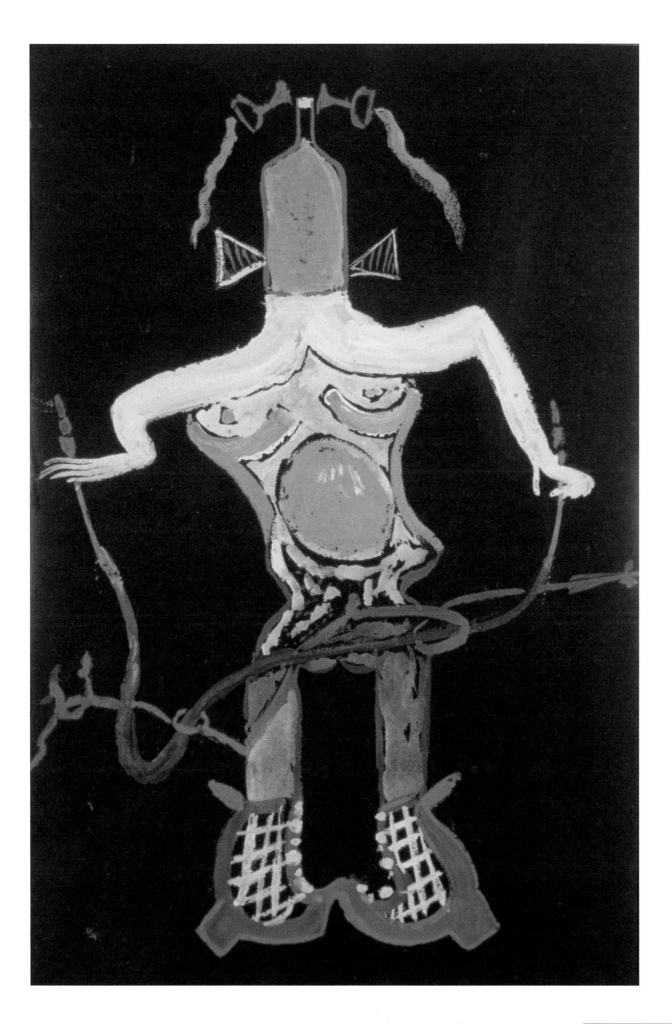

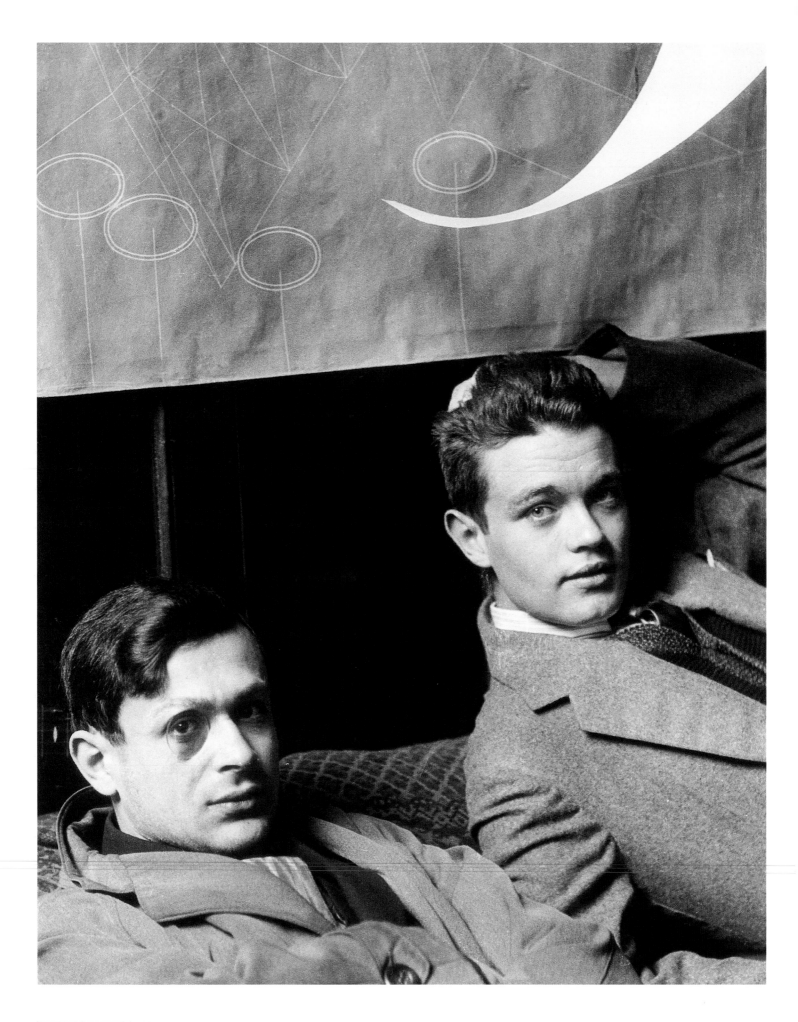

hand. Artaud, the director of the Centre de Recherches Surréalistes (Center for Surrealist Experimentation), would find in Balinese theater a source of inspiration for his "Théâtre de la Cruauté (Theater of Cruality)." Desnos was also fascinated by the Orient – all the Surrealists were – as N° 3 of their review demonstrates.

Nothing like a few public scandals to consolidate a group – thus the sabotage of the Banquet Saint-Pol Roux. The "magnificent" (Catholic) poet – much admired by the Surrealists for his dazzling rhetoric – was being honored at the Closerie des Lilas in July 1925. The Surrealists disliked some of the guests. Madame Rachilde having loudly asserted that "No Frenchwoman could marry a German," Breton stood up and solemnly informed the woman that she had just insulted his friend Max Ernst, present at the banquet. Tumult followed with cries of "Long live Germany!" Philippe Soupault, hanging from the chandelier, swept the entire table. Saint-Pol Roux whined in a corner. Fists were flying. The police arrived and kicked out everyone. Michel Leiris, leaning out the window screamed "Down with France!" The crowd outside dared him to come down. He came down, and had his face smashed in before being manhandled at the police station. Later, texts of this major writer and ethnologist would be found in schoolbooks…

The press unanimously condemned these Surrealist hoodlums. At the same time they published *Une Lettre Ouverte à Paul Claudel, Ambasadeur de France* (An Open Letter to Paul Claudel, French Ambassador) – in which one could find jewels such as: "We declare having discovered treason and all that in one way or another could endanger state security, which is finally more compatible with poetry than the sale of 'large quantities of lard' for the benefit of a nation of pigs and dogs…"

L'Action Française, a royalist newspaper of "*nationalisme intégral*" (militant nationalism), called for the imprisonment of the Surrealists – all the more so given that in a gloomy political context, Abd el-Krim in Morocco had started the "War of the Rif." War over and over again! The Surrealists' political conscience was awakened by this colonial affair, and they then rallied around *Clarté*. Old differences were forgotten and they joined the "comrades" of the French Communist Party. They published a manifesto *La Révolution Encore et Toujours* (The Revolution Now and Forever). The signatories declared that the idea of national identity was an "*concept bestial*" (brutal concept), that they were "in revolt against history," that they admired Asia and called for "the Mongols, to camp on our sites." They added: "We will never accept to put on the abject 'blue-horizon' cape – we are not utopians. We can only conceive of this revolution in social terms." Nearly ten years later, in 1934, Breton would note that this text, "ideologically rather confused," had nonetheless marked a considerable turning point. The Surrealists had let go of a certain anti-rationalist idealism, and tried to advance to "reasoning" and materialist phase. However, along with this political statement was a "*Lettre aux Voyantes*" (Letter to Clairvoyants) by Breton and a "*Nouvelle Lettre à Moi-même*" (New Letter to Myself), a dark, tortured work by Artaud. Later Artaud would publish (N° 8) "*Lettre à la Voyante*" (Letter to the Clairvoyant) – "*plus proche de moi que ma mère*" (closer to me than my own mother). The clairvoyance of women, in the mystical sense, was one of Surrealism's principal values. In defending this position, the groundwork was laid for what would later be called the two level theory – the simultaneous adherence to political discipline imposed by a political party and the personnel freedom for experimentation and creativity… For the moment, the Surrealists hoped to be able to act on both levels in spite of Naville's position, which demanded that a choice be made between subjective anarchy and dialectic materialism.
Aragon, Breton, Eluard, Péret and Unik joined the Communist Party. Breton found himself in the gas unit…

Love, the Tragic and the Sexual
Fortunately, Surrealism, as such, was in the course of transforming art, if not life itself, with works such as *Le Paysan de Paris* (The Peasant from Paris), by Aragon, *Capitale de la Douleur* (The Capital of Grief), by Eluard, *Nadja*, by Breton and the famous *Traité du Style* (Treatise on Style), by Aragon (Gallimard, 1928). Masson fabricated his first sand paintings. The Galerie Surréaliste opened in Paris. Soupault and Artaud were excluded because of their refusal to become committed

Man Ray
TRISTAN TZARA AND RENÉ CREVEL
About 1928, silver salt print.
Centre Pompidou-MNAM-CCI, Paris

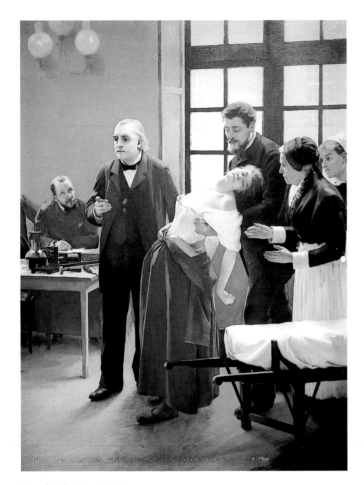

Pierre-André Brouillet
**A CLINICAL LESSON ON HYSTERIA
AT THE SALPÊTRIÈRE HOSPITAL
WITH DR JEAN-MARIE CHARCOT
(DETAIL)**
1887, oil on canvas.
Musée de l'Assistance publique, Paris

politically… Let's name some of the great poems that have survived the test of time: in *Capitale de la Douleur*, one can sense the suffering hidden beneath the celebration of love and woman:

> *"La Dame de Carreau" (The Queen of Diamonds)*
> *Tout jeune, j'ai ouvert mes bras à la pureté. Ce ne fut qu'un battement d'ailes au ciel de mon éternité, qu'un battement de cœur amoureux qui bat dans les poitrines conquises. Je ne pouvais plus tomber.*
> (As a young man, I opened my arms to purity. It was only a flutter of wings in the sky of my eternity, only the beating of a heart in love which beats in won-over bosoms. I could no longer fall.)

Shortly after in *L'amour, la Poésie* (1929), Eluard expanded his incantation of love to a cosmic dimension:

> *Je te l'ai dit pour les nuages*
> *Je te l'ai dit pour l'arbre de la mer*
> *Pour chaque vague pour les oiseaux dans les feuilles*
> *Pour les cailloux du bruit*
> *Pour les mains familières*
> *Pour l'œil qui devient visage ou paysage*
>
> (I told you in regard to the clouds
> I told you in regard to the tree of the sea
> For each wave, for the birds in the leaves
> For the pebbles of noise
> For the familiar hands
> For the eye that becomes face or landscape)

With Nadja, Breton wrote his only novel, which was in fact an essay. He had already published his autobiographical poem, "Tournesol" (Sunflower) in *Clair de Terre* (1923): "The lady traveler, crossing Les Halles at nightfall…" And here it's he who falls upon – Rue Lafayette, then Place Dauphine (which must surely be the sexual organ of Paris) – a mysterious woman, Nadja, of whom he asks himself on what inner abyss fell her slightest words. From the Hôtel des Grands Hommes, Place du Panthéon, where Breton stayed, to the statue of Etienne Dolet, which created for him "an unbearable uneasiness," Breton listens to Nadja, and makes the tragic enter the supernatural:

> "…I saw her fern-like eyes *open* one morning onto a world where the beating wings of immense hope could barely make out the other noises, which were the sounds of terror…"

In the meantime, polemics became enflamed with Artaud, who was to publish in 1929 *L'Art de la Mort* (The Art of Death), in which one could already sense the heartbreaking nuances that would distinguish him as the poet of physical misfortune as a category of the mind: "This flux, this nausea – it's here that begins the Fire. The fire of tongues. The fire woven into tresses of tongues, in the reflection of the earth that opens like a belly in labor, with entrails of honey and sugar."

Artaud had already been excluded from the group when he founded the Alfred Jarry Theatre, an extraordinary enterprise. He had responded to the manifesto *Au Grand Jour* (In Broad Daylight, 1927), that proposed social revolution in a rather severe pamphlet, *A la Grande Nuit, ou le Bluff Surréaliste* (To the Big Night, or the Surrealist Bluff). Thus, breaking-up. And in 1938, in the preface to *Théâtre et Son Double* (Theater and Its Double), he wrote this sentence, a declaration of his personnel vision of art and the world: "If there is still something infernal and veritably cursed in our times, it is the artistic lingering over form, instead of being like the victims of torture that are burned, who make the sign of the cross on their funeral pyres." (**O.C.**, Gallimard, vol. IV, p. 14). The Surrealists never really liked the theatre. The breaking-up with Artaud was consummated during the presentation of *The Dream Play* by Strindberg, on 7 June 1928.

La Révolution Surréaliste was doing brilliantly. The appearance of a defrocked priest lent a humorous note to N° 8. The priest wore his robe, garnered with a red carnation in order to show off with the hussies at the Dome. He ended up accusing Breton of being the devil's helper... In N° 11 (March 1928) the fiftieth anniversary of hysteria was celebrated (1878-1928), "the greatest poetic discovery of the end of the twentieth century," with the famous photos of Madeleine de Charcot, during a seizure... In addition, it dedicated nine full pages to "Experiments in sexuality," the fruit of the group's discussions. What is remarkable in this text is its aspect of being both libertarian and limited at the same time. For example, Breton stands up against male homosexuality, which is not very libertarian, yet he demonstrates a certain freedom in his answer to the question:

"What does Breton think about sodomy between men and women?"
"Only the best."
"Have you already indulged in it?"
"Of course."

Once again we can conclude that in love, bodily freedom is in fact, spiritual freedom. This quest for truth within the meanders of physical love culminates in N° 12 (December 1929) with the famous enquiry "What sort of hope do you place in love?" This number opens with the *Seconde Manifeste du Surréalisme*. A year earlier *Le Surréalisme et la Peinture* (Surrealism and Painting) was published. Let us examine the movement's relationship with visual arts.

Painting, Photography and Cinema
In the fourth issue of *La Révolution Surréaliste* Breton began the series of articles that would figure in the 1928 publication, *Le Surréalisme et la Peinture*. In the third issue (April 1925), Naville had denied the existence of Surrealist painting: if one barters technique in the name of pure spontaneity, how can one really paint? Co-director of the review at the time, Naville decided that "Everyone knows that there is no Surrealist painting. Obviously, neither random free-flowing sketches, nor dream reproductions nor pure products of the imagination can qualify." Breton wasn't the slightest bit worried about this problem; his articles set out to prove that Surrealist painting truly existed. As of the second page of the review he clearly stated his point of view: "It is impossible for me to look at a painting without seeing it as a window. The first thing I want to know is, " *What do you see through the window*?" It must look upon some "outrageous spectacle," something marvelous.
Picasso, (who participated in the 1925 Surrealist exhibition in the Galerie Pierre) and Braque were warmly congratulated, whereas the precursors of the expressionist and Dada movements, were completely ignored. Francis Picabia was cited for his "Perfect lack of unders-

Pablo Picasso
BATHER PLAYING BALL
30 August 1932, oil on canvas.
Private Collection.

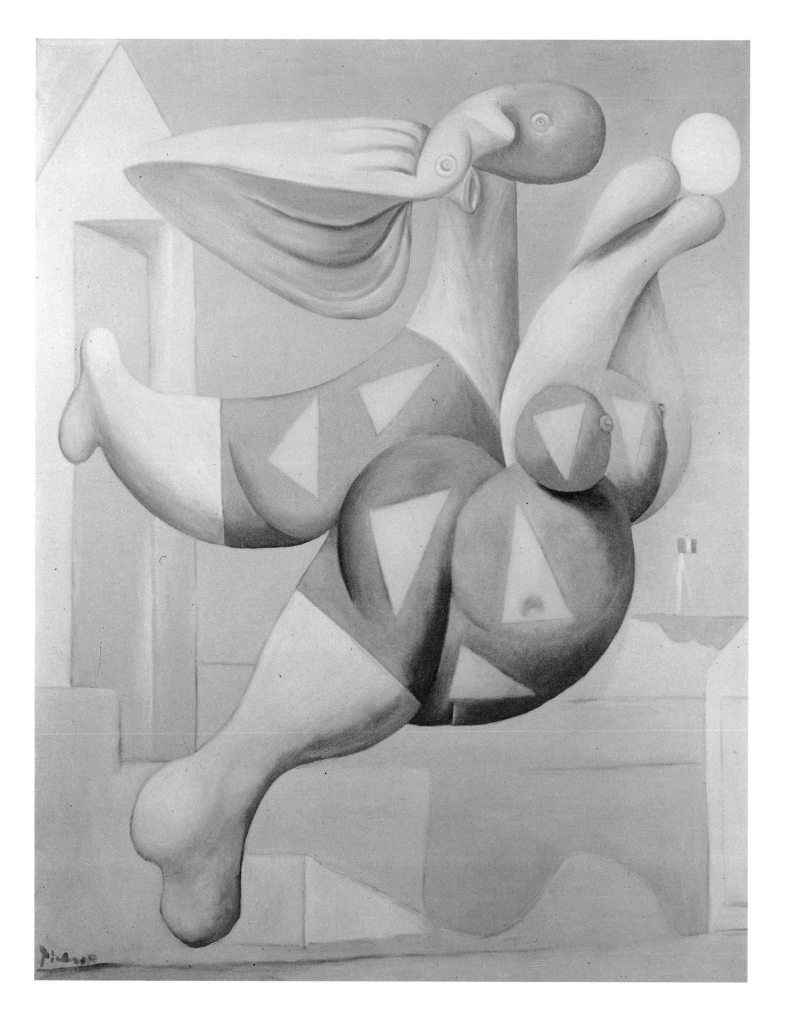

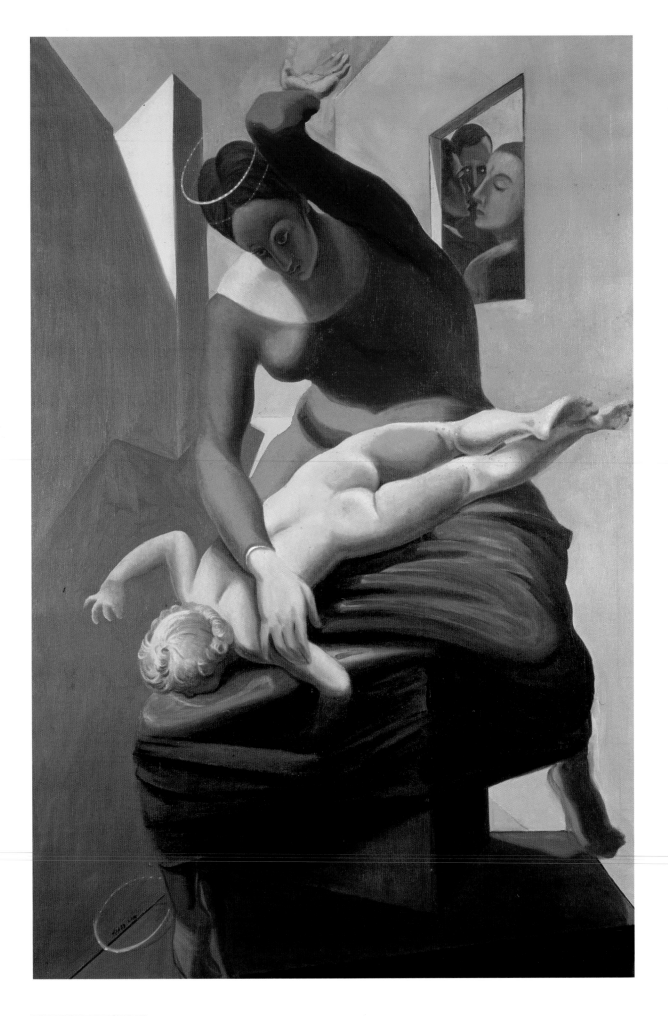

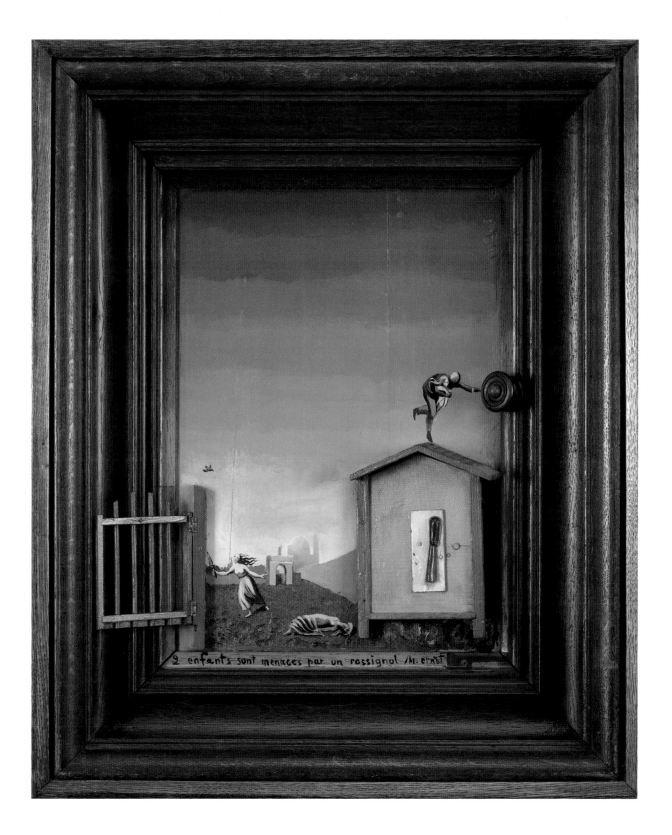

2 enfants sont menacés par un rossignol /M. ernst

Max Ernst
THE VIRGIN MARY PUNISHING
BABY BEFORE THREE WITNESSES :
A. B., P. E. AND THE AUTHOR
1928, oil on canvas.
Ludwig Museum, Cologne.

Max Ernst
DEUX ENFANTS SONT MENACÉS
PAR UN ROSSIGNOL
1924, huile sur bois.
The Museum of Modern Art, New York
Crédit : The Museum of Modern Art, New
York/Adagp, Paris 2001

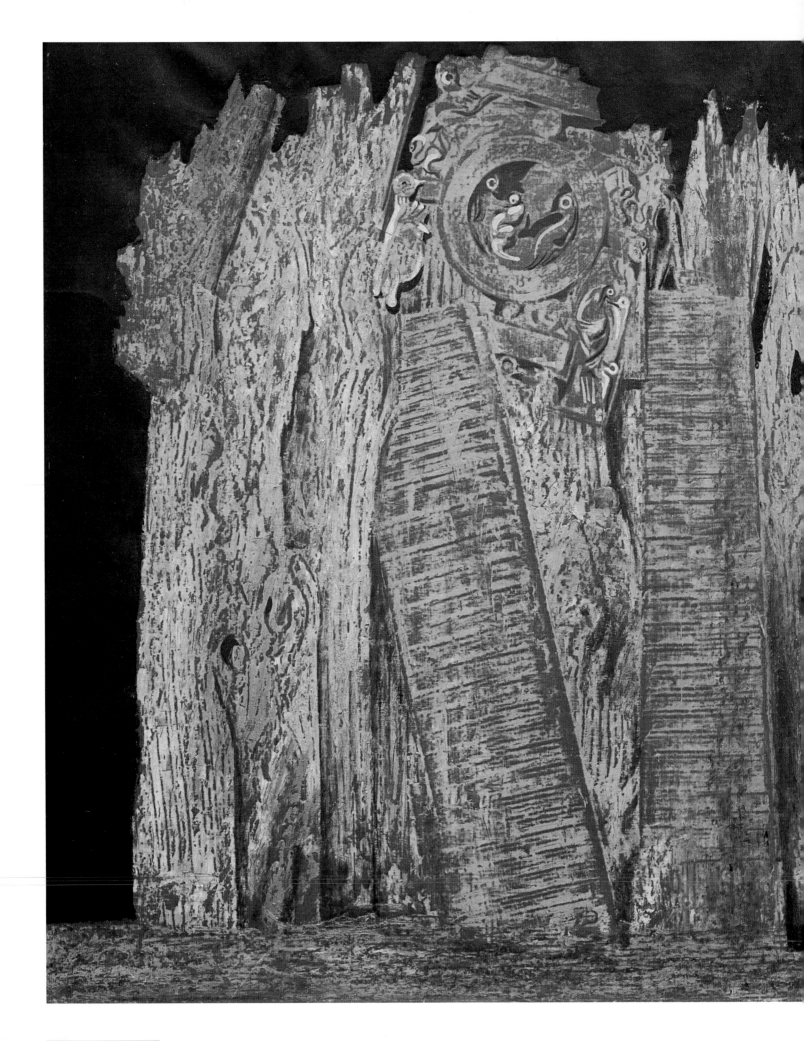

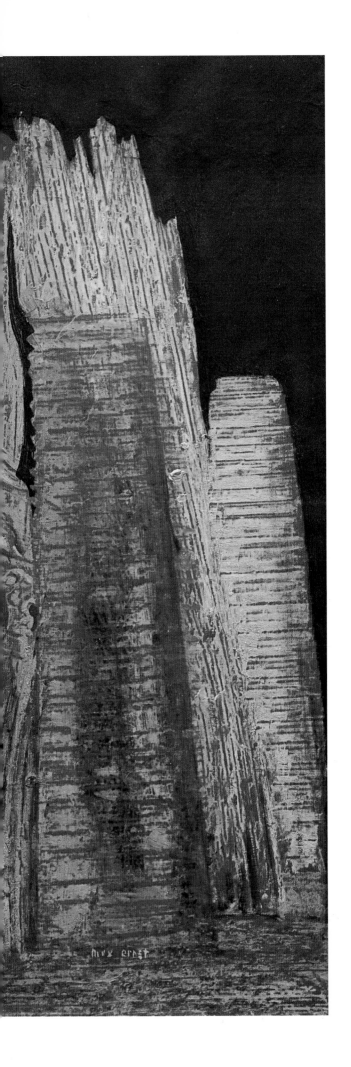

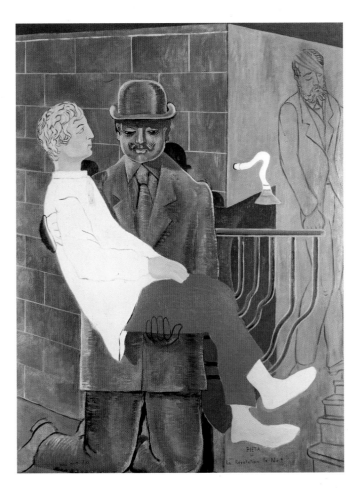

Max Ernst
**VISION PROVOKED BY THE
NOCTURNAL ASPECT OF THE PORTE
SAINT-DENIS**
1927, oil on canvas.
Private Collection.

Max Ernst
PIETÀ OR RÉVOLUTION AT NIGHT
1923, oil on canvas.
Penrose Collection, Londres

tanding of Surrealism." Breton brutally panned Georgio De Chirico's new style: "What greater folly, than this man's, lost among the besiegers of the very city that he built, that he made impregnable." A diatribe against the relationship between painting and money followed. The Surrealists were in fact avid collectors and, far from rich, didn't hesitate to sell their works, sometimes even paintings that had been gifts. There *was* a market for Surrealist painting; the paradox was in making use of it, while all the time playing the game, whether through opening galleries or by brokering paintings on a second-hand market.

Max Ernst
SURRÉALISM AND PAINTING
1942, oil on canvas.
Menil Collection, Houston

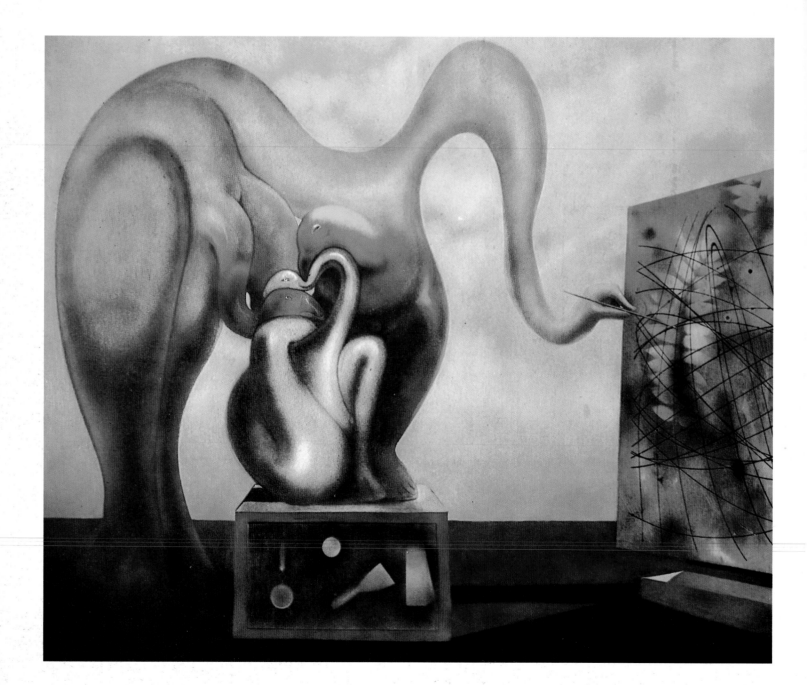

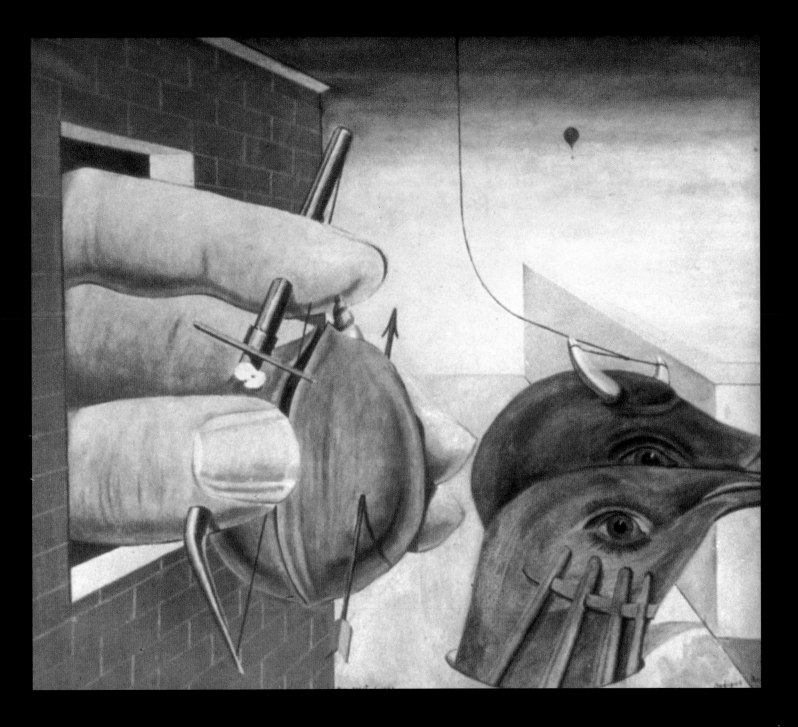

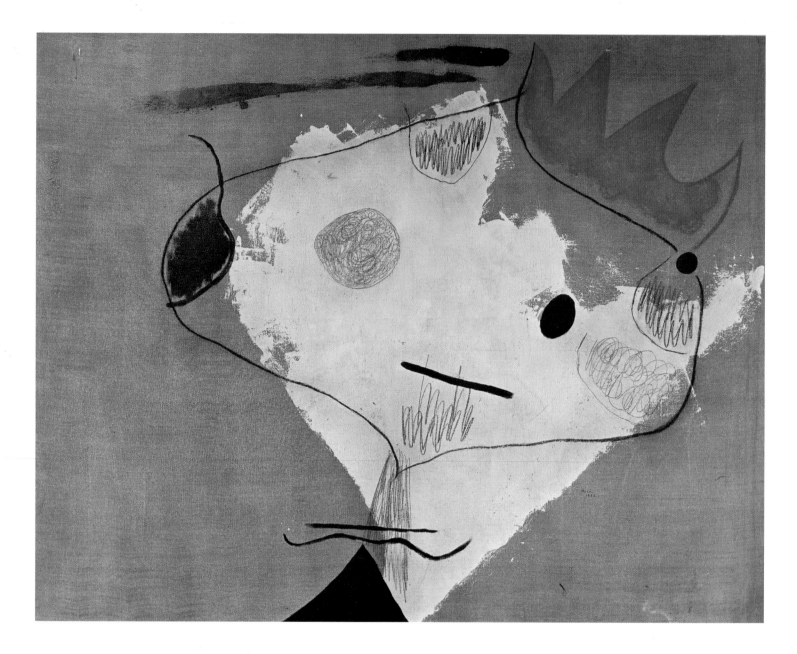

Joan Miró
LE FOU DU ROI
1926, oil on canvas.
André Lefèvre Collection, Paris

André Masson
AUTOMATIC DRAWING
1925-1926, inch on paper.
Centre Pompidou-MNAM-CCI, Paris

Max Ernst was one of the first to prove that Surrealist painting really existed. In his collages from 1918 and his paintings from 1921 – he was living in Saint Brice near Paris at the time – to his *raclages* (scrapings) from 1927, Breton often mentioned numerous works reproduced here. Nick-named the "the Superior of the birds," Ernst left the Surrealist movement in 1942 having painted a canvas called, appropriately, *Le Surréalisme et la Peinture.* The painting rightly takes up Naville's arguments. A viscous monster sitting on a case containing artist's

tools, draws automatic "abstract" forms with his tentacle-paint-brush. The forms bear no relation to his vague inner impulses. This symbolic self-portrait of the artist at work, as on a stage-set, presents a critical and pictorial awareness of the principles of Surrealist painting. It shows the image of a creative work, distorted by stylistics which are culturally founded and not "*sauvage*" (wild) in the sense Breton intended in the first sentence of his book: "*L'œil existe à l'état sauvage,*" (The eye exists in a wild state). Was this wishful thinking, more than a

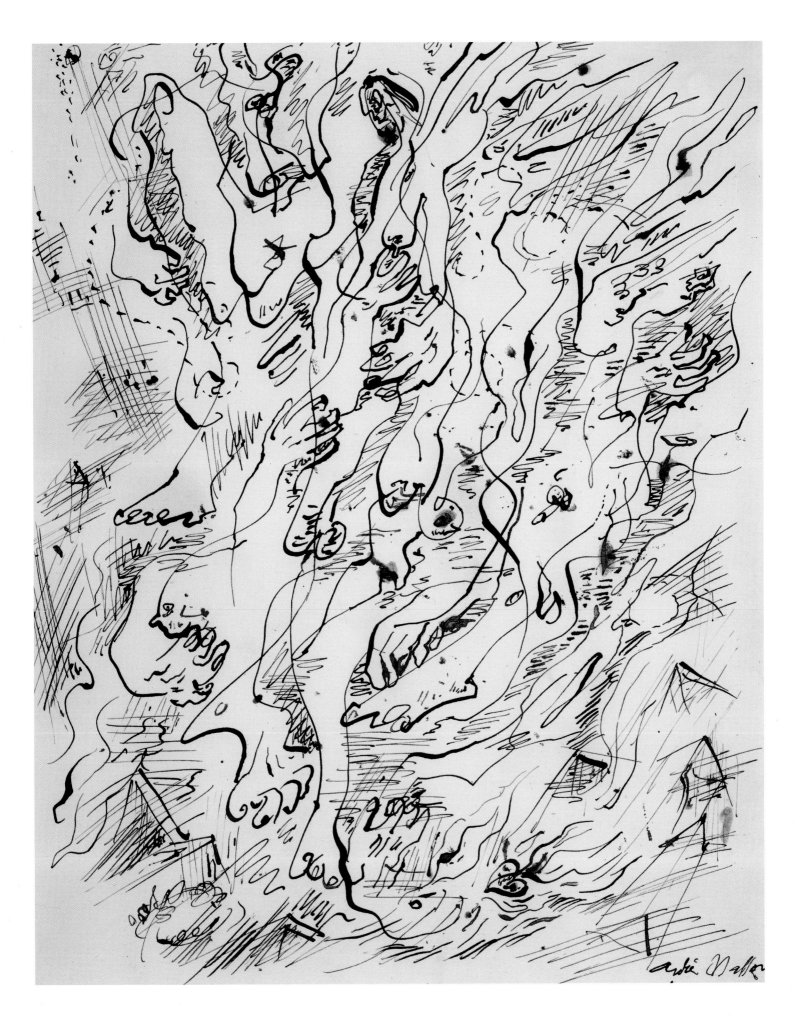

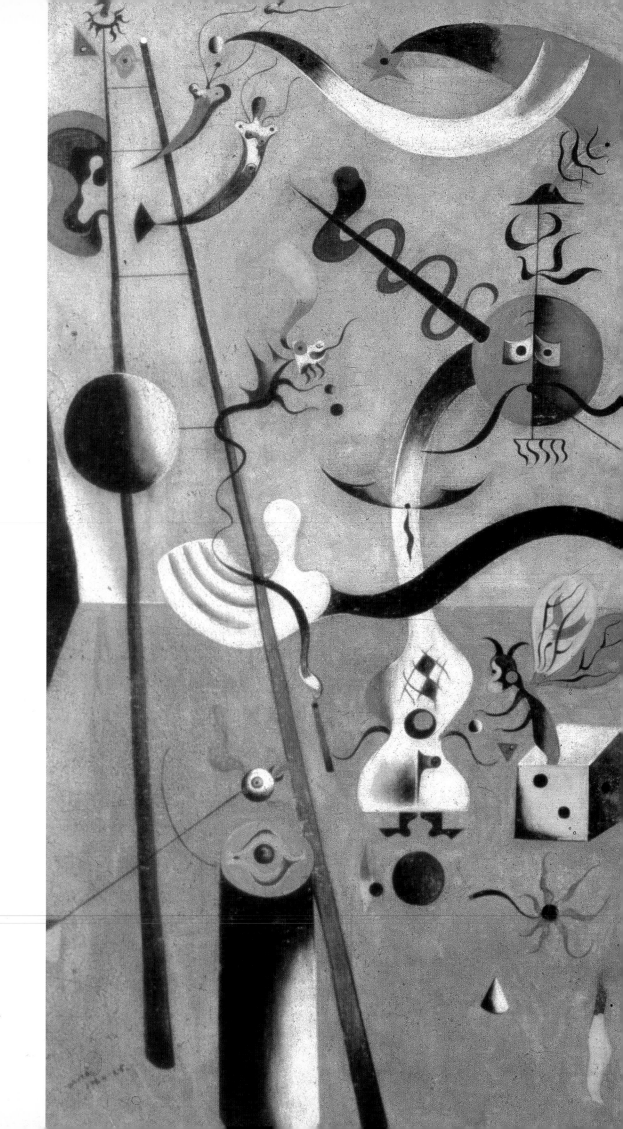

Joan Miro
HARLEQUIN'S CARNIVAL
1924-1925, oil on canvas.
Albright Knox Art Gallery, Buffalo, New York.

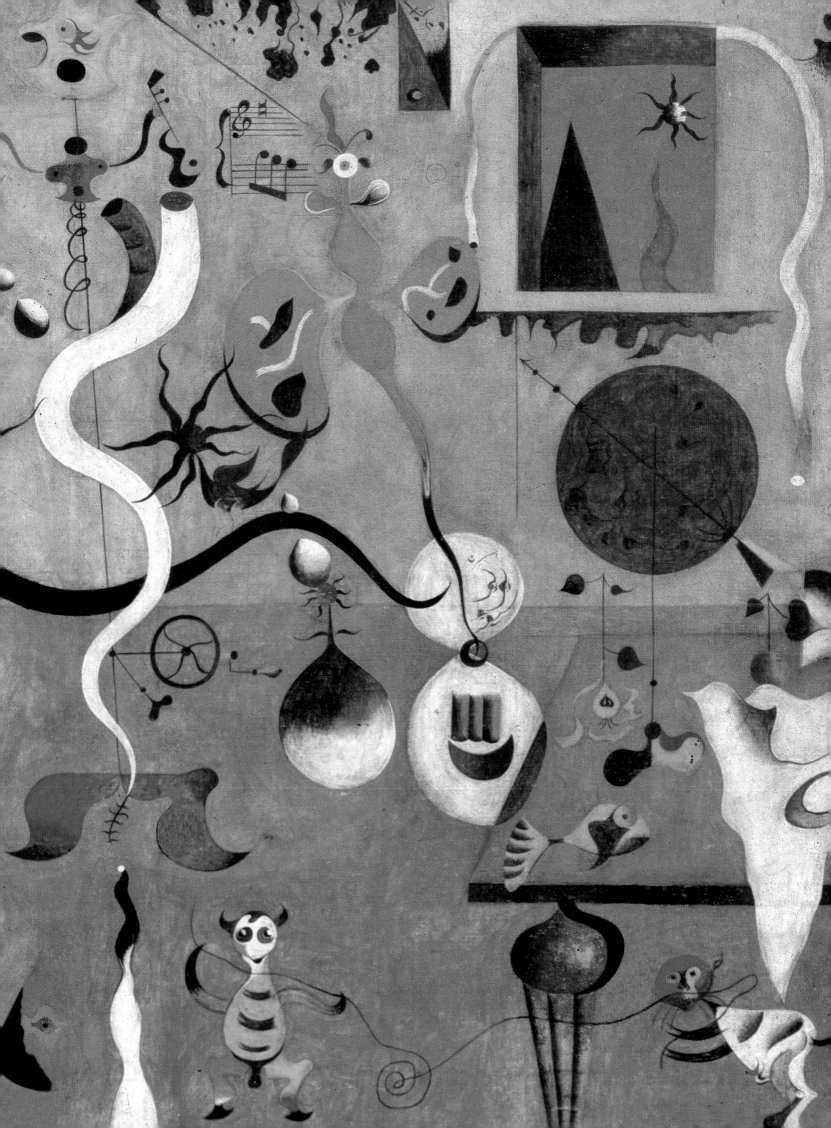

observation – no eye exists in a wild state. In spite of this lucid satire, if remains that Max Ernst's painting is Surrealism itself.

Joan Miró, a Catalan, moved to Paris in 1920. First of all he was a realist meticulous painter who took no part in Parisian polemics. However, he quickly shed his traditional style with *Terre Labourée* (Plowed Earth, 1923-1924) – the canvas becomes a space upon which objects are juxtaposed. The style is still angular, yet dreamlike. Miró lived on the Rue Blomet, and would soon become a part of the group. Under the influence of Paul Klee, his painting attained, according to Michel Leiris, "the understanding of emptiness." It was Miró who brought another Catalan to the group in 1929, Salvador Dali.

André Masson, another Rue Blomet artist, was trying to find a liquid "automatic" style in his drawing while his painting still tended towards Cubism. In 1927 he invented his sand pictures, perhaps as a way of reaching the same level of spontaneity that he had achieved in his drawings. Breton saw in Masson "the chemistry of intelligence" and would write in this regard in 1941: "The painter's hand is *tied* part and parcel to him…" In 1928 Masson illustrated Sade's *Justine*. More Surrealist than ever, he was nonetheless among those excluded from the *Second Manifesto of Surrealism…*

René Magritte's name appears only at the end of the 1965 edition of Breton's book. And yet this enigmatic Belgian figurative painter of the absurd was all the same a major figure in pictorial Surrealism. The emotional shock he felt upon seeing De Chirico's canvases led him to paint his first Surrealist work, *Le Jockey Perdu* (The Lost Jockey, 1925). He then produced one painting a day, and in 1928 met the Surrealists in Paris. Breton and Eluard encouraged him, but his first quarrel with Breton dates from 1929. There the Belgian Surrealists were often at loggerheads with the French ones. It seems to me that Magritte's thematic material can be reduced to five leitmotifs: the great cold open spaces, the night interior, woman gazed upon, and metamorphosis, as a search for a surreal coming out of the depths, enlightened by the laws of absurdity. Magritte refuted Psychoanalysis, but a painting such as *La Poitrine* (The Bosom – a pile of empty houses) appears to evoke his mother's suicide. She had thrown herself into the Sambre River when he was fourteen. His thought processes, deliberately directed toward an *outside model*, would bring a philosophy of "looking" to Surrealism that would contradict Breton's dogma for "little reality."

Yves Tanguy began to paint in 1924 after the scandal at the Banquet Saint-Pol Roux drew him to the Surrealists. He quickly found his niche in this world that would remain his own until his death in America in 1955. Breton spoke of the village Ys, hidden away along the Brittany coast, whatever – once the painter had plunged into his world of milky luminosity, he would never leave it.

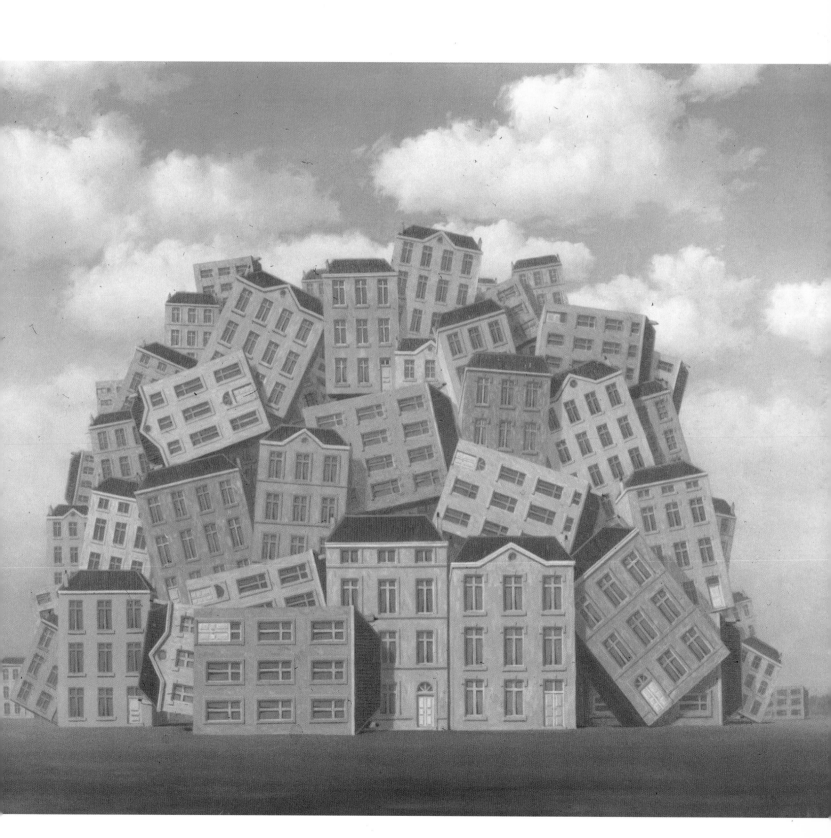

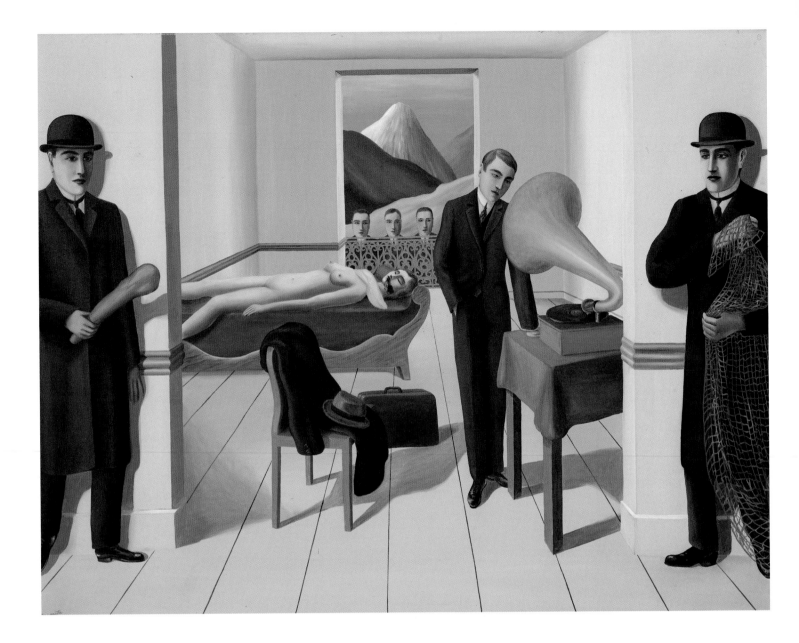

René Magritte
THE MENACED ASSASSIN
1926, oil on canvas.
The Museum of Modern Art, Kay Sage
Tanguy Fund, New York.

Yves Tanguy
A GREAT PAINTING WHICH
REPRESENTS A LANDSCAPE
1927, oil on canvas.
Private Collection.

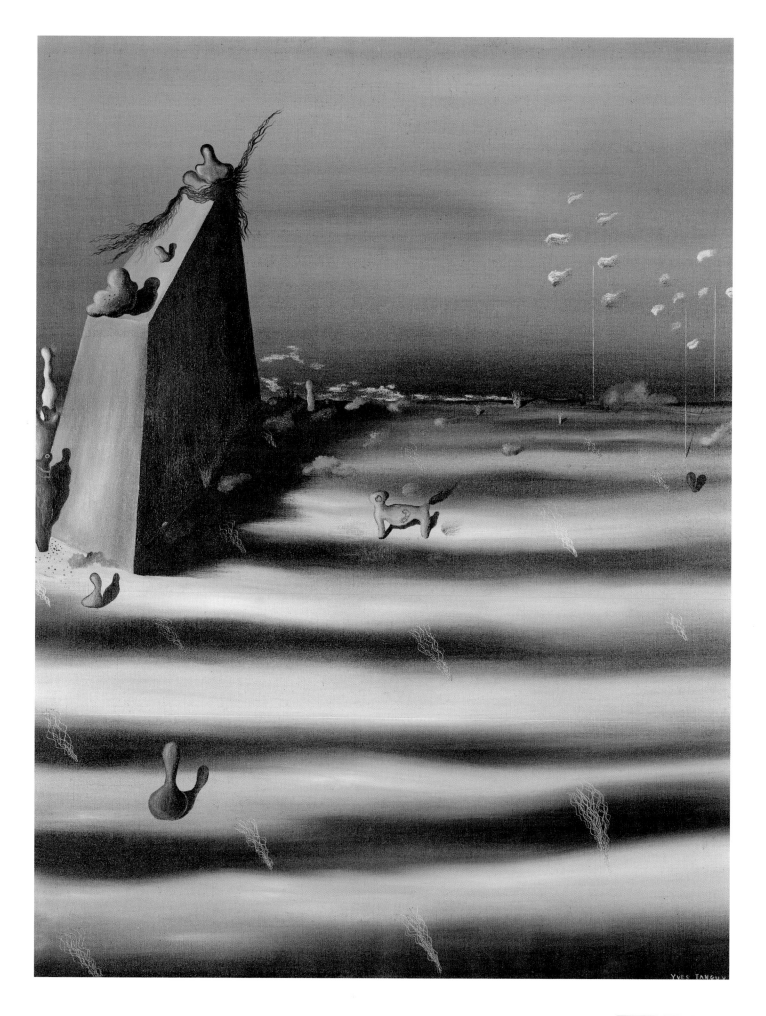

Hans Arp
DANCER
1925, oil on cut-out wood
glued on woods
Centre Pompidou-MNAM-CCI, Paris

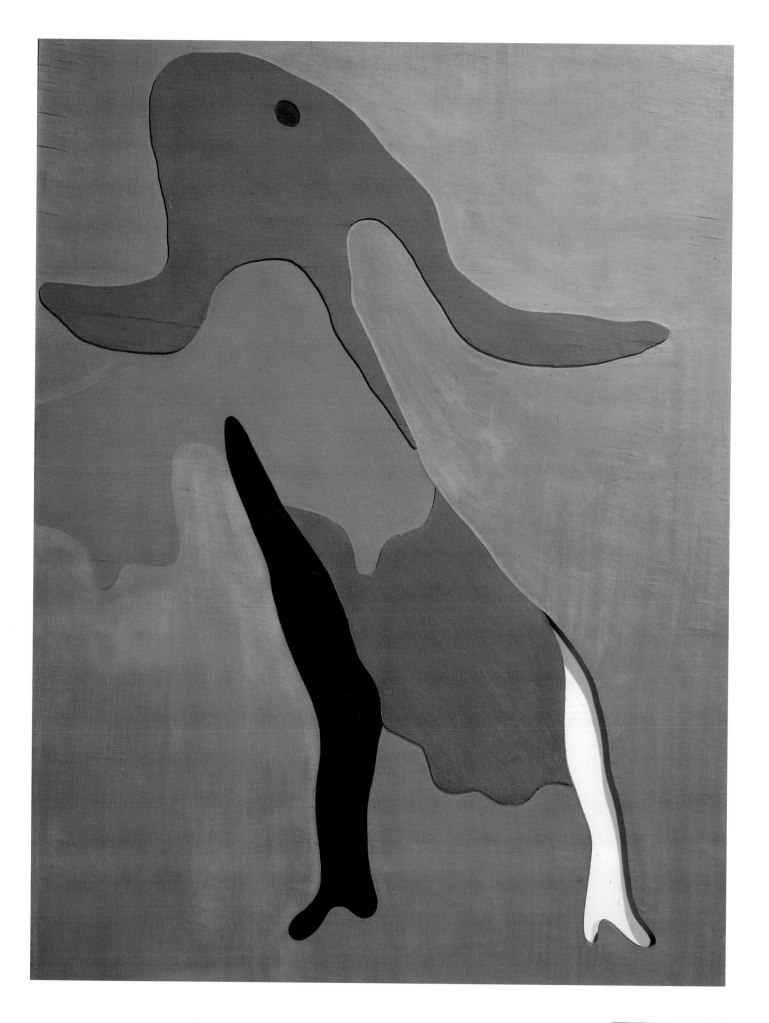

The Surréalists
around Germaine Berton
Illustration published in
La Révolution surréaliste
n°1, 1st December
1924.

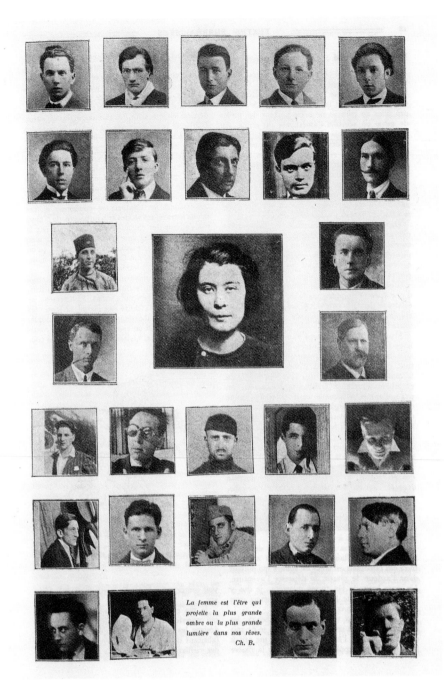

Man Ray
and René Magritte
**I DON'T SEE THE
[WOMAN] HIDDEN
IN THE FOREST**
Illustration
by René Magritte and
photographed
by Man Ray, Published in
La Révolution surréaliste
n° 12, December 1929.
From top left :
Alexandre, Aragon,
Breton, Bunuel,
Caupenne, Éluard,
Fourrier, Magritte,
Valentin, Thirion, Tanguy,
Sadoul, Nouqué,
Coemans, Ernst and
Dali.
Bibliothèque littéraire Jacques
Doucet, Paris.

Breton had great esteem for Hans Arp's sculpture in spite of the fact that certain critics called him an abstract artist. A friend of Kandinsky's, linked with the Expressionist review *Der Sturm* in Berlin, 1913, Arp met Ernst in Cologne and came to Paris after the war. It was in 1915 that he met Sophie Tauber, whom he would marry in 1922. Entangled in the uprising at the Cabaret Voltaire, he delved into a Dadaist form of spontaneity, inventing the shapes that would define his work throughout his life. With a pure, refined style, he presented works that were always linked to something lifelike.

Breton's notes on Man Ray, Victor Brauner, Oscar Dominguez, Salvador Dali, Wolfgang Paalen, Frida Kahlo, Diego Rivera, Wilfredo Lam, Maria Toyen, etc. (which were often prefaces for exhibitions) only referred to their works sometime after 1934. We will come back to this. Painters contributed greatly to the development of Surrealism in the world, for the very simple reason that painting goes beyond language barriers.

The same could be said about photography, having already been in the limelight with the Dadaists' photomontages. Let us mention two famous Surrealist photos

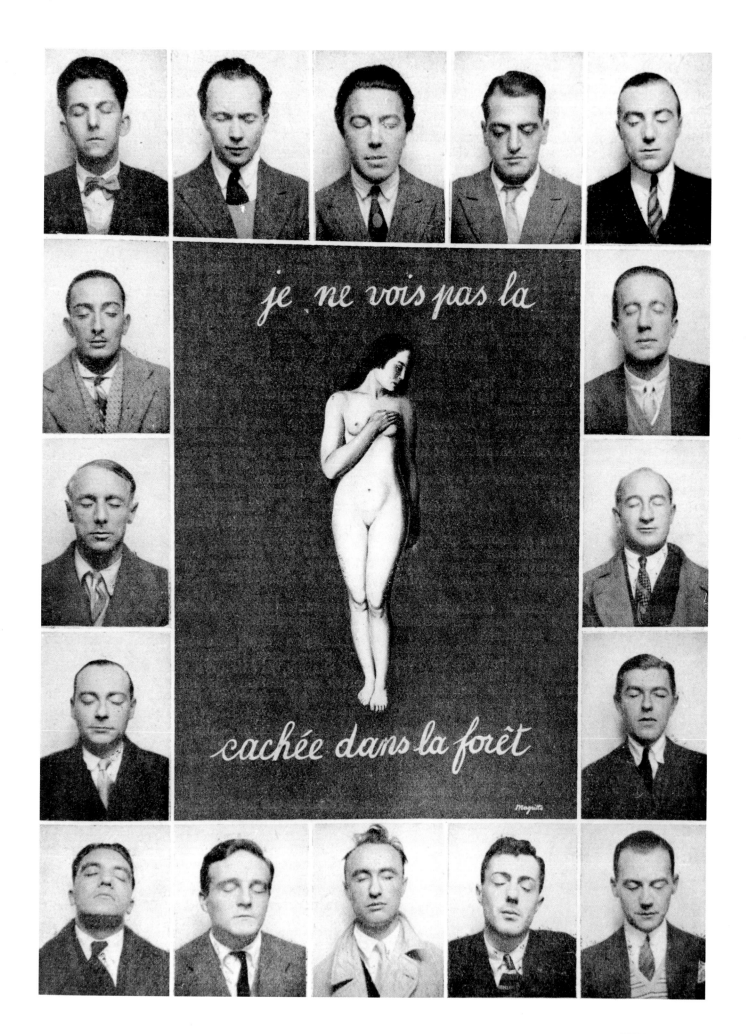

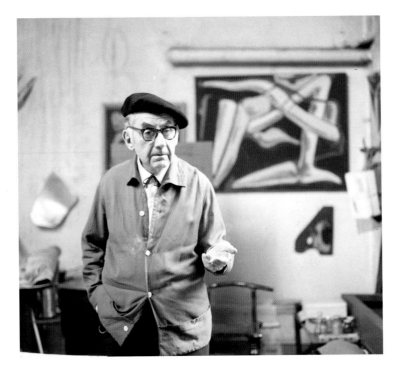

Man Ray in his studio
in Paris in 1960.

Man Ray
Jacqueline Goddard as a Nun
Solarisation about 1934,
gelatin silver print.
Centre Pompidou-MNAM-CCI, Paris

Below
Raoul Ubac
Fossil of the Bourse, Paris
1937, photo relief
Published in *Le Minotaure*
n° 12-13, October 1938.

of members of the group which appeared in *La Revolution Surréaliste*. In N° 1, the face of Germaine, who had just assassinated a militant royalist; and in N° 12, there is a female nude by Magritte with the inscription: "*Je ne vois pas la femme nue cachée dans la forêt* (I don't see the nude woman hidden in the forest). All the Surrealists closed their eyes in perfect contentment.

There were two tendencies emerging in Surrealist photography:
1/ The *insolite* or outrageous on the street or in everyday life. Bellmer's nudes bordering on the indecent (1946) (cf. Catalogue: *Explosante Fixe, Photographie Surréaliste*, p. 101), numerous portraits, unsettling sometimes in the case of Man Ray.

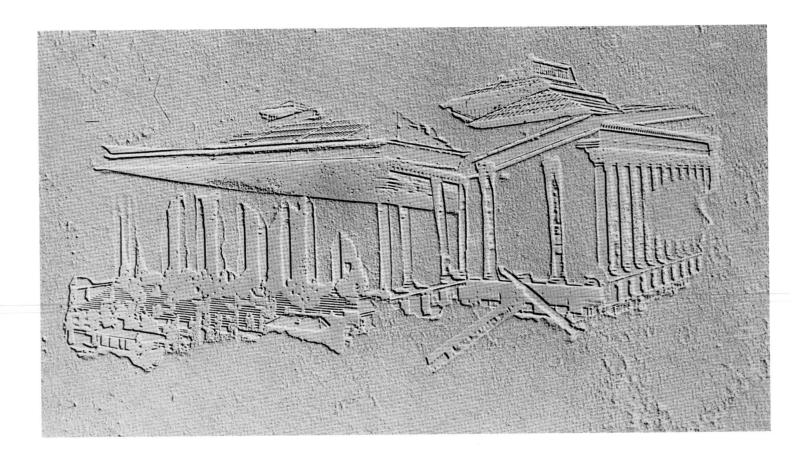

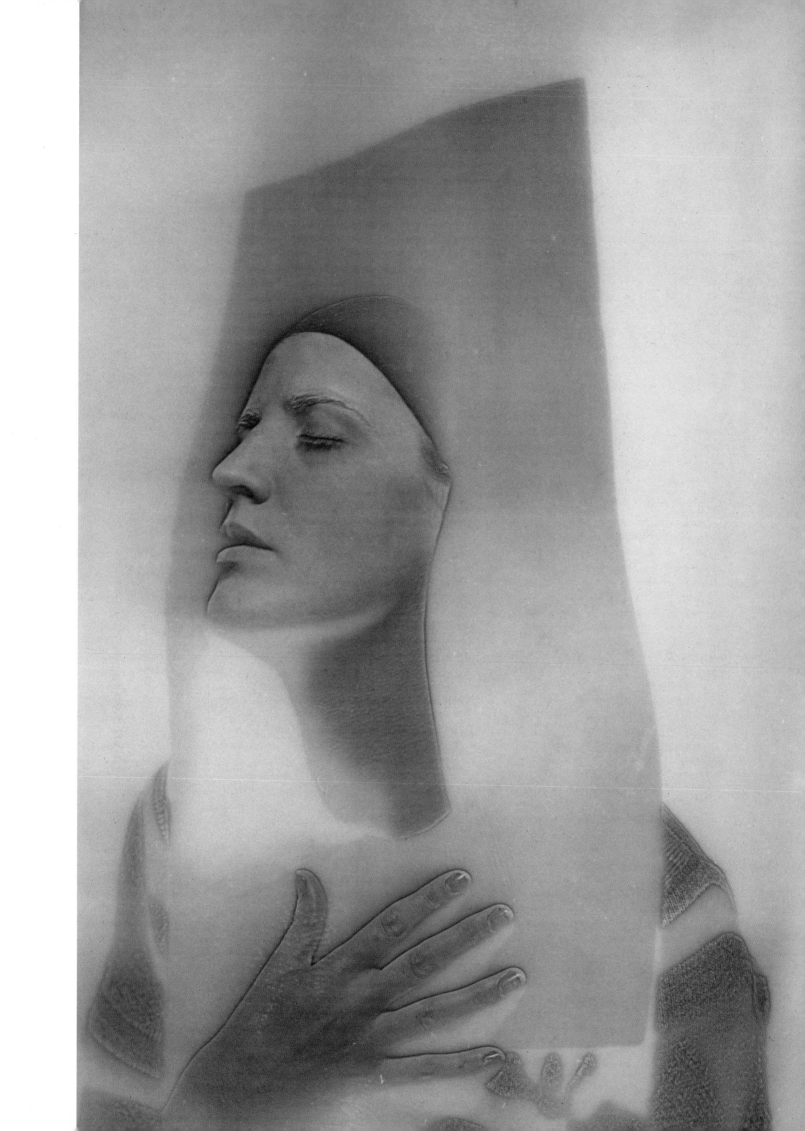

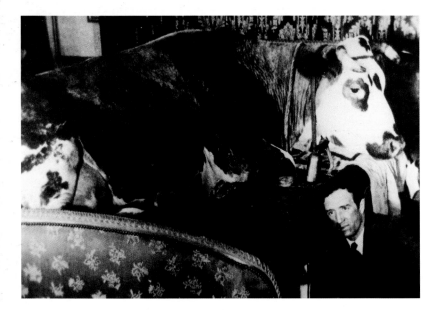

DELICIOUS FIELDS
1ST RAYOGRAM
1922, gelatin silver print.
Centre Pompidou-MNAM-CCI, Paris

Scene from *L'Âge d'or*
by Luis Buñuel, 1931.

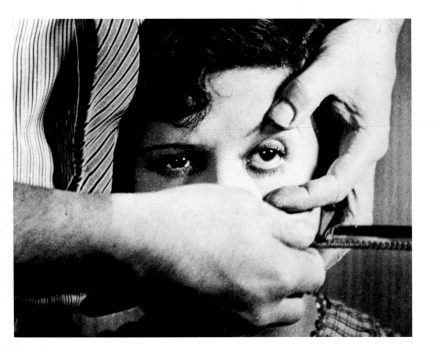

Scene from *Chien andalou*
de Luis Buñuel, 1929.

2/ Experimentation with direct work on the film as matter, having nothing to do with the lens of the camera. This led to numerous technical inventions including *solarisation*, (Man Ray) and *photo-relief* (*Les Fossiles* [Fossils], by Raoul Ubac)…

There were a considerable number of Surrealist photographers in the world even if we only refer to an article by Edouard Jaguer in the *Dictionnaire Général du Surréalisme et de Ses Environs* (General Dictionary of

Surrealism and Its Surroundings, P.U.F., 1982). Its abundant documentation was read the world over.

As for cinema, it was the contrary – the Surrealists were spectators more than creators. Darkened movie theaters were sanctuaries of the outrageous for wandering city dwellers. They went to working-class movie houses where Feuillade and the first Charlie Chaplin films were shown. They were particularly fond of *Les Mystères de New York* and *Les Vampires.* Of course they applauded Sergei Eisensteins's *Potemkin*, and their taste even evolved to the point of enjoying Alain Renais's *Marienbad* and *Les Abysses* by Nico Papatakis. For them, Murnau's expressionism (*Nosferatu, le Vampire*), was the nightmare of sinister Surrealism. In fact, they were totally enamored with actresses such as Marlène Dietrich, Louise Brooks and later, Ava Gardner. In *L'Amour Fou* Breton spoke of the film *Peter Ibbetson*, where every night in his dreams, the hero finds the same woman. *Anicet* and *Le Paysan de Paris* by Aragon, *Poisson Soluble* (Soluble Fish) by Breton, *La Liberté ou l'Amour* (Liberty or Love) by Desnos – all contain allusions to cinema.

The Surrealists' film creativity? But all cinema, as Ado Kyrou would write, "is of Surrealist essence…" And yet there were two films that created an uproar because of their extreme Surrealism, *Un Chien Andalou* (An Andalusian Dog) and *L'Age d'Or* (The Golden Age) by Salvador Dali and Luis Buñuel. In the first, it is impossible to explain the plot, but certain images remain, such as a razor blade cutting an eye, or the palm of a hand teeming with ants… After the scandal over *Chien Andalou*, Buñuel began *L'Age d'Or*, financed by Charles and Marie-Laure de Noailles. The film came out in 1931. A kind of a dream, which first of all should make you dream, the film defies all logic, even symbolic. It sets an example of an absolute and gratuitous freedom of the imagination. Presented in Paris at Studio 28 in 1930, it greatly annoyed the Croix de Feu (extreme right-wing

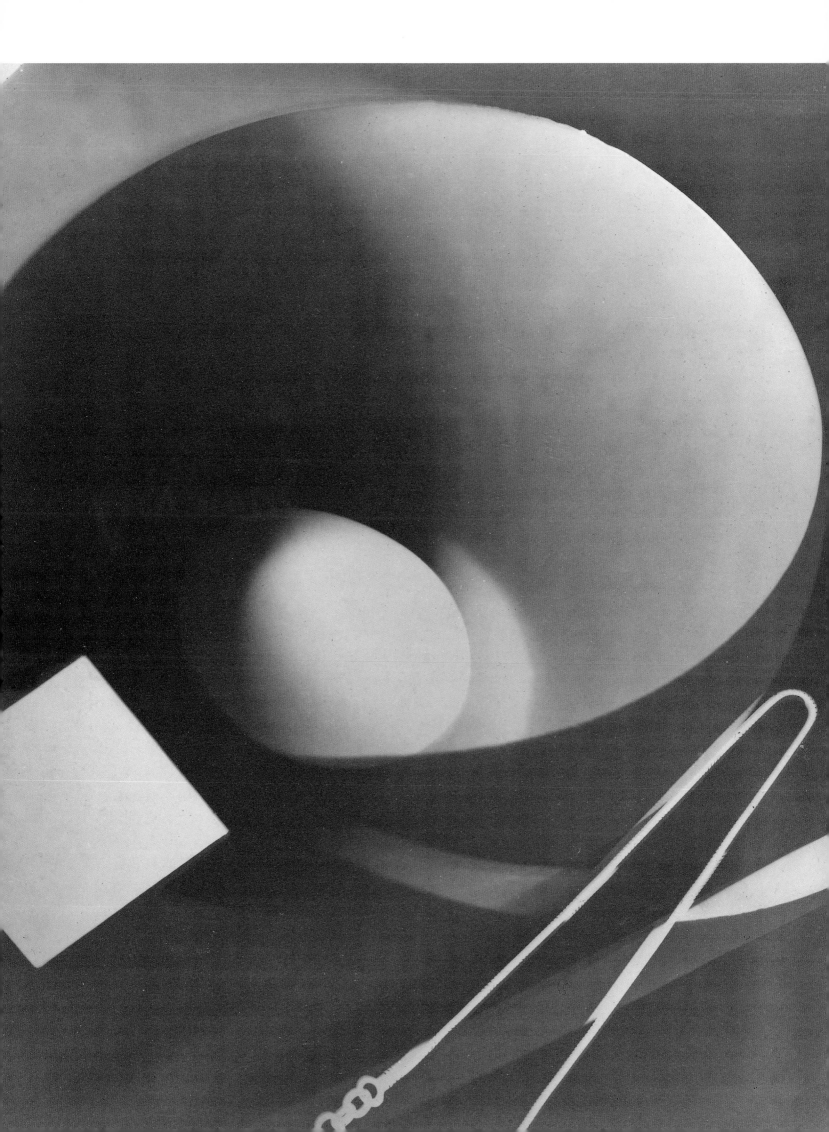

political movement). The locale was trashed and paintings by Miró, Ernst, Dali, shown in the lobby, were slashed. The film was banned for disturbing the peace, and would only be rehabilitated (by a *visa de sortie)* in 1981! (It was recently shown, with sound, on Arte, the Franco-Germain television channel.)

Far from any political involvement, but violently anti-Christian, these films were an affirmation of Surrealism in its fundamental purity. The *Second Manifesto of Surrealism* would do as much in terms of pure doctrine.

The Second Manifesto of Surrealism

The group had swelled with a certain number of new arrivals, more concerned with their own future than with the fate of Surrealist thought. The most loyal among them regretted the exclusion of Artaud, Soupault and Vitrac – old comrades. Breton's very tone had become that of a politician. The November 1926 meeting's order of the day included the "Examination of individual opinions: (a) Are all these opinions justifiable in a revolutionary context...? (b) To what extent are they tolerable...?" A call for self explanation was broadly announced, and resulted in a meeting on 11 May 1929, concerning the fate of Trotsky, recent exiled by Stalin.

A painful occasion. Letters were read from those who defended purely Surrealist individual acts – Masson, Miró, Ernst among others (the painters gathered strength in their studios). Then, putting aside Trotsky's fate, Breton, backed by Raymond Queneau, asked that the assembly "vote on the degree of qualification of each member, moral or otherwise." Members of the group and the review, *Le Grand Jeu,* were accused of the worst – collusion with journalists. Faced with this inquisition court, a number of people started to leave in order not to get sick. The meeting was a failure.

The purists took stock. Breton was depressed by these incidents as well as by his divorce in 1929. He wrote the *Second Surrealist Manifesto,* which was first published in the review, then in 1930 as a volume by the publisher Kra.

The latter contained additions taking into account the responses to Breton by those who had been excluded, *Un Cadavre* (A corpse).

Reading this work today, one can understand why in the 1946 edition *(Sagittaire)* Breton attempted to excuse himself for the "regrettable nervous traces" that it contained. Nevertheless, this *Manifesto* cannot be reduced to the violent upheavals caused through purification of the group. There are certain large key ideas:

1. "In spite of the specific efforts of each of those who claimed to or claims to represent Surrealism, one must ultimately admit that, more than anything else, Surrealism attempted to provoke, from the intellectual and moral point of view, a *crise de conscience* (crisis of conscience), of the most general and serious kind...a question of testing by any and all means, and of demonstrating at any price, the meretricious nature of the old antinomies hypocritically intended to prevent any unusual ferment on the part of man... The horror of death, the simplistic theatrical portrayal of the hereafter... The insurmountable silver wall splattered with brains... These all too gripping images of human catastrophe are, perhaps, only images. Everything would lead one to believe that there is a certain point within the mind where life and death, the real and the imagined, past and future, the communicable and the incommunicable, the high and the low, cease to be perceived as contradictions. So, it was in vain that one sought any other motivating force in Surrealist activity than the hope of determining this point."

2. This attitude needs no antecedents. Except for Lautréamont there are none. But personal attacks began against Antonin Artaud, Jean Carrive, Georges Limbour, André Masson and Roger Vitrac. "A policeman, a few rascals, two or three lightweight pimps, several unhinged madmen, an idiot, to whose number no one would mind our adding a few sensible, stable, and upright souls who could be termed energumens – is this not the making of an amusing, innocuous team, a faithful replica of life, a team of men paid piecework, winning on points? *MERDE* (shit)."

3. Breton defends his predilection for dialectic materialism over the old materialism. It is a question of applying the dialectic to the realm of conscience, not only to economics. One must "separate the good from the bad, the false from the sincere" by means of "control of ideas," according to the Surrealists.
(The idea of synthesis, inherent in dialectics and the search for the "sublime moment" seem to have been forgotten here.) Such is the revolutionary attitude.

4. Hence Surrealism's self criticism, which refused rational logic without revealing the logic of dreams. One must combine Freud and Marx in order to study the complex phenomenon of inspiration. "It is for the innocence and the anger of a few men yet to come that one should free Surrealism of all that is not really alive, and restore it to its initial goals, even if the price to pay is a good ransacking..." In fact individual failures take nothing away from the movement in general, proof being the Romantic movement. Although Breton rejected Desnos, Duchamp, and Picabia, he found Tzara.

5. Then came ideas that the future would develop. Surrealism through "the alchemy of the word" by Rimbaud, is quite close to the alchemy of the fourteenth century and that of Nicolas Flamel. There was no fear of malediction, and Breton's assimilating different aspects of the occult – even to the extent of applying astrological predictions in a note – that "orders the real and profound eclipse of Surrealism."

6. One could easily imagine that this text is over. No. Breton came back attacking Georges Bataille, whom he reproaches for having a taste for corruption. He rejected him on the grounds of physical and moral correction because "the Surrealist operation can only succeed in a state of moral asepsis that few men want to hear about."
The text concludes by a desperate call. "The key to love that the poet claimed to have found, he too, he should look well: he's found it. It is up to him to rise above the passing feeling of living dangerously, and dying. He should employ against all prohibition the ultimate weapon, the avenging arm of the *idea,* to fight against the bestiality of all the people and things and that one day, vanquished – but vanquished only *if the world is world* – he will welcome the firing of his sad rifles like a wave of salvation."

It was in the appendix to the *Second Manifesto* that the publication of a new review was announced which would be the follow-up to *La Révolution Surréaliste.* The title was explicit: *Le Surréalisme au Service de la Révolution* (Surrealism at the Service of the Revolution), abbreviated as *SASDLR* (1930). Participants included Maxime Alexandre, Aragon, Joe Bousquet, Luis Buñuel, René Char, René Crevel, Salvador Dali, Paul Eluard, Max Ernst, Marcel Fourrier, Camille Goemans, Paul Nougé, Benjamin Péret, Francis Ponge, Marco Ristitch, Georges Sadoul, Yves Tanguy, André Thirion, Tristan Tzara, Albert Valentin.

1930-1940
Expansion

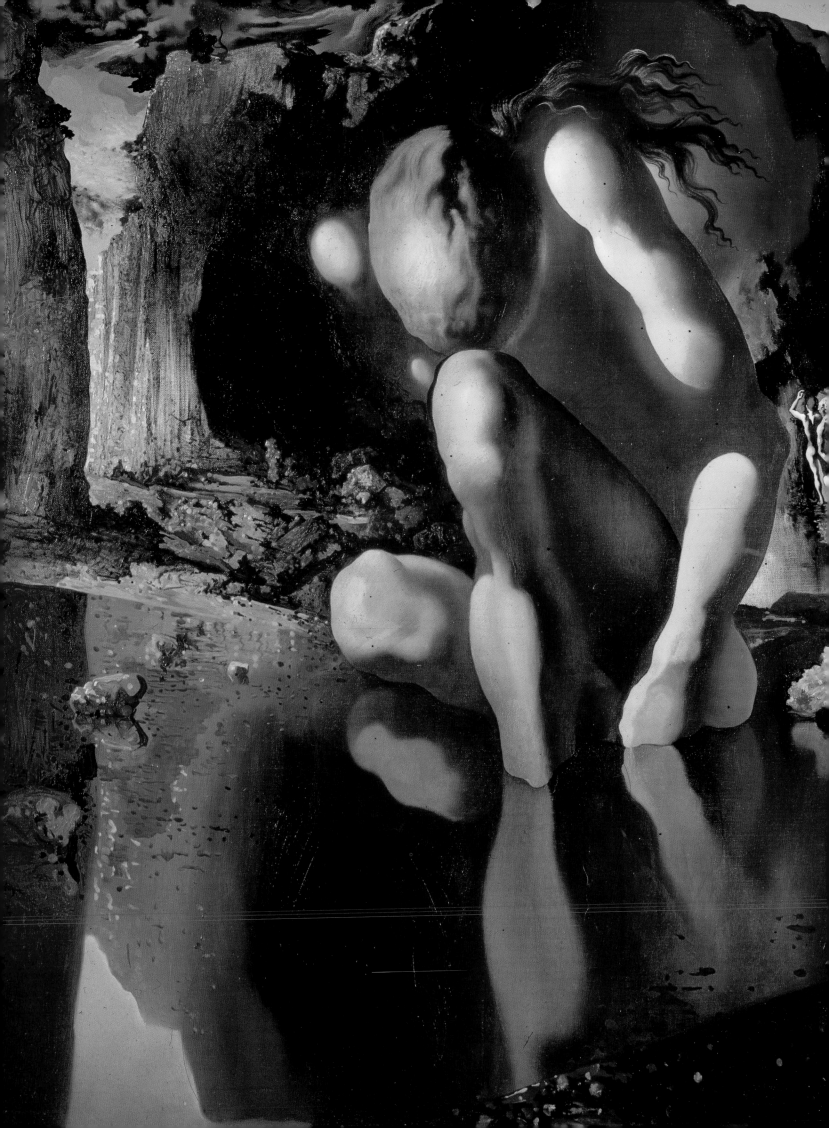

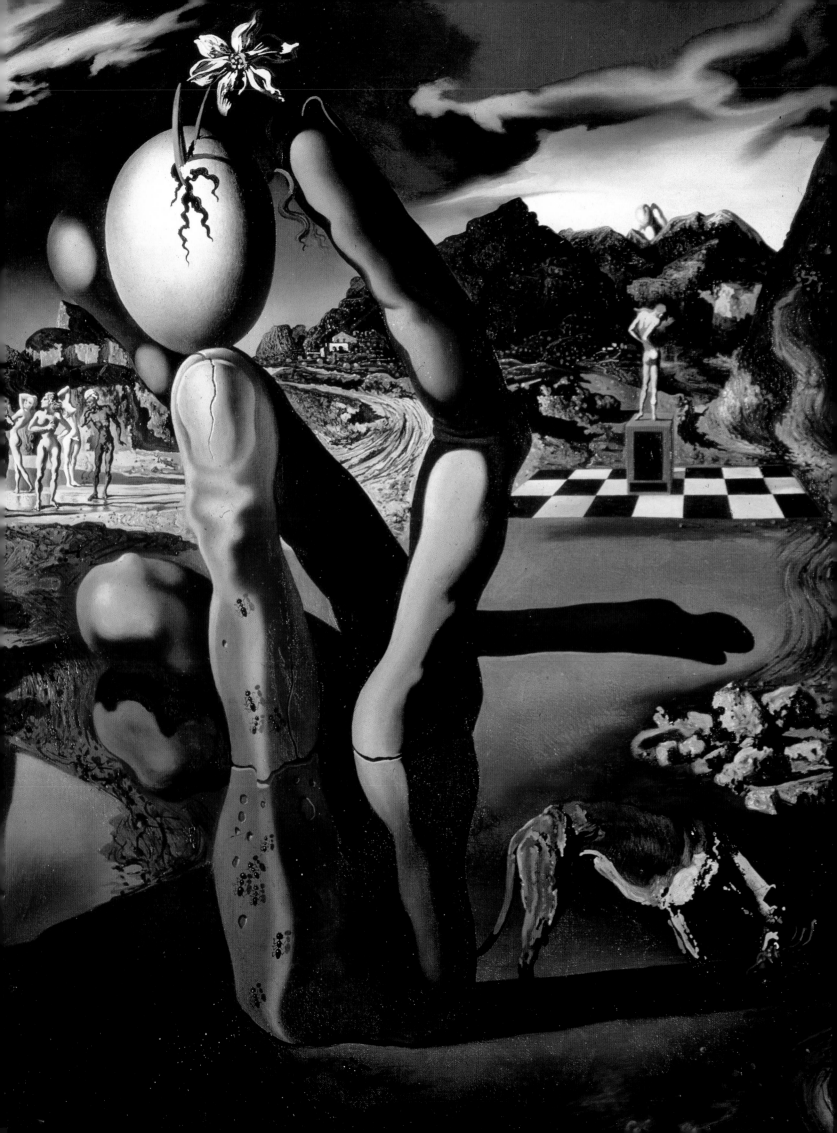

The creation of *SASDLR*, the title of which is already a political statement, could be misleading. In fact after the upheaval of the *Second Manifesto*, Surrealism returned to one of its sources, mental pathology. "Dream states," and "automatism" had not really shed any light on the real nature of creative inspiration.

Back to Mental Pathology

In the second issue of this magazine, we find a review of Freud's book on *Le Mot de l'Esprit dans ses Rapports avec l'Inconscient*, one of Breton's important works, "Mental Health in the Light of Surrealism," where the author attacks the psychiatrists'"misuse of power" and establishes what would later be called, anti-psychiatry. Two major events marked this return to original sources:
1. The publication of Breton and Eluard's *L'Immaculée Conception* (Immaculate Conception), late in 1930, a masterpiece of Surrealistic research, going far beyond esthetic and political concerns.
2. The development of "Salvador Dali's paranoid-criticism."
Published by Les Editions Surréalistes, *L'Immaculée Conception* is an account of an experiment where the authors plunged into their own unconscious through "forms of possession" mental debility, manic behavior, general paralysis, interpretive delirium and precocious dementia. These "simulations," preceded by an allusion to the immaculate conception of the Virgin Mary, lead to a resurgence of "anti-religion," and talk of inter-uterine life (under the influence of Rank), of birth, of life and death – followed by a prolongation, where the concept of "ediations" intervenes, for example, force-of-habit, surprise, and love. The end of the book is a collection of aphorisms, where one can see, according to Hegel's dialectic, the synthesis of the two preceding movements. *Thesis*: a plunge into psychic obscurity; *antithesis*: the negation of obscurity in favor of reflection; *synthesis*: poetry seen as an ethic of clairvoyance. This is the moralist's style, imposing maxims like the book's last two lines:

Frappe à la porte, crie: Entrez, et n'entre pas.
Tu n'as rien à faire avant de mourir.
Knock on the door, scream:
Enter, and don't come in.
You have nothing to do before dying.

Take the beginning of this simulation, which refers to the most visionary syndrome of all: *Essai de Simulation de la Paralysie Générale* (Attempt at Simulating General Paralysis).

Ma grande adorée belle comme tout sur la terre et dans les plus belles étoiles de la terre que j'adore ma grande femme adorée par toutes les puissances des étoiles belle avec la beauté des milliards de reines qui parent la terre l'adoration que j'ai pour ta beauté me met à genoux pour te supplier de penser à moi je me mets à tes genoux j'adore ta beauté pense à moi toi ma beauté adorable ma grande beauté que j'adore je roule les diamants dans la mousse plus haute que les forêts dont tes cheveux les plus hauts pensent à moi – ne m'oublie pas ma petite femme sur mes genoux à l'occasion du coin du feu sur la sable en émeraude – regarde-toi dans ma main qui me sert à me baser sur tout au monde pour que tu me reconnaisses pour ce que je suis ma femme brune-blonde ma belle et ma bête pense à moi dans les paradis la tête dans mes mains.

My cherished one, beautiful as everything on earth and in the most beautiful stars on earth that I adore my great cherished woman adored by all the powers of the stars beautiful with the beauty of billions of queens who adorn the earth the adoration that I feel for your beauty brings me down on my knees to beg you to think of me I put myself at your feet I adore your beauty think of me you my adorable beauty my great beauty whom I adore I rub diamonds in moss higher than the forests of which your highest hair thinks of me – don't forget me my little woman sometimes on my knees around the hearth on emerald sand – look at yourself in my hand that allows

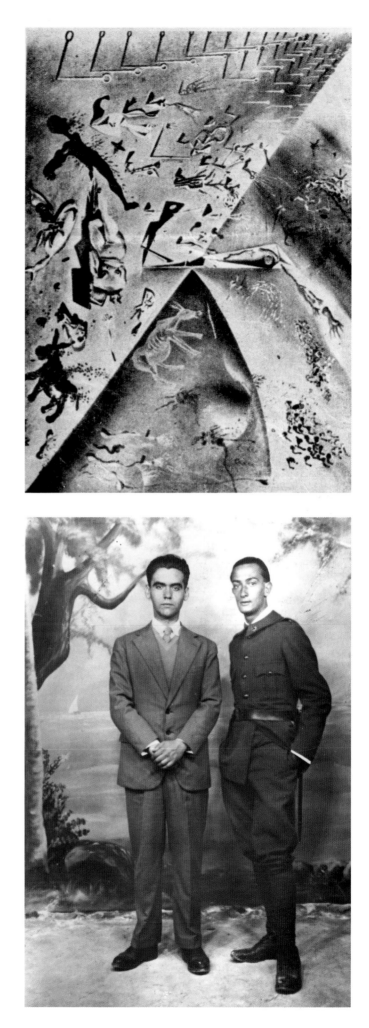

Salvador Dali
HONEY IS SWEETER THAN BLOOD
1927, oil on canvas.
Private Collection.

Salvador Dali and Federico Garcia
Lorca in Figueras in 1927.
R. Descharnes Collection.

me to base my judgement on everything in the world so that you can recognize me for what I am my brunette-blond my beauty and my beast think of me in paradise my head in my hands.

We should add the end of the *Essai de Simulation du Délire d'Interprêtation* (Attempt at Simulating Interpretive Delirium), because we shall be very much dealing with paranoia in the years to come.

> *Vous avouerez que vos lits-cages, et vos barreaux tor-dus, et vos planchers mordues, et vos muscades, et vos épouvantails à la dernière mode, et vos fils télégra-phiques, et vos voyages en compartiment de pigeon, et le socle d'agneaux de vos statues de proie, et vos courses de haies faites au crépuscule de rouges-gorges qui s'envolent... Ne comptez plus sur moi pour vous faire oublier que vos fantômes ont la tournure des paradisiers.*
>
> *Au commencement était le chant. Tout le monde aux fenêtres! On ne voit plus, d'un bord à l'autre, que léda. Mes ailes tourbillonnantes sont les portes par lesquelles elle entre dans le cou du cygne, sur la gran-de place déserte qui est le cœur de l'oiseau du nuit.*

You have to admit that your bed-cages, and your twisted prison bars, and your **bitten** floor boards, and your **conjurer's balls**, and your stylish fans and your telegraph wires, and your travels in **pigeon** cages, the pedestal of sheep for your statues of prey, and your obstacle courses of hedges made in the dusk of robins who fly away... Count no longer on me to make you forget that your ghosts resemble birds of paradise.

In the beginning was song. To your windows everyone! From one end to the other all we can see is Leda. My fluttering wings are the doors through which she enters into the neck of the swan, on the great deserted square that is the heart of the bird of the night.

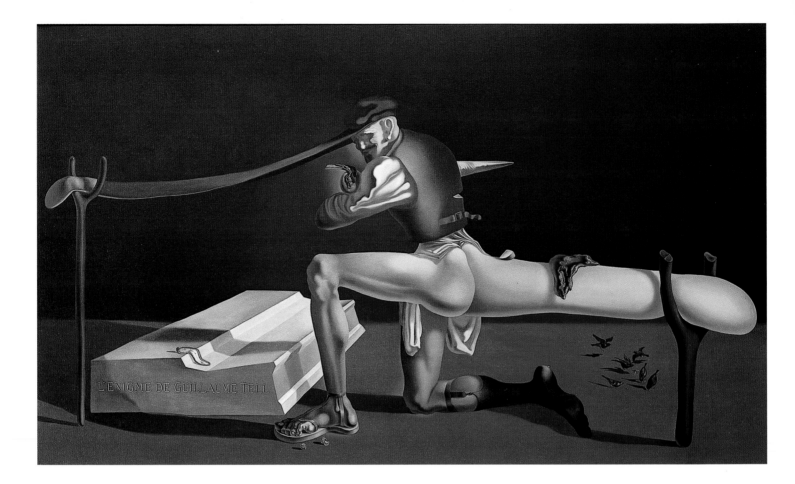

Salvador Dali
THE ENIGMA OF WILLIAM TELL
1933, oil on canvas.
Moderna Museet, Stockholm.

Salvador Dali
**IMPÉRIAL MONUMENT
TO THE CHILD-WOMAN, GALA (UTOPIAN FANTASY)**
1929, oil on canvas.
Centro de Arte Reina Sofia, Madrid.

In 1899, the well-known psychiatrist Kraepelin had defined interpretive delirium (paranoia) as "the insidious development, dependant on internal causes and following a constant evolution, of a system of long-lasting and impossible-to-eradicate delirium, that takes over without affecting one's clarity and order in thought, will and action." Most often it's question of the famous persecution complexes and delusions of grandeur that the patient doesn't want to let go of.

In his medical thesis *De la Psychose Paranoïaque dans Ses Rapports avec la Personnalité* (Le François, publisher, 1932) Jacques Lacan studied the case of a young woman, Aimée, who became paranoid during her pregnancy. The woman believed both that the Prince of Wales was her lover and that a mob was persecuting her, wanting to harm her child. Finally, she stabbed an actress, and wound up in prison. Lacan published a detailed account of this case, and in an annex, published Aimée's storybook writings. He diagnosed a "curable self

punishment psychosis," based on the single fact that once in prison, Aimée seemed freed of her delirium – the real punishment erased the imaginery one… In fact Aimée returned to the mental hospital several months later, and Lacan's conclusions – based on this one case study – were nevertheless validated by the Surrealists who read this thesis with passion.

In 1932 the translation of an important work by Freud on paranoia appeared in Paris, in which Lacan was credited with "bringing a lateral contribution to Surrealism." Lacan published two articles in *Minotaure* in 1933: "Paranoid Forms of Experience" and "Paranoid Criminal Motivations," using the example of the Papin sisters. But it was Dali who first brought the notion of paranoia into the group, as well-noted by José Pierre (Catalogue Dali, Centre Pompidou, vol. II, p.138).

Jacques Lacan spoke of paranoia after reading "*L'Ane Pourri*" by Dali in *SASDLR*, N°1, July 1930. It was in *La Femme Visible* (The Visible Woman, Editions

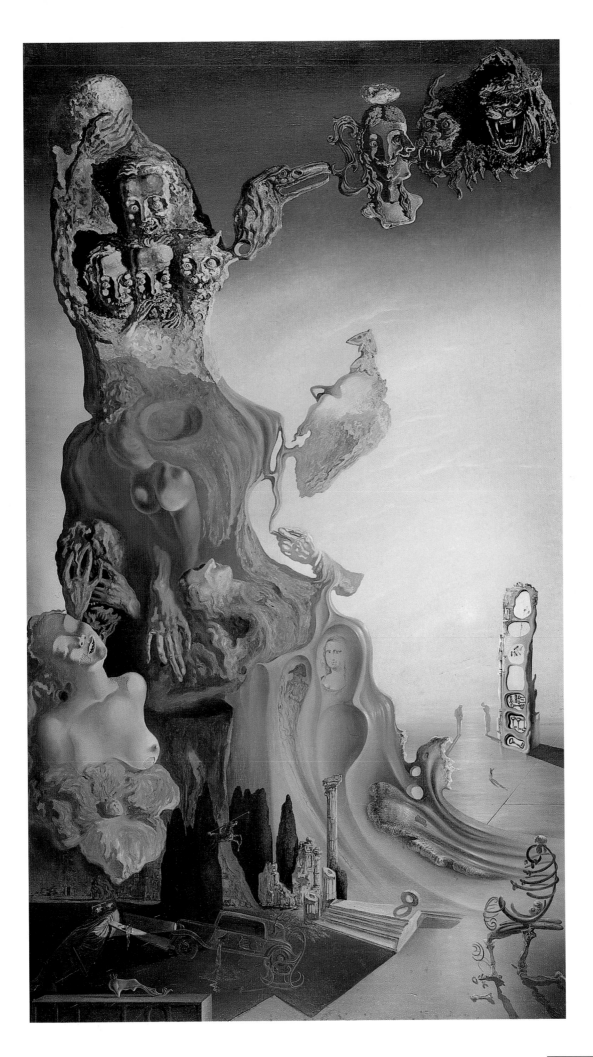

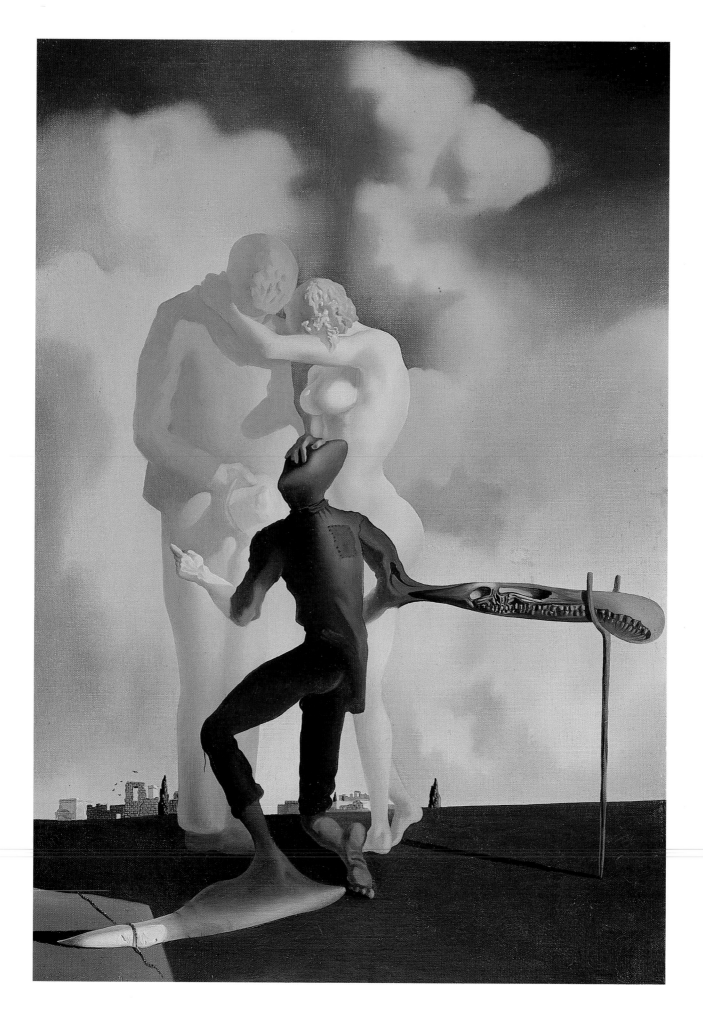

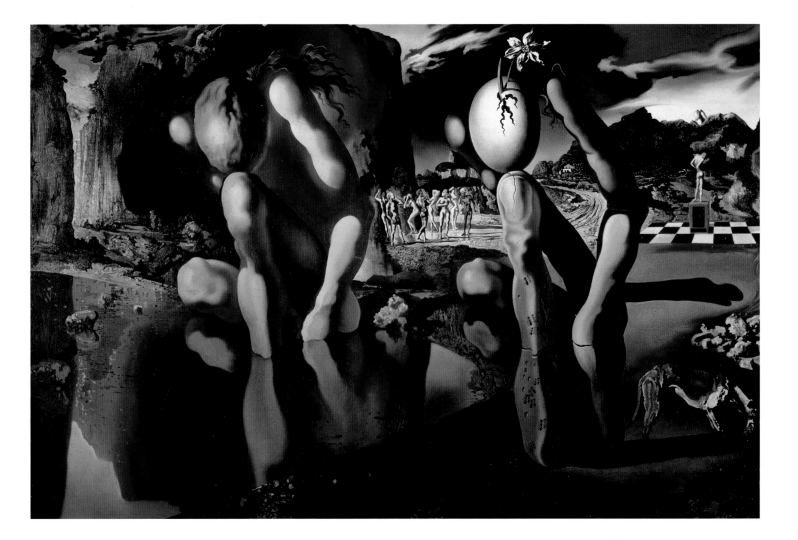

Salvador Dali
MEDITATION ON A HARP
About 1932-1934, oil on canvas.
Former André Durst Collection, Morse Charitable Trust,
On loan Salvador Dali Museum, Saint-Pétersbourg

Salvador Dali
METAMORPHOSIS OF NARCISSUS
1937, oil on canvas.
Tate Gallery, London.

Surréalistes, 1930) that the term "paranoia-criticism" appeared. This method is an "first class instrument" Breton wrote. We know where this comes from, in the case of Dali, this idea of integrating paranoia into the artist's creative, and thus critical, activity. He recounts in his *Vie Secrète* that as early as 1927 in Cadaquès, he had as neighbor a women of the fishermen, who believed that Eugenio d'Ors was writing about her in his books and sending her love letters. This interpretive delirium particularly struck Dali, who was constantly terrorizing himself with the dead bodies of hedgehogs, grasshoppers and ants – therein lies the "fusion of reality and the imaginary," the very basis of Surrealism. The title of the painting *Le Miel est Plus Doux que le Sang* (Honey is Sweeter than Blood) is simply Lydia's wording.

In his book, *La Conquète de l'Irrationnel* (Conquering the Irrational, 1935), Dali returned to the exposé of his method underlining its active nature. Dali's fantasizing would develop throughout his life, upon the theme of the lost paradise of the prenatal world. Nothing, regarding his creative activity, really permits us to divide Dali's life into two parts: a first Surrealist part lasting until 1939, then a betrayal of Surrealism with "*Avida Dollars.*" His public eccentricities never interfered with his solitary concentration at Port Lligat (Catalonia), as his obsession with dollars and Gala's avarice didn't prove that he was capable of managing a fortune…

For Dali, the inter-uterine paradise is "soft, immobile, warm, symmetrical, duplicitous and sticky." Throughout his life his painting would respond to this

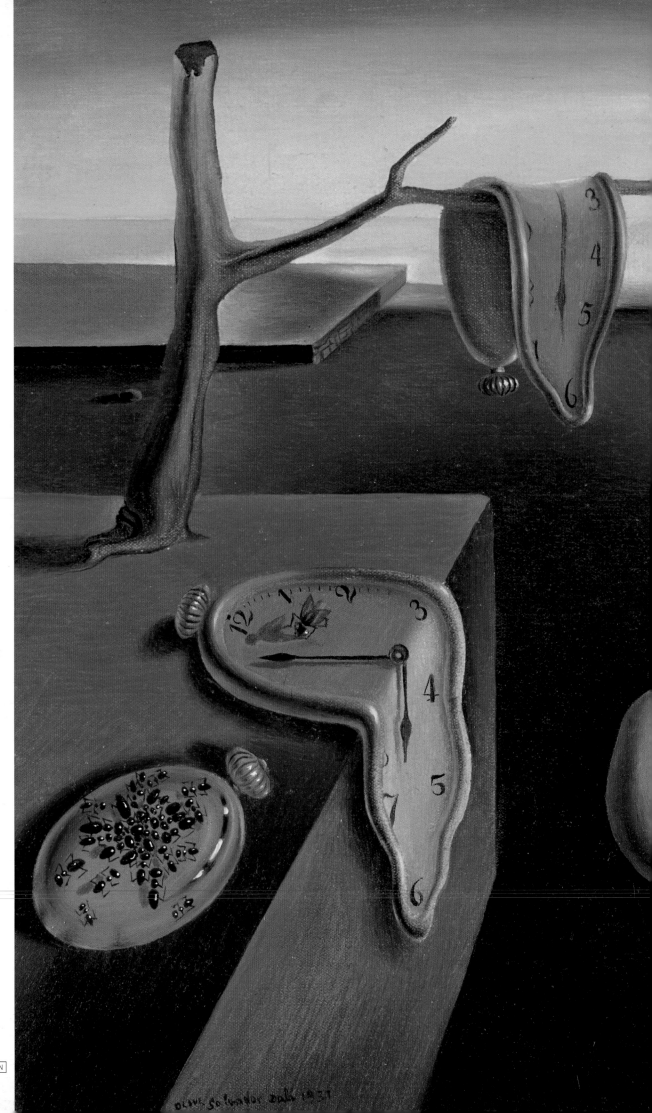

Salvador Dali
**PERSISTENCE OF
MEMORY**
1931, oil on canvas
The Museum of Modern Art,
New York

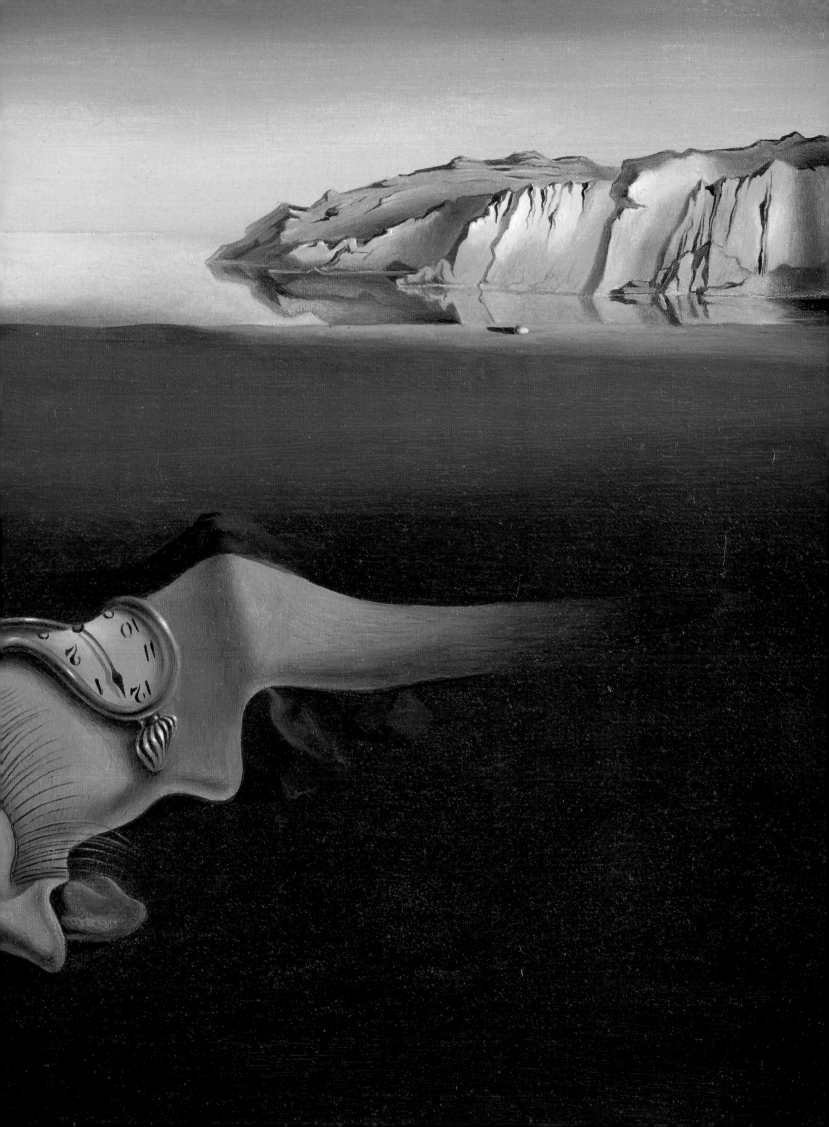

vertical inspiration, oriented toward the depths, (like Baudelaire in "La Charogne") which counters Breton's "ascendant." Reproduced here are some examples of his major works. Later, his obsession with viscosity would be combined with a fear of explosions, due to the anxiety surrounding the atomic bomb.

In fact, Dali was not paranoid. Whereas a patient obstinately believes in his delusions, Dali played, and never stopped playing with his dreams, attempting to bring them into his painting. In his *Vie Secrète* he wrote: "At dawn I woke up, and without washing or dressing, I would sit in front of the easel placed in my bedroom, opposite my bed. The first image of the morning was my canvas, which would also be the last thing I saw before going to bed. I tried to go to sleep staring at it in order to keep the drawing during my sleep, and sometimes in the middle of the night I would rise to look at it for a moment in the moonlight. Or, between two naps, I turned on the electricity and contemplated this work that never left me. All day, sitting in from of my easel, I stared at my canvas like a medium trying to bring elements out of my own imagination. When the images were precisely placed in the painting, I painted them immediately. But sometimes I would have to wait for hours, passive, the paintbrush immobile in my hand, before seeing anything suddenly appearing." (p. 169)

This procedure is the product of a highly nervous individual whose passion for perfection, capricious narcissism and "divergent" intelligence made for dilettante effervescence. The painter's ultimate goal was simply to paint his "inner model," in solitude. This desire can be seen in the surprising pages recounting the "cut-off hand," (horrible nightmare for a painter) in *La Vie Secrète de Salvador Dali* (The Secret Life of Salvador Dali). In my opinion the *Métamorphose de Narcisse* (Narcissus's Metaporphosis, 1936) is the painting that resumes all Dali – of which Dali would write in *Oui*, "[This is] the first painting entirely produced by the strict application of the critical-paranoiac method." In the middle of a nocturnal orgy we see the reflection of Narcissus's body multiplying in the water, while a giant wrinkled hand holds out a narcissus blossom, in a sign of fragile hope... We will return to Dali later.

The Conquest of Objects

Paranoia-criticism would be a source of stimulation in the creation of dream objects. Freud's "transitional objects" heavily sexual – finding quite out-of-the-ordinary objects in the flea market, driftwood, discolored by salt, found on the beach, the use of everyday objects in some humorous or absurd manner, the call for objects from the far end of the earth...this world, infinitely rich, was periodically revisited by the Surrealists.

We have already mentioned Duchamp's *readymades* and the *cadeau* (gift) by Man Ray. Dada had already toyed with the *Tete Mécanique* (Mechanical Head) by Raoul Haussmann, and Kurt Schwitters had already composed his *Mertz* objects out of garbage. But it was starting in 1930, and especially in 1935, that the first truly Surrealist objects would appear. And this, all over the world. To such an extent that one could consider this "*chosiste*" ("thingist") activity (the word is Bachelard's) like a determining factor in the cosmopolitan character of the great International Exhibitions of Surrealism. (London in 1936, Paris in 1938 etc...)

Let us first say a word about the Surrealist texts relative to the question. They tell us specifically what makes an object Surrealist. In 1931 (N° 3 of *L.S.A.S.D.L.R*), Salvador Dale proposes a "general catalogue of Surrealist objects," where one can find *L'Heure des Traces* by Alberto Giacometti prominently placed. This was one of the first fully Surrealist objects. In the same issue we find Breton's text on "*L'Objet Fantôme*, (excerpt from his book, *Les Vases Communicants*). In N° 5 (May 1933) Marcel Duchamp's text which was supposed to explain *La Mariée Mise à Nu par Ses Célibataires, Même* (this *Grand Verre* contains a graphic fantasy touching on obsessional subjects such as "*la broyeuse de cholat*" [the chocolate grinder]) – and an article by Roger Caillois on the "Specification of Poetry," where we read, " It is clear that the utility of an object never completely justifies its form, in other words, the object always goes beyond the instrument. In this manner, it would be possible to discover in every object an irrational residue, determined among other things by the inventor's or the technician's unconscious representations." It would be in this residue (which is undoubtedly a plus) that can be found the essential for a Surrealist.

A few pages later Dali mentions "anamorphic psycho-atmospheric objects" (anamorphosis is the deformation of an image, or of the form of an object, through the use of an angle of vision taken from the edge of the perspective – very popular in the Renaissance). And in N° 6, a long account of experiments involving "irrational knowledge" of objects such as a cristal ball, indeed, involving the "possibilities of the beautification of a city." In answer to the question: "How can one improve upon the Panthéon?" Tzara replied: "Split it down the middle and separate the two halves by 50 cm…"

In *Le Surréalisme et la Peinture* (1965 edition) we find Breton's texts "*Crise de l'Objet*" where he calls upon modern science to validate Surrealism, and "Du Poème-Objet", where it is simply a question of replacing words by tiny things stuck together. Surrealism wouldn't be satisfied with detecting the "residue" that Caillois describes, it creates it like a surplus of the marvelous, it

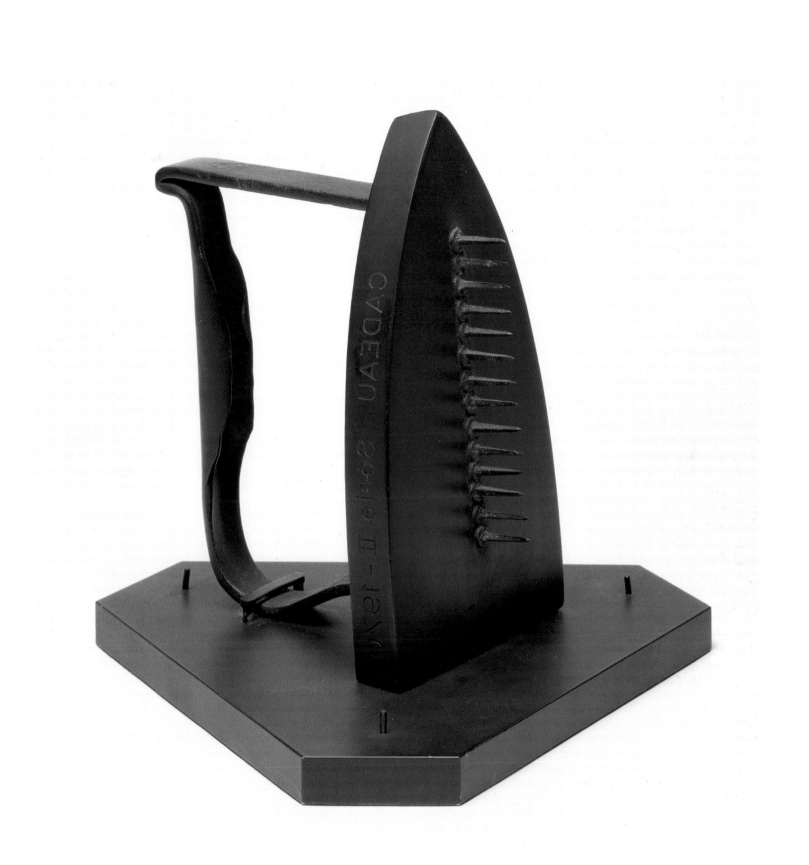

Man Ray
GIFT
1921, gelatin silver print.
Centre Pompidou-MNAM-CCI, Paris

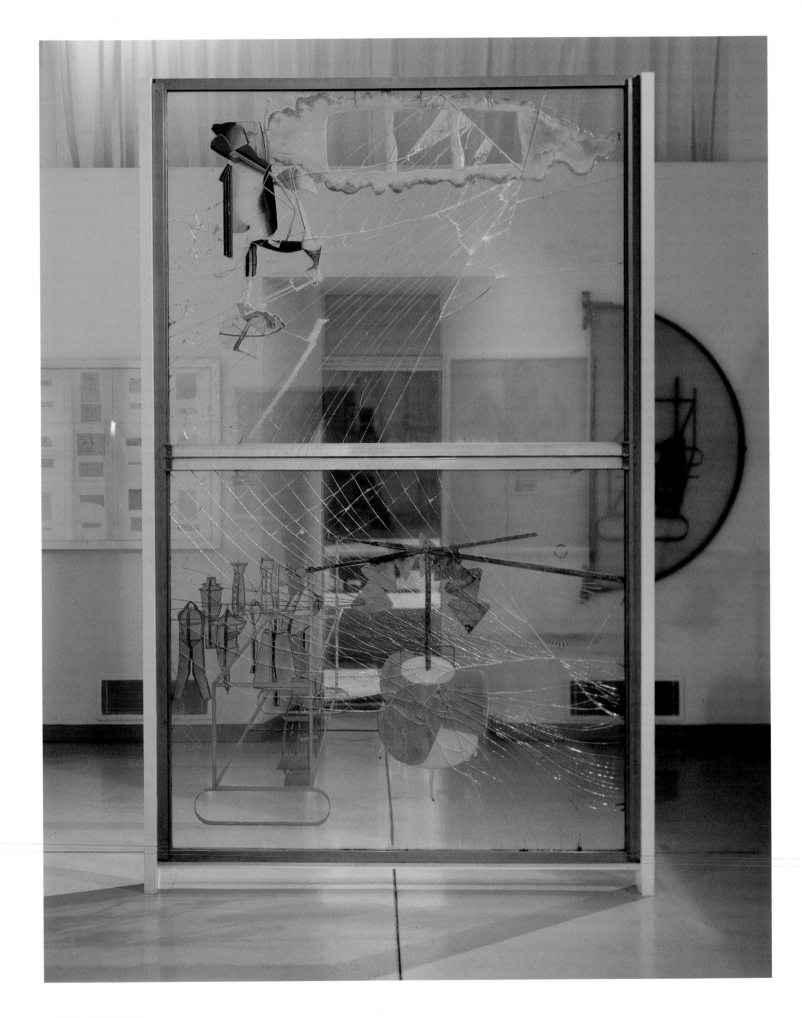

makes a poem out of an object, by displacing and modifying it. Giacometti explains that he dreams of an object in minute detail long before he actually creates it. In this manner *Le Palais à Quatre Heures du Matin* (The Palace at Four in the Morning, 1932) is simultaneously the fulfillment of a dream and what Freud calls a "dream gear shift" he inspires us. *L'objet Invisible* (The Invisible Object – the title Breton gave to this sort of statue, which seems to be holding something missing between its hands) is Giacometti's last Surrealist object; he then concentrated on his sculpture. Beginning in 1935, he repudiated his Surrealist period; one wonders why…

It was in 1936, at the home of Charles Ratton, that the first major exhibition of Surrealist objects took place, to which the *Cahiers d'Art* devoted a special issue which furnishes the nomenclature of the Surrealist objects exhibited: *objets naturels* (natural objects – including a stuffed ant-eater), *naturels interprétés* (interpreted natural objects), *naturels incorporés* (incorporated natural objects), *objets perturbés* (perturbed objects, works of glass melted by volcanic lava), *objets trouvés* (found objects), *objets trouvés interprétés* (interpreted found objects), *objets amérindiens and océaniens* (American Indian and Oceanic objects), plus the *Porte-bouteilles* (readymade) by Duchamp, des *objets mathématiques* (mathematical objects, pedagogical) and finally *objets Surréalistes*, created from scratch: *Trousse de Naufragé* (Instrument Case for the Drowned) by Arp, *Veston Aphrodisiaque* (Aphrodisiac Jacket) by Dali *Arrivée de la Belle-Epoque* (Arrival of the Belle-Epoque) by Dominguez, the objects by Giacometti, *Hommage à Paganini* by Maurice Henri (fantastic!), a version of *Cadeau* by Man Ray (sadistic), poem-objects by Breton and all his friends, and finally the most famous of all, the *Couvert en Fourrure* (Fur Place

Alberto Giacometti
THE INVISIBLE OBJECT
1934-1935, bronze.
Fondation Maeght, Saint-Paul-de-Vence

Marcel Duchamp
THE BRIDE SRIPPED BARE BY THE BACHELORS, EVEN
1913-1915, painting on glass.
Philadelphia Museum of Art, Philadelphie

Alberto Giacometti
**THE PALACE AT FOUR IN THE
MORNING**
1932-1333, construction
in wood, glass, metal, string.
The Museum of Modern Art, New York.

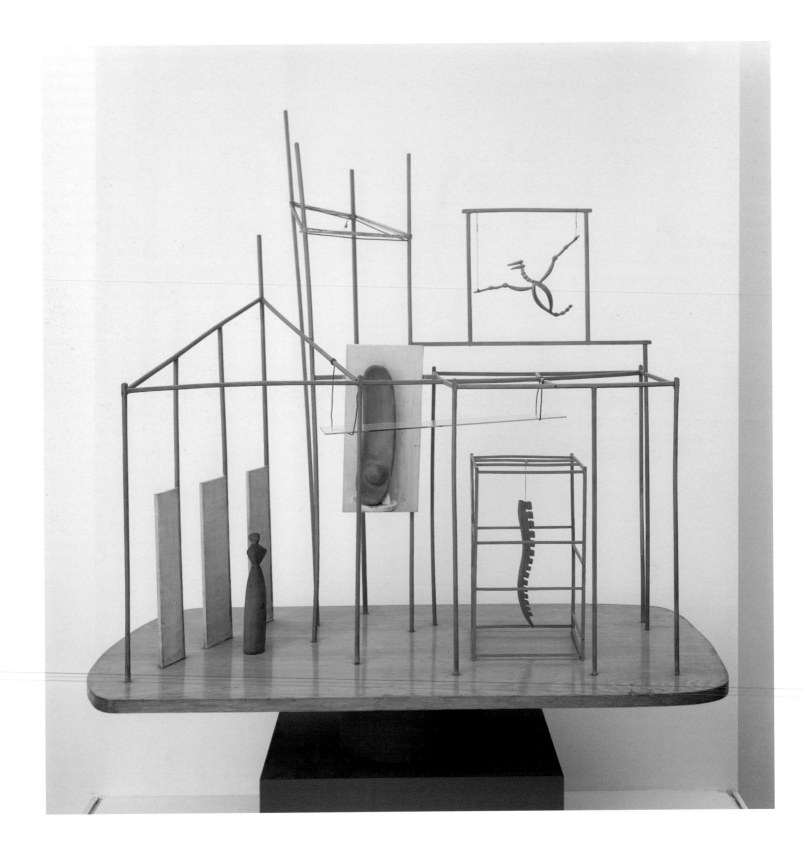

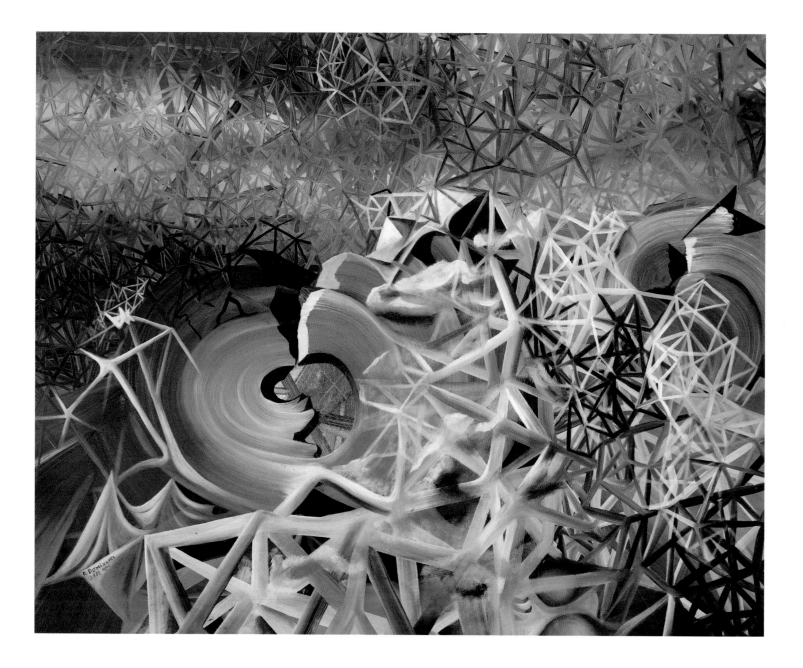

Oscar Dominguez
NOSTALGIA FOR SPACE
1939, oil on painting.
The Museum of Modern Art, New York

Setting) by Meret Oppenheim (who would later invent the disturbing *Chaussures Siamoises* [Siamese shoes], sewn together at the tip).

Many of these objects were exhibited at *L'Exposition Internationale du Surréalisme* in 1938 (Paris). Instead of exhibiting the objects in a traditional manner with works juxtaposed, the Galerie des Beaux Arts itself was treated like a kind of architectural object fitted-out for the occasion. At the entrance one was greeted by Dali's *Taxi Pluvieux (*Rainy Taxi), in which a beautiful blond woman (wax) is assaulted by a squad of live snails. Then comes the *Rue Surréaliste* lined with mannequins, each pretty woman had been dressed by an artist according to his most intimates fantasies. (Léo Malet's goldfish in a bowl placed in a mannequin's belly had been judged too risqué…) The *Couvert de Fourrure* was shown in the main room, in which the ceiling had been decorated with coal sacks (by Duchamp) and everywhere, hands, especially in Dominguez's composition, *Jamais*, where the bell of a gramophone swallowed up a woman's legs while the arm of the record-player had been replaced by a hand… Following the exhibition's catalogue came out a *Dictionnaire Abrégé du Surréalisme* which consisted of "discoveries" from the *Cadavres Exquis* (Exquisite Corpses).

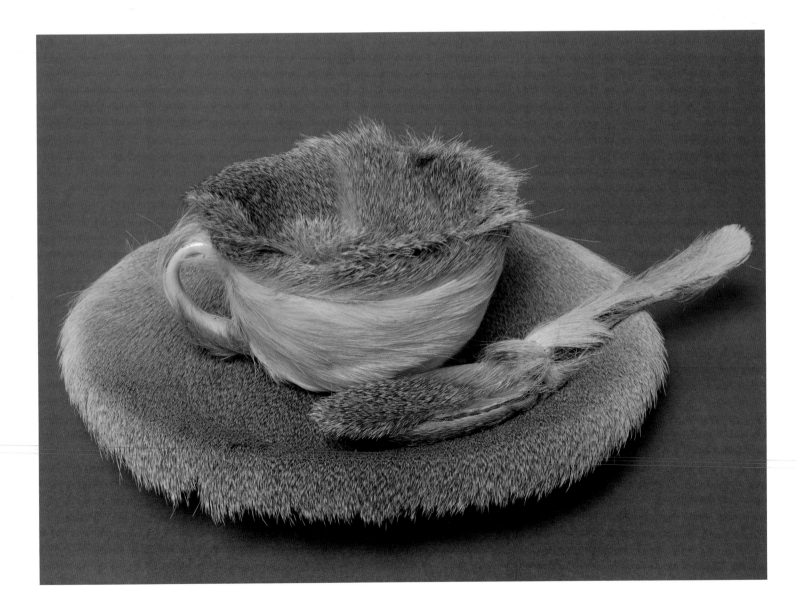

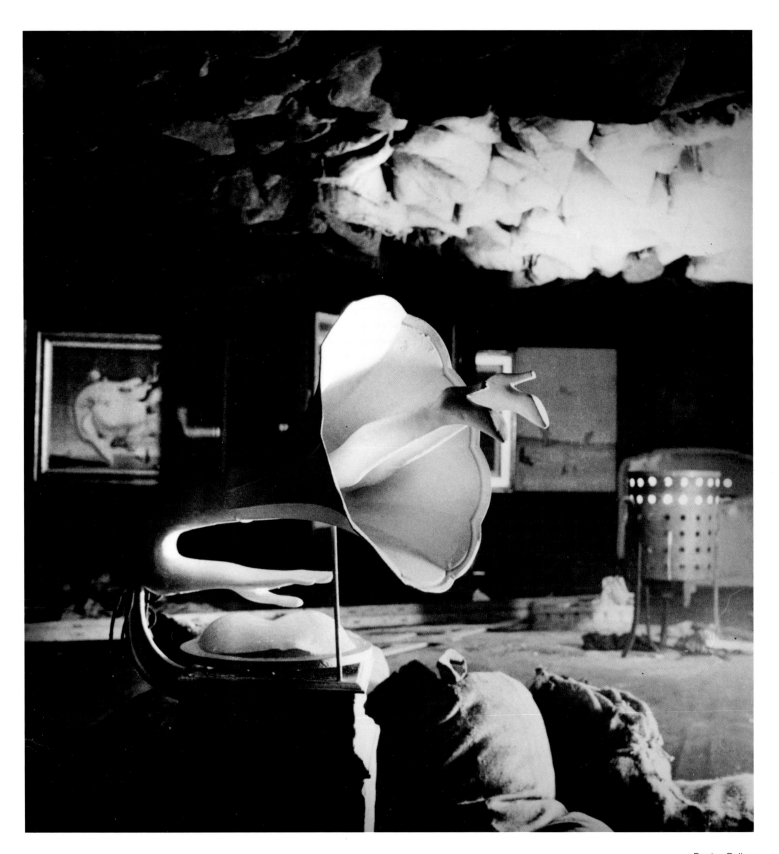

Meret Oppenheim
FUR-COVERED TEA CUP, SAUCER AND SPOON
1936.
The Museum of Modern Art, New York

Denise Bellon
NEVER
Oscar Dominguez, at the
Exposition
Internationale du Surréalisme,
galerie des Beaux-Arts,
Paris, 1938.
Galerie Claude Oterelo, Paris

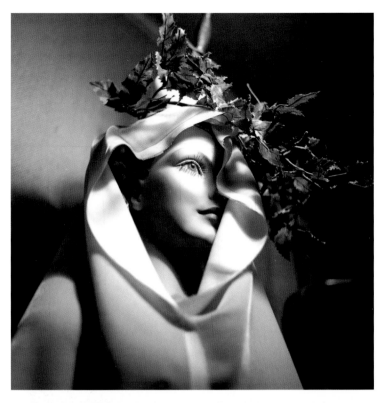

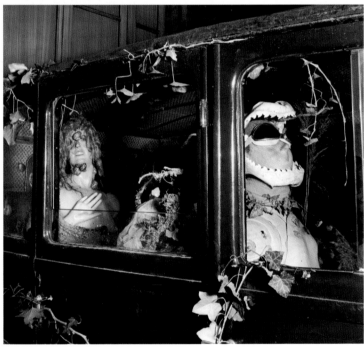

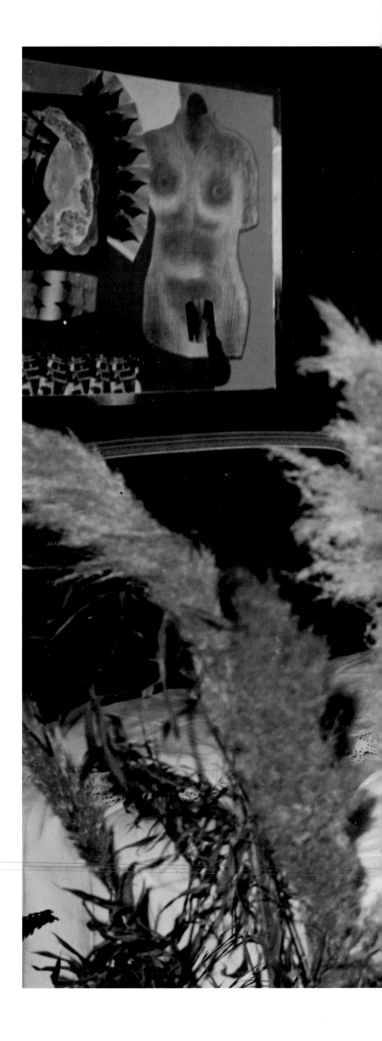

Rue surréaliste at the Exposition
Internationale du Surréalisme,
galerie des Beaux-Arts,
Paris, 1938.

P. 110 haut
Denise Bellon
THE RAINY TAXI
by Salvador Dali at the
Exposition Internationale du
Surréalisme,
galerie des Beaux-Arts,
Paris, 1938.
Galerie Claude Oterelo, Paris

Mlle Vanel in a tragic stance in
her *danse macabre*
at the Exposition Internationale
du Surréalisme,
galerie des Beaux-Arts, Paris,
1938.

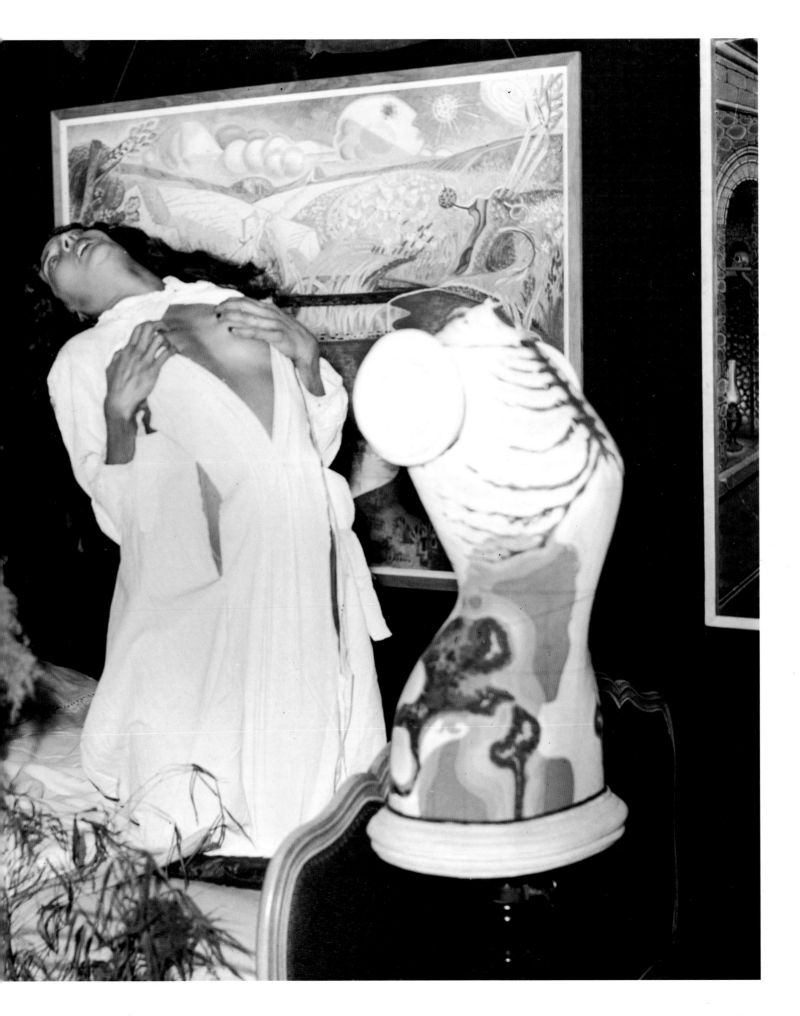

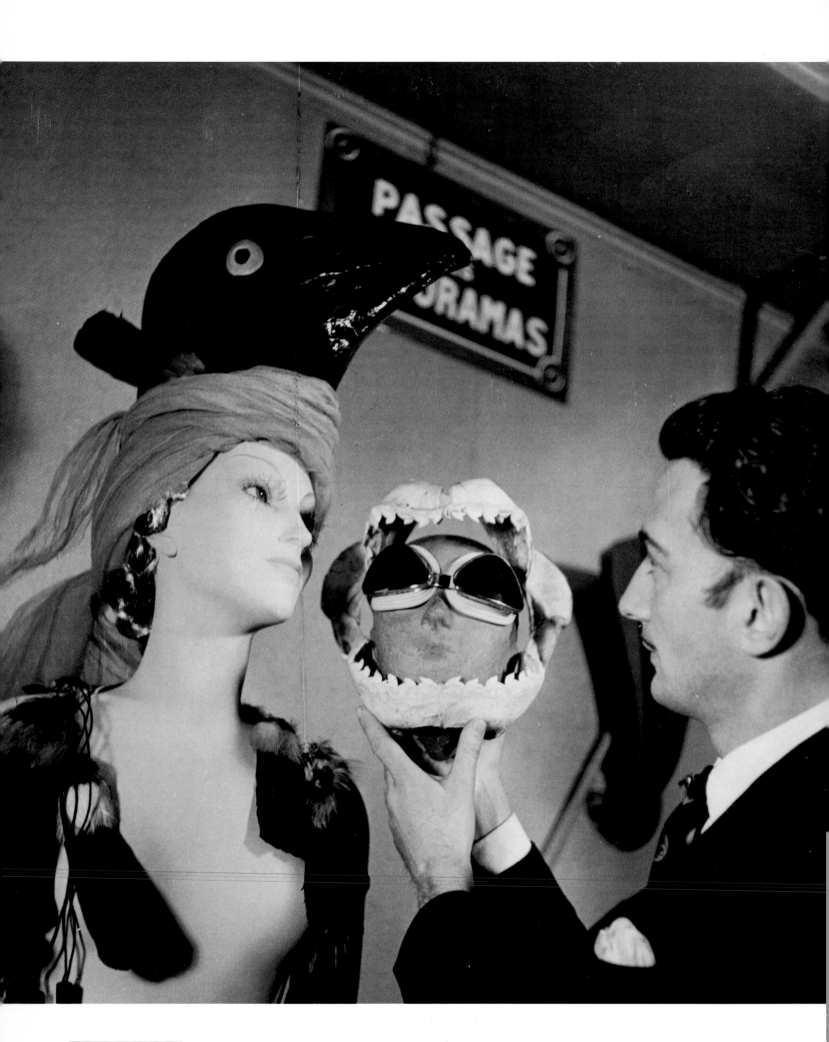

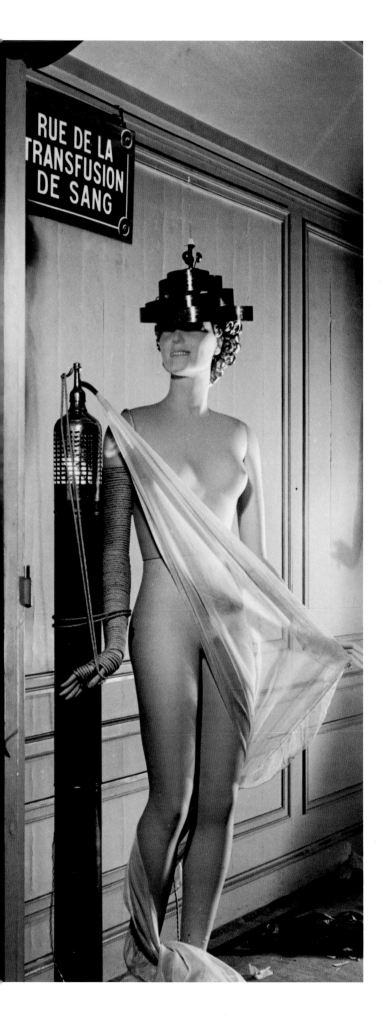

Denise Bellon
Salvador Dali at the Exposition
Internationale du Surréalisme,
galerie des Beaux-Arts, Paris,
1938.
Galerie Claude Oterelo, Paris.

Denise Bellon
The Street of Blood transfusion
at the Exposition Internationale
du Surréalisme,
galerie des Beaux-Arts,
Paris, 1938.
Galerie Claude Oterelo, Paris.

We will later encounter other major exhibitions where
the poetic dream-state will know how to impose
Surrealist sensitivity on the general public. For the
moment we are in 1938 and André Breton's group is still
in the midst of their political crisis. Let's back up a bit.

Political Problems

A few pages after Dali's "*L'Ane Pourri*" in N° 1 of
SASDLR a letter by Mayakovski was published at the
time of his suicide, where the line "Love's raft was broken to pieces running up against everyday life," serves as
the title of a long article by Breton about the relationship
between revolutionary fervor and love. Women supposedly "detest everything that isn't done for the sake of
their beauty," for Mayakovski killed himself both out of
despair in love and out of deception in politics. The problem being that in spite of Engel's reservations, a person's right to love, like death, is absolute. The ambiguity
of Breton's position is that of a diplomat attempting to
maintain an equal balance between the two options offered by Surrealism at that time – commitment to the
Third International and Communist ideal, and individual artistic creativity. These two ideals which were to
become distorted from a historical perspective, would be
fundamentally, indissolubly linked.

However, while Breton maintained this balancing act,
Aragon and Sadoul gave in and left for Kharkov, USSR,
for the Second Congress of Revolutionary Writers and
Intellectuals. In *SASDLR* N° 3, Aragon, back from
Kharkov, attempts to put things into place theoretically.

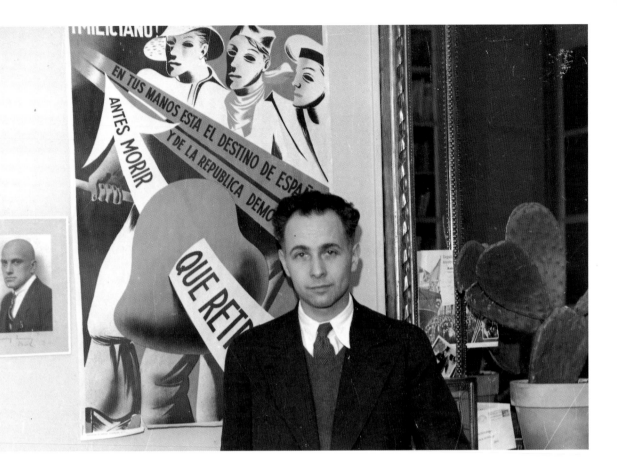

Louis Aragon at the time of the
Spanish War.
(On the wall portrait of Mayakovski).

"Don't Visit the Colonial Exhibition"
1931, surréalist tract

His article "Le Surréalisme et le Devenir Révolutionnaire" (Surrealism and Revolutionary Evolution) states that in the realm of action, the final word must come from the 3rd International Communist Committee. Noting that the bourgeoisie – who had just condemned Sadoul to three months of prison for having sent an insulting letter one drunken evening, to majors at Saint-Cyr (Caupenne, guilty of complicity, formally apologized and was let off) – subtly undermines and handicaps the Surrealists, forcing them into the arms of high society snobbish patrons, managing to distance them from intellectuals sympathetic to the USSR And yet, Aragon maintained that he went to the Congress out of pure pleasure…

In fact, once there he gave in to everything that was asked of him. He went as far as calling psychoanalysis "idealist" (horrors!) and signing a petition against Trotsky. In order to justify his adherence to Stalinist Communism, he wrote a violent poem, "*Front Rouge*"

(The Red Front) in which one can read some fairly wretched "party line" insults, such as, "I fire upon the trained bear of social democracy…" Aragon is then accused of inciting murder and the Surrealists, with Breton leading some 300 intellectuals, sign a petition in defense of Aragon… and of poetry.

One can see the difficulty. If poetry does not assume the consequences of its existence, and in the name of the poet's unconscious drives, relieves him of all notion of responsibility, where is its place in a revolutionary context? One accepts one's responsibilities or one does not. Breton's position is ambiguous. He did not like this "poem of circumstance." And Aragon had been placed in a difficult position with this manifestation of support. If he approved, or so it seemed – at least until the day that a tiny line in *L'Humanité* revealed that Aragon "entirely disapproved" of the contents of the document written in his defense. A few jolted Surrealists – trying to maintain their faith in the French Communist Party, as

Ne visitez pas l'Exposition Coloniale

A la veille du 1ᵉʳ Mai 1931 et à l'avant-veille de l'inauguration de l'Exposition Coloniale, l'étudiant indo-chinois Tao est enlevé par la police française. Chiappe, pour l'atteindre, utilise le faux et la lettre anonyme. On apprend, au bout du temps nécessaire à parer à toute agitation, que cette arrestation, donnée pour préventive, n'est que le prélude d'un refoulement sur l'Indo-Chine. * Le crime de Tao ? Etre membre du Parti Communiste, lequel n'est aucunement un parti illégal en France, et s'être permis jadis de manifester devant l'Elysée contre l'exécution de quarante Annamites.

L'opinion mondiale s'est émue en vain du sort des deux condamnés à mort Sacco et Vanzetti. Tao, livré à l'arbitraire de la justice militaire et de la justice des mandarins, nous n'avons plus aucune garantie pour sa vie. Ce joli lever de rideau était bien celui qu'il fallait, en 1931, à l'Exposition de Vincennes.

L'idée du brigandage colonial (le mot était brillant et à peine assez fort), cette idée, qui date du XIXᵉ siècle, est de celles qui n'ont pas fait leur chemin. On s'est servi de l'argent qu'on avait en trop pour envoyer en Afrique, en Asie, des navires, des pelles, des pioches, grâce auxquels il y a enfin, là-bas, de quoi travailler pour un salaire et cet argent, on le représente volontiers comme un don fait aux indigènes. Il est donc naturel, prétend-t-on, que le travail de ces millions de nouveaux esclaves nous ait *donné* les monceaux d'or qui sont en réserve dans les caves de la Banque de France. Mais que le travail forcé — ou libre — préside à cet échange monstrueux, que des hommes dont les mœurs, ce que nous essayons d'en apprendre à travers des témoignages rarement désintéressés, des hommes qu'il est permis de tenir pour moins pervertis que nous et c'est peu dire, peut-être pour éclairés comme nous ne le sommes plus sur les fins véritables de l'espèce humaine, du savoir de l'amour et du bonheur humains, que ces hommes dont nous distingue ne serait-ce que notre qualité de *blancs*, nous qui disons hommes de couleur, nous hommes sans couleur, aient été tenus, par la seule puissance de la métallurgie européenne, en 1914, de se faire crever la peau pour un très bas monument funéraire collectif — c'était d'ailleurs, si nous

---

* Nous avons cru devoir refuser, pour ce manifeste, les signatures de nos camarades étrangers.

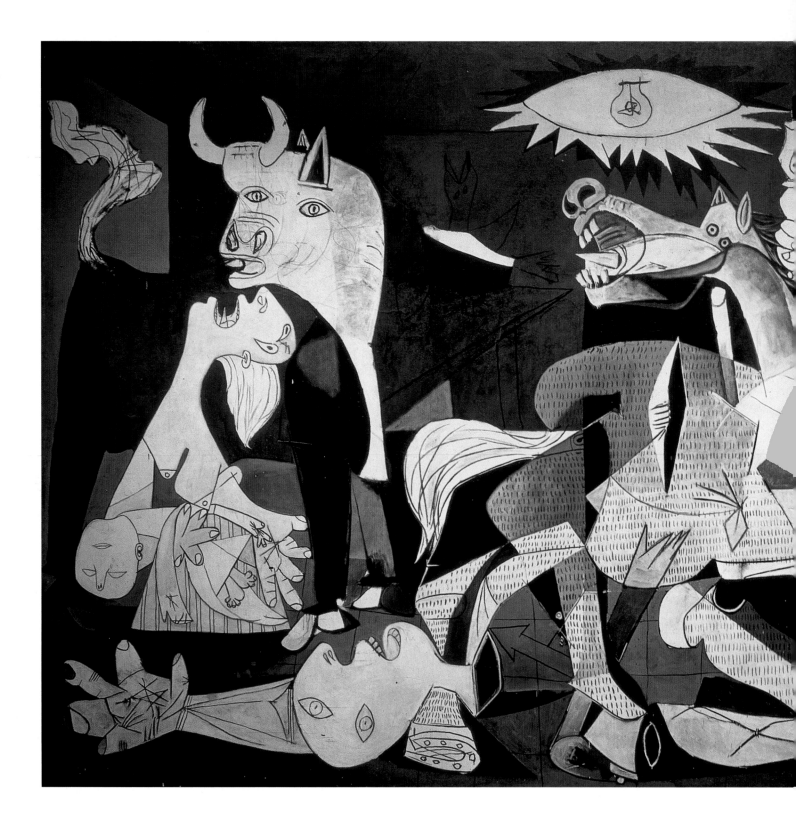

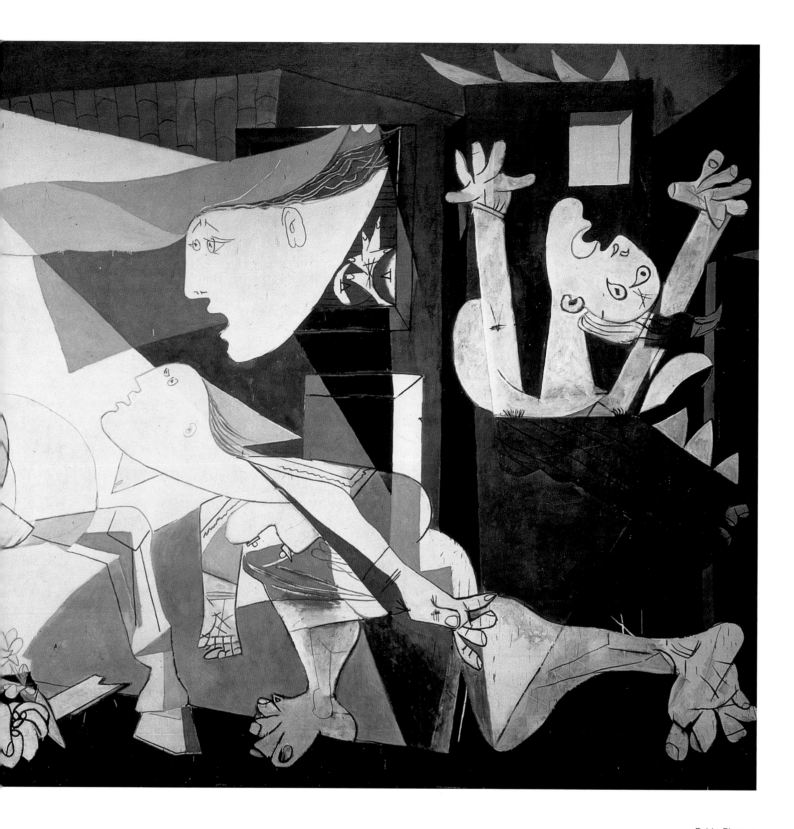

Pablo Picasso
GUERNICA
1937, oil on canvas.
Centro de Arte Reina Sofia, Madrid

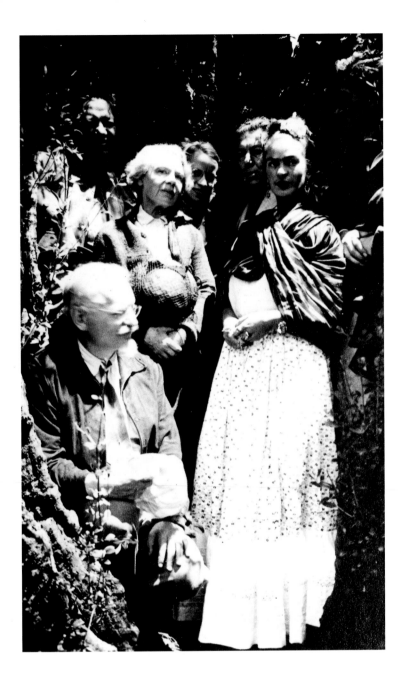

André Breton with Diego Rivera,
Frida Kahlo, Trotski in Mexico
City, in 1938.

rather quickly not only to the Party, but also to the lyricism of love. She became his idol, and during years Aragon would "sing" his love in poems such as *Les Yeux d'Elsa* (The Eyes of Elsa). Was Aragon won over to Stalin out of the love of Elsa? So, is there really nothing pure, even among the pure of heart?

Aragon, who at the time of the "Naville affair" considered political action "dishonoring," became a member of the French Communist Party in 1936 after several trips to the USSR Adopting Zhdanov's theory of "Socialist Realism," he published his poem "Hourra l'Oural" (Hurrah the Ural!) in 1934. Breton for his part, was drawing nearer to Trotsky, founder of the Red Army and then "glorified" with the "prestige" of having been sent into exile. The five Surrealists who were members of the French Communist Party were excluded in 1933, a dark year, the year of Hitler's ascension, the burning of the Reichstag and the founding of the Gestapo...

The Surrealists had participated in the counter-exhibition aimed at the 1931 Exhibition of the Colonies, (where Artaud had discovered Balinese theater). Not inclined to support Henri Barbusse and Romain Rolland in their pacifist undertakings, the Surrealists published their pamphlet *La Mobilization Contre la Guerre n'est pas la Paix,* in 1933. One can read: "If you want peace, prepare for civil war." *SASDLR* N° 5, in May, 1933, published a letter addressed to Breton by the philosopher Ferdinand Alquié, in which he rages against "the wind of 'idiotization'that is blowing from the USSR" The personality cult of Stalin, in fact, was paving the way for films that would appear completely ridiculous to the Surrealists... In the face of the movements of the extreme right in France, which would culminate on 6 February 1934, the Surrealists intoned slogans such as "War on war." After their text *Appel à la Lutte* (Call to Fight, 10 February), they joined the "Comité de Vigilance des Intellectuels Antifascistes" (Vigilant Committee of Antifascist Intellectuals) and signed their manifesto.

Laval's pact with the USSR brought the French Communist Party closer to the government, and the Surrealists could only distance themselves from this line of national unity. At a pacifist meeting for the defense of culture, René Crevel would be the only Surrealist tolerated. But, he committed suicide. It was Eluard who would read a text by Breton (no longer allowed to take the floor since having slapped Ilya Ehrenburg). Breton objected to the "about-face" that allowed Communists to defend the idea of national identity. But all this fell on deaf ears and it was in vain that he attempted to distinguish living art from that of the conservatives.

In an attempt to show that a disengagement with Stalin was not a disengagement with the revolution, Breton, who in 1931 had published *Les Vases Communicants*

far as action's concerned, but what action? – couldn't hide the evidence: Aragon had left.

We cannot ignore that this political-emotional abduction was of a passionate nature that insured Aragon's loyalty to Surrealism at the very moment of his departure. In fact, it was in Kharkov that Aragon found again Elsa Triolet (they had first met in Paris in 1928), sister of the Lili to whom Mayakovski wrote, in his last letter, "Lili, love me." Elsa, who would only be a "sympathizer" with Communism seems to have converted Aragon (in which he shows that desire, in a waking state, leads to revolution and, in a dreaming state, to poetry) – wrote *Position Politique du Surréalisme* (Political Position of Surrealism), where he announced the formation of the group *Contre-Attaque* (Counter-Attack), "the intellectual revolutionaries' union for struggle." Bataille would be the leader of this group. Their leftist position would leave them on the outskirts of the mass movements of 1936 and the Popular Front. Worried to see that in Europe revolutionary movements often turned into fascism, they proclaimed that the defense of revolution should be "aggressive." However a text in *Contre-Attaque* having indicated that they preferred "in all events and without being taken in, Hitler's anti-diplomatic brutality, less surely mortal for peace than the slobbery excitation of diplomats and politicians," the Surrealists withdrew their signatures, refusing to fight fascism with a "super-fascism." The group was shaken by this contradiction, and disbanded on its own.

1937 was the year of the Universal Exhibition "*Arts et Techniques*" in Paris. For the first time one could see Picasso's large wall painting *Guernica* in the Spanish Republic's pavilion. The Spanish Civil War (and the non-intervention of France) lead to a hardening of the left. Péret, among others, joined the "Durutti Column" along with the anarchists. He would come back only in 1939. Artaud had left for Mexico in 1936. He discovered the Tarahumara Indians and their " dance of peyote," a hallucinogenic in which he recognized with exaltation the discovery of this own psyche. Returning to Europe in 1937, he suffered seizures on the ship that resulted in his confinement to a mental hospital upon arrival in Le Havre. This was the beginning of a long martyrdom in several psychiatric hospitals, ending with the Rodez Hospice in 1942. We will return later to Artaud, who lived out in his own skeletal body the experience that others only knew through simulation or out of curiosity.

André Breton and Benjamin Péret with friends in 1935

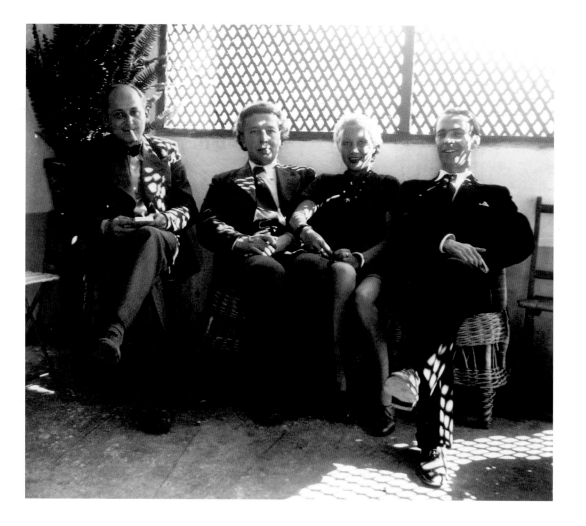

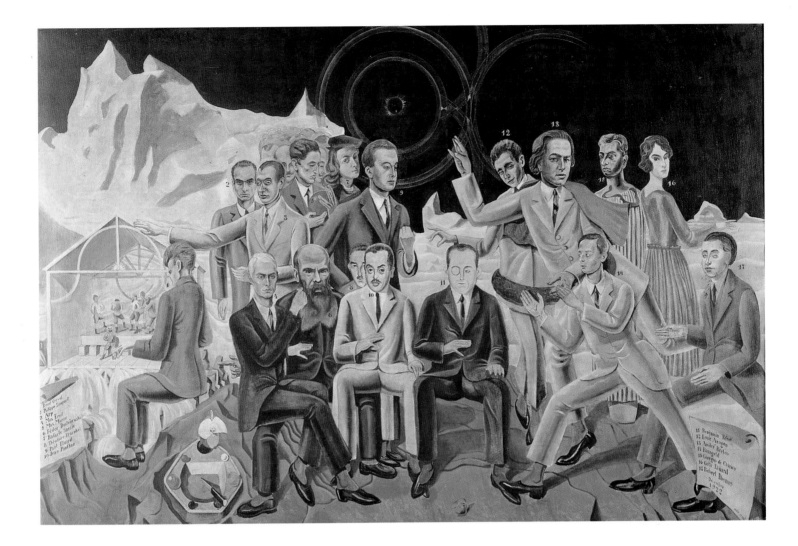

In 1938, the year of Munich, Breton went to Mexico where he met Leo Trotsky at the home of the painter Diego Rivera. He found to his pleasant surprise that they shared similar ideas about art. The artist participates in the future of permanent revolution if he is truly faithful to his inner voice. Breton then founded the *Fédération Internationale des Artistes Révolutionnaires Indépendants* (F.I.A.R.I.) and in the manifesto (another one) *Pour un Art Révolutionnaire Indépendant* repeats that art should be beyond national identities. Back in France, he published the bulletin *Clé:* "Art no more has a national identity than do workers." In the second and last number he presented a text by Trotsky. Dissention within the inner circle – Eluard, having moved closer to the French Communist Party, was excluded from the group – soon led to its breaking up.

When mobilization was announced, the contradiction between verbal jousting and real action was flagrant. The Surrealists went to their assigned posts without hesitation. Jean Louis Bédouin noted: "The refusal to serve in the military, which remains the rule in Surrealism, doesn't suit certain leaders of the movement, going as far as to the will to *de-serve.*" (*Vingt Ans de Surréalisme* [Twenty Years of Surrealism] Denoël, 1961, p.31).

It is obvious that the political discords that shook the Surrealist group left their scars. The painters, especially, were never particularly interested in doctrine, and maintained a certain distance from the revolutionary fervor. The ambiance surrounding Breton was becoming insufferable. Ernst was fed up and wanted to leave the group. He recounts, "The opportunity was presented to me when a perfectly candid Benjamin Péret, acting as the chief's emissary, came to my illegal lodgings, 12 Rue Jacob, one day in December 1938, in order to inform me that for political reasons, each member of the Surrealist group was called upon to 'sabotage Paul Eluard's poetry, using any and all means at their disposal.' Orders from the top. Refusal would mean exclusion." (Max Ernst, Gonthier-Seghers III, p. 27-28). In fact Breton's intellectual authority wasn't the only cause for dissention within the group during this period of expansion. Individual notoriety took its toll. Robert Lebel wrote, "It was a fact that they ran up against a paradox – Surrealism attempted to stay out of the public eye, at the very moment that Surrealist painters were becoming famous."

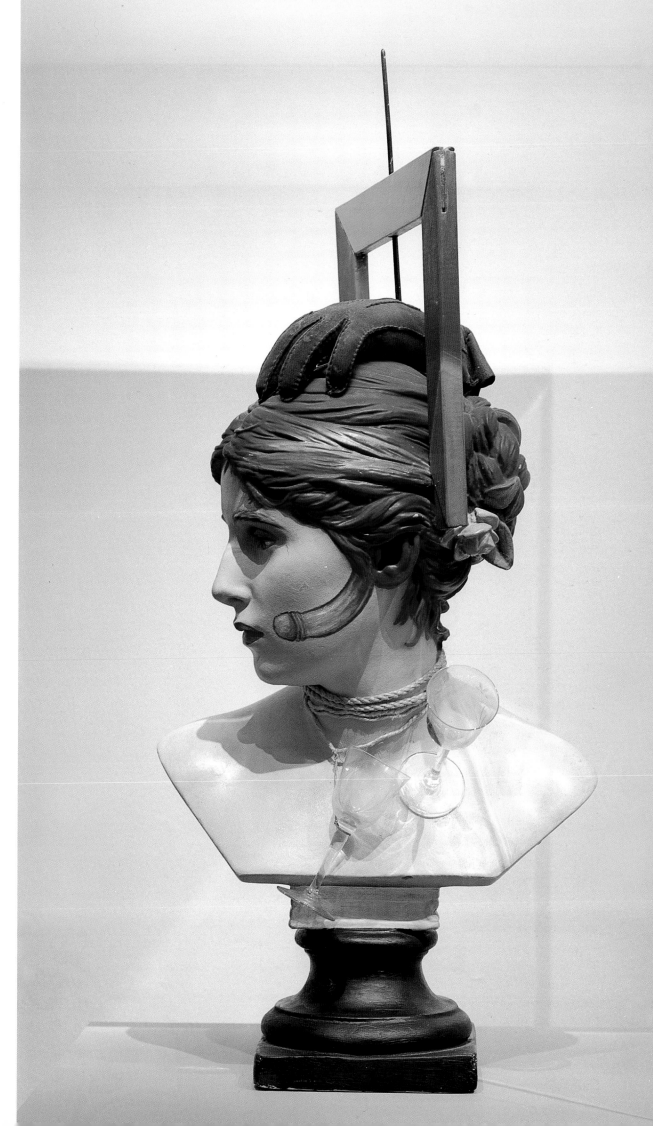

Wilhelm Freddie
SEX-PARALYSAPPEAL
1936, sculpture
Moserna Museet, Stockholm.

Max Ernst
**AT THE RENDEZ-VOUS
OF FRIENDS**
1922, oil on canvas.
Ludwig Museum, Köln

Page 116 et 117
Surréalism
around the World
Double spread
of the review
Minotaure n° 10,
December 1937.
Private Collection.

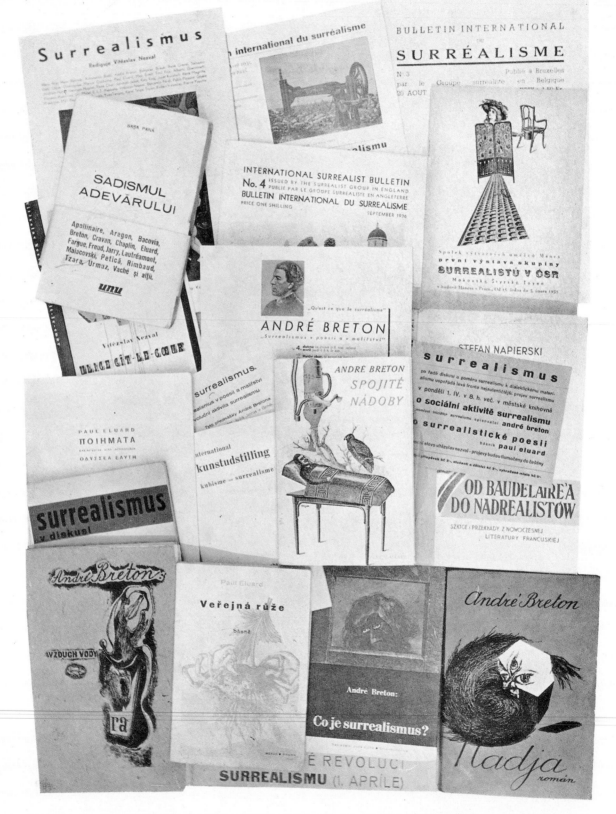

ANGLETERRE, BELGIQUE, DANEMARK, GRÈCE, POLOGNE, ROUMANIE, TCHÉCOSLOVAQUIE

UTOUR DU MONDE

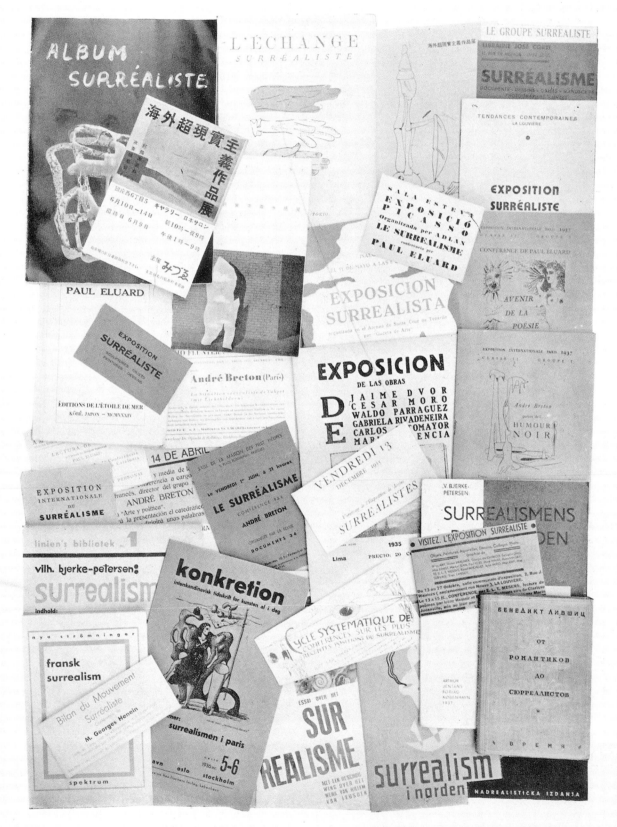

BELGIQUE, DANEMARK, ÉGYPTE, ESPAGNE, FRANCE, JAPON, PÉROU, SUÈDE, SUISSE, U. R. S. S., YOUGOSLAVIE

SASDLR folded in 1933 and was immediately replaced by the review *Minotaure*. It is interesting to note that the word *revolution* was no longer found in the titles of Surrealist reviews, and would only reappear briefly in the ephemeral attempt with *Surréalisme Révolutionnaire* in 1946. Implicitly for the moment, the motto in the thirties seemed to be: "Surrealists of the world, unite!"

Around the World

Surrealism's first expansion was paradoxically centripetal. We know that as of the beginning of the century numerous artists from every horizon came to Paris from all over. The phenomenon would continue would continue between the two world wars. Dada and Surrealism brought notably Francis Picabia (Cuba and Paris), Hans Arp (Switzerland), Joan Miró and Salvador Dali (Catalonia), Maria Germinova, called "Toyen" (Czechoslovakia), Roberto Matta (Chile), Hans Bellmer (Poland), Victor Brauner and Jacques Hérold (Rumania), Man Ray, Kay Sage, Joseph Cornell and William Copley (United States), Oscar Dominguez, Esteban Francès (Spain), Wilfredo Lam (Cuba), René Magritte, Paul Delvaux, Félix Labisse, Raoul Ubac (Belgium), Wolfgang Paalen (Austria), Kurt Seligmann (Switzerland), Max Walter Svanberg (Sweden), Abdul Kader El Janaby (Iraq), not to mention Picasso, De Chirico or Chagall. The Dane Wilhelm Freddie would be remarked for his anti-Nazi violence. His exhibition *Surreal-Sex* (Copenhagen, 1938) brought him death threats. He sought refuge in Sweden, and would later live in France. All these artists came to Paris to find what Chagall called an "astounding light – freedom." The great international exhibitions, such as the one held in Paris in 1938, proved to the general public that the Surrealists were not only international, but also eminently cosmopolitan.

Later, in a completely opposite movement, Surrealism spread to other countries. Major exhibitions took place: starting with Hartford (U.S.) in 1931. And in New York in 1936, "Fantastic Art, Dada, Surrealism" was organized by Alfred Barr at the Museum of Modern Art. Followed Zurich, Santa-Cruz de Tenerife, and Tokyo in 1937, London 1936, Santiago du Chili, Mexico City (1940), etc. Surrealists books were translated: note in *Minotaure* N° 10 a double-page spread of photos, " Le Surréalisme Autour du Monde" (Surrealism Around the World). Other groups were forming, information circu-

lated thanks to the *Bulletin International du Surréalisme,* which was first published in Prague in 1935, N° 2 in Brussels and N° 3 in London in 1936. In 1934 Dali met with great personnel success in New York. This was the same year that the Czech chapter would form, becoming one of the most active, followed by England, Portugal and Japan (several reviews), Brazil… It was in Yugoslavia that Marco Ristic led the Serbian Surrealist group beginning in 1924. It is noteworthy that in spite of the 1932 repression, the Surrealists integrated Tito's government. The Czechs, who had warmly welcomed Breton and Eluard in 1938, would suffer several waves of repression; however, in the end they were the only people not to have given in to Stalin's reign of terror.

The political repression often led to exile for example the Iraqi Abdul Kader El Janaby, or the Egyptian Ramses Younnane (founder of the review *La Part du Sable*, along with Georges Hénein). This phenomena however involuntary, led to the international diffusion of Surrealism. This said, the new avant-garde review in France, *Minotaure*, founded by a Swiss, Albert Skira, was simultaneously cosmopolitan and very open to cultural diversity. From 1933 to 1939, the thirteen successive issues were luxuriously presented, with front pages created by great painters, (Picasso, Duchamp, Magritte, Ernst, Masson, among others). The review was not only a beautiful object, it was also meant to be "state of the art" with regard to what we now call social studies, then represented by psychoanalysts or ethnologists. The science of art is integrated with general anthropology and the second issue of *Minotaure* was entirely dedicated to the Dakar-Djibouti mission. This expedition, led by Marcel Griaule, seconded by Michel Leiris, brought back objects ("stolen," maintained Leiris, in order to prove the cultural existence of the populations they encountered). These objects were left in what would become *Le Musée de l'Homme*, in Paris in 1936.

With regard to psychoanalysis, we have quoted works by Lacan, and Breton attempts a self-analysis in his poem "La Nuit du Tournesol" (Night of the Sunflower – N° 7). This perspective is widened to include sexology, with Caillois ("La Mante Réligieuse," N° 5) and Maurice Heine, a specialist on Sade, likewise for the study of the esoteric element in myths and rituals. In "L'Oeil du peintre" (N° 12-1") Dr. Mabille studies the strange phenomena of premonition. In the course of a fight, Victor Brauner was struck and blinded in one eye by glass shards. Ubac maintains that he saw Brauner's right eye

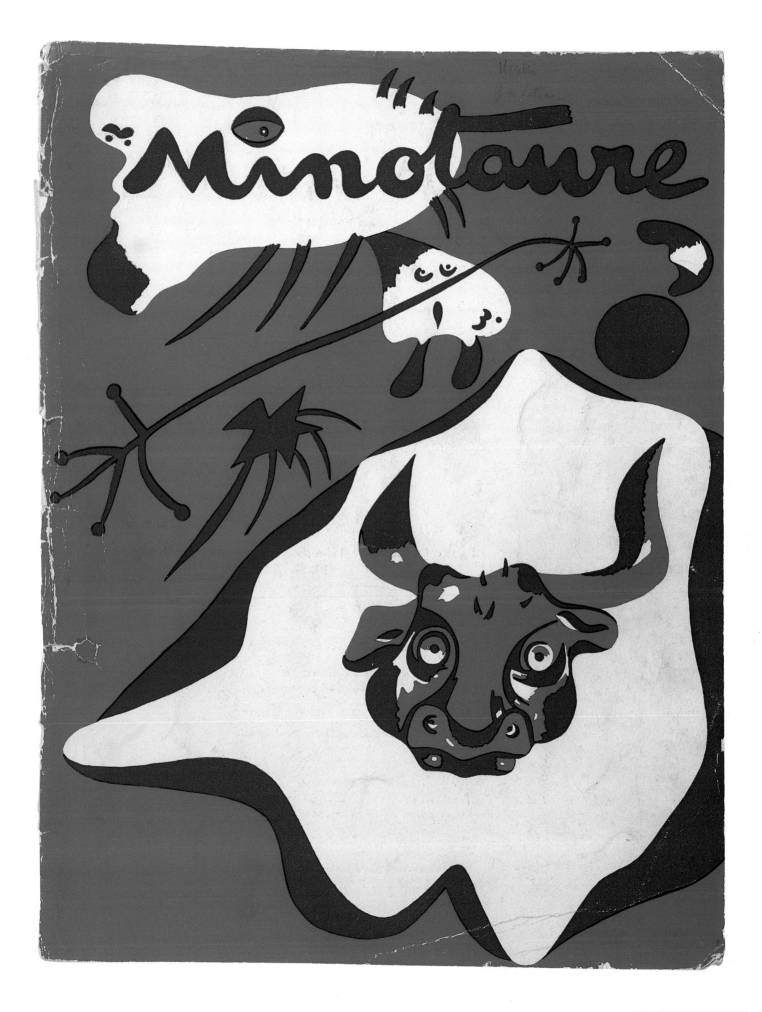

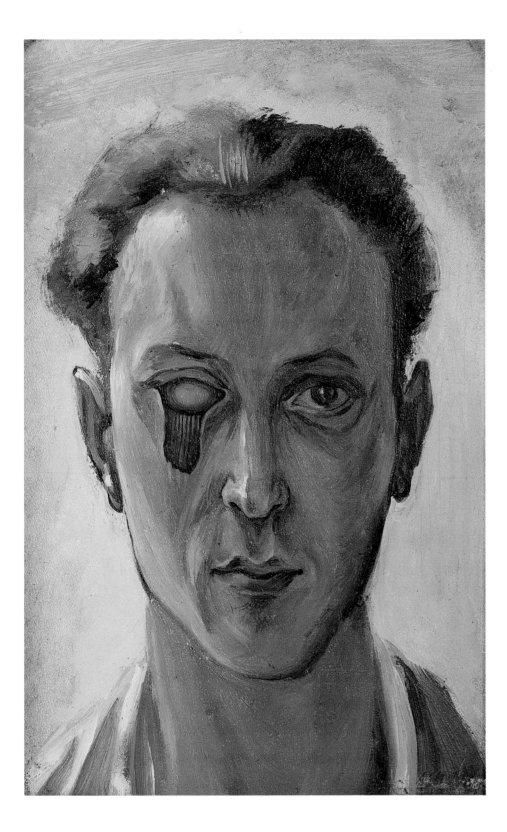

Victor Brauner
SELFPORTRAIT WITH PITTED EYE
1931, oil on canvas
Centre Pompidou-MNAM-CCI, Paris

Victor Brauner
CHIMERA
1939, oil on canvas.
Former Thyssen-Bornemisza Collection.

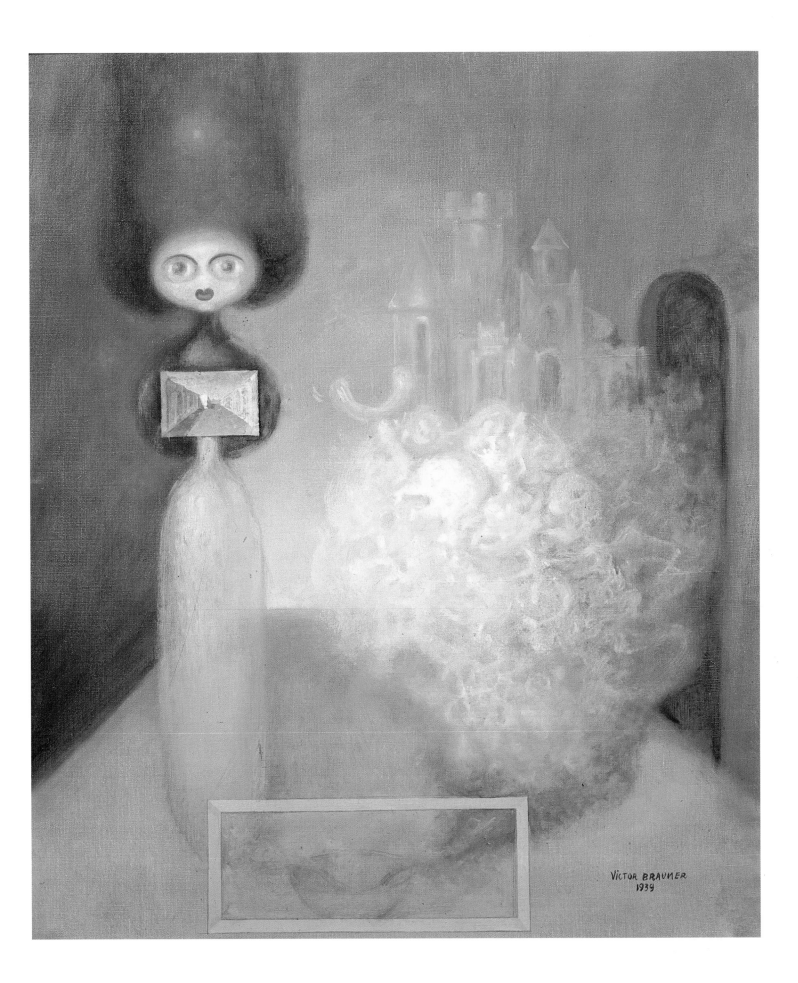

hanging on his cheek. Now Brauner had painted the *Autoportrait à l'Oeil Enuclée* (Self-portrait with Pitted Eye) in 1931. Mabille tries to explain this phenomena with psychoanalysis. It is impossible to really know, so the enigma is exacerbated. Dali figures in *Minotaure* with several snappy articles: "Interprétation Paranoïaque-Critique de l'Image Obsédante *L'Angélus* de Millet," (Critically-Paranoiac Interpretation of the Obsessive Picture *The Angelus* by Millet) "De la Beauté Terrifiante et Comestible de l'Architecture Modern Style" (About the Terrifying and Edible Beauty of Modern Style Architecture, N° 3-4), "Le Sex-appeal Spectral" (Ghostly Sex-appeal, N°5) and "Le Surréalisme Spectral de l'Eternel Féminin Préraphaélite" (The Ghostly Surrealism of the Eternal Feminine Pre-Raphaelite, N°8, 1936).

Breton presents several important texts: "Picasso dans son Elément" (Picasso in His Element, illustrated by Brassaï), "Le Massage Automatique" (The Automatic Massage), "La Beauté Sera Convulsive" (Beauty Will Be Convulsive, N°5), a text that will be used again in *L'Amour Fou*, "Phare de la Mariée" (The Lighthouse of the Married Woman), where he attempts to understand Duchamp's *Grand Verre*, "Le Merveilleux Contre le Mystère" (The Marvelous as Opposed to the Mysterious), in which Breton praises the 19th century Symbolists. There are notes about black humor, "André Masson's prestige" and an essay recounting his meeting with Trotsky.

Added to all of the above were abundant illustrations that mixed Picasso with Cranach and Boticelli with Dogon masks, as well as initiating a survey: "What was the most important encounter of your life?" The plethora of responses evidenced the broad circulation of the review. Skira later reprinted it in three volumes.

One can wonder at the little importance accorded to film, and the total absence of theater. Artaud was not even mentioned. Strange gaps. While Europe was seething, politics were rarely mentioned with the exception of the editors' attack on art critics who called for the censorship of what was referred to as "degenerate art" (*Entartete Kunst*, Munich, 1938).Dali had himself

Victor Brauner
NEEDLES OF ICE
1938, oil on canvas.
Private Collection

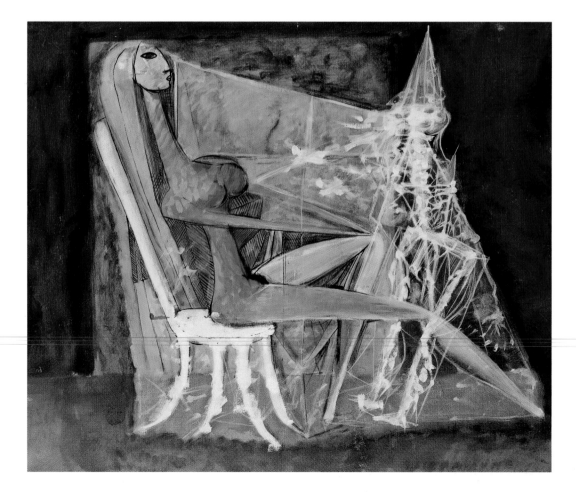

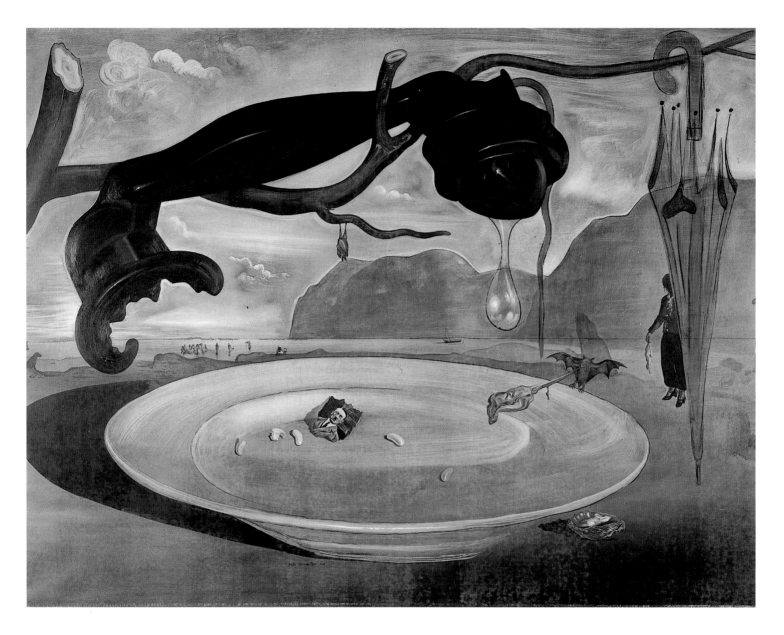

Salvador Dali
THE ENIGMA OF HITLER
About 1939, oil on canvas.
Centro de Arte Reina Sofia, Madrid

Page 126
Salvador Dali
PARANOID-CRITICAL INTERPRETATION
OF THE OBSESSIVE IMAGE OF MILLET'S "L'ANGÉLUS" DE MILLET
Page in *Minotaure* n° 1, 1st June 1933.

Page 127
Salvador Dali during a « bed-making contest »
at the Hotel Warwick in New York
le 26 April 1939.

excluded from the Surrealist group in 1939. As early as 1934, he seemed to see in Hitler another Maldoror. He was summoned before the entire group, and explanation was demanded. He answered, clowning about with a thermometer in his mouth, arguing about the orthodoxy of the movement: He dreamed of Hitler… the events of 1934 created a diversion, but his exclusion was only a question of time. In fact, Dali was no more a catholic than an admirer of Hitler, nor even of Franco – his only true allegiance was to himself.

The Surrealists discharged at the end of 1939 would mostly flee Europe and pursue Surrealist transformations in America, where he movement was essentially more artistic than political. *Minotaure*, "the review with a beast's head" ceased publication in 1939. The world was entering into a dark labyrinth, the battle of Theseus against the men with beasts'heads.

Interprétation Paranoïaque–critique
de l'Image obsédante
"L'Angélus" de Millet

par SALVADOR DALI

PROLOGUE

NOUVELLES CONSIDÉRATIONS GÉNÉRALES
SUR LE MÉCANISME DU PHÉNOMÈNE PARANOÏAQUE
DU POINT DE VUE SURRÉALISTE

Antagonisme entre les états passifs (rêve, automatisme psychique) et des états actifs systématisés. — Actualité expérimentale de l'automatisme. — De l'irrationalité, aspiration générale née de l'expérience critique de l'automatisme, à l'irrationalité concrète pré-paranoïaque. — Affirmation, contre l'attitude contemplative de l'évasion poétique, du principe productif d'action-intervention des rêves dans la vie réelle. — Rappel du principe de « vérification » formulé par Breton lors de l'invention capitale des « objets oniriques ». — Le mécanisme paranoïaque confirme la valeur dialectique de l'activité surréaliste dans les domaines de l'automatisme et du rêve. — Il illustre et réalise d'une manière tangible, matérielle, le principe de « vérification » des contenus délirants (loin des régressions coercitives que la présence « systématique » pourrait déceler en accord avec la notion de « folie raisonnante »). — Le phénomène paranoïaque, contrairement aux idées générales des théories constitutionnalistes, serait en lui-même un délire *déjà* systématisé. — Le phénomène paranoïaque, de par sa valeur de force, de pouvoir et ses caractéristiques de productivité, de permanence et d'accroissement inhérents au fait systématique, objectiverait avec évidence l'intégration de toutes les notions dynamiques fondamentales de « processus » au « délire dialectique » du surréalisme.

Dès 1929 et les débuts encore incertains de *La Femme visible**, j'annonce comme « proche le moment où, par un processus de caractère paranoïaque et actif de la pensée, il sera possible (simultanément à l'automatisme et autres états passifs) de systématiser la confusion et de contribuer au discrédit total du monde de la réalité ».

Le « drame poétique » du surréalisme résidait à ce moment pour moi dans l'antagonisme (appelant la conciliation dialectique) des deux types de confusions qui implicitement étaient prévus dans cette déclaration : d'une part la confusion passive de l'automatisme, d'autre part la confusion active et systématique illustrée par le phénomène paranoïaque.

★

On ne saurait trop insister sur l'extrême valeur révolutionnaire de l'automatisme et l'importance capitale des textes automatiques et surréalistes. L'heure de telles expériences, loin d'être passée, peut sembler plus actuelle que jamais au moment où s'offrent à nous des possibilités parallèles, résultant de la conscience que nous pouvons prendre des manifestations les plus évoluées des états passifs et de la nécessité d'une communication vitale entre les deux principes expérimentaux qui nous sont apparus plus haut comme contradictoires.

Après les coactions intellectuelles que, sous une grande charge d'émotion sthénique, Dada avait revendiquées sous la forme mécaniste d'un programme d'attitude réactionnelle (comportant, il est vrai, l'intuition de presque toutes les principales imminences), l'assimilation de l'automatisme par les surréalistes liquide toute possibilité d' « attitude » à adopter, qui serait nécessairement incompatible avec leur passivité, avec leur capitulation sans réserves devant le fait même du fonctionnement réel et involontaire de la pensée, cette capitulation à l'automatisme, cette soumission totale à la pensée en dehors de tout contrôle coercitif ne pouvant manquer d'apparaître, chaque jour davantage, comme la tentative la plus sensationnelle de tous les temps en vue d'atteindre à la liberté de l'esprit.

D'une manière plus cohérente, par suite plus grave que par la simple intuition des imminences dont il vient d'être question, l'automatisme dépasse et libère, dans les strictes limites du phénomène psychique, les aspirations latentes auxquelles Dada imposait pour contrainte les réactions mécaniques des dernières situations et attitudes «intellectuelles».

C'est dans le cours même, dans le cours le plus involontaire de la pensée, et en dehors de toute « obligation » poétique que cette fois en la démoralisation va s'incorporer de fait aux hiérarchies neutres, voraces et autoritaires des documents scientifiques. L'autorité ne pourra laisser d'être officiellement reconnue à la trépanation pisseuse du petit principe de contradiction, à l'érosion fine, en forme de sonnette, d'une diminuante vieille cul-de-jatte, enrhumée, bretonne et électrique, merdoyant les nostalgies finies des localisations spatiales et temporelles, à la nouille-nonnade générale, à la légère morve de toupie de merde de la « causalité » molle et lamentable, pareille à une misérable montre de cendre mélangée à la nourriture et projetée avec elle par une des narines du bureaucrate moyen, confit et méditatif, à la suite d'une toux saccadée et asphyxiante et des convulsions bruyantes d'un étouffement accidentel et mécanique, provoquées par une mauvaise déglutition, survenue à la fin médiocre d'un repas solitaire achevé sans conviction sous la lumière très avancée du soir d'été filtrant irisée à travers les timides et convalescents vitrages en couleurs au motif de cigognes habillées en nourrices dans la salle vide d'un restaurant grandiose, modeste et perpendiculaire.

Considérant l'état lamentable où nous trouvons les notions fondamentales de la pensée logique, nous devons nous attendre à ce que les restes des bases mécaniques de défense des catégories décrépites du raisonnement souffrent également de cette haute et souveraine dépréciation involontaire et généreuse qui inonde fécondement, d'un regard irréparable, les terrains rassurants et confortables de l'esthétique et de la morale. Après cette submersion totale de l'abstrait-censure par l'inactivité même de la libération, comment peut-on prendre encore en considération l'évidente mauvaise foi des générations mécanistes arguant des nécessités de limitation de la productivité ainsi que de la cohérence interne non évolutive des résultats automatiques ? Comment peut-on accepter de voir mettre en balance ce prétendu manque de processus automatique et ses inconvénients épisodiques avec la déroute réelle qu'il entraîne dans la pensée — phénomène de toutes les hiérarchies coercitives du monde pratique — rationnel, de toutes les sales « combinaisons » clandestines et transférées du désir dans le domaine crapuleux de l'esthétique, de tous ces agents provocateurs, en somme, de la pensée réaliste ? Comment hésiter, je

---

* Éditions surréalistes, Paris, 1930.

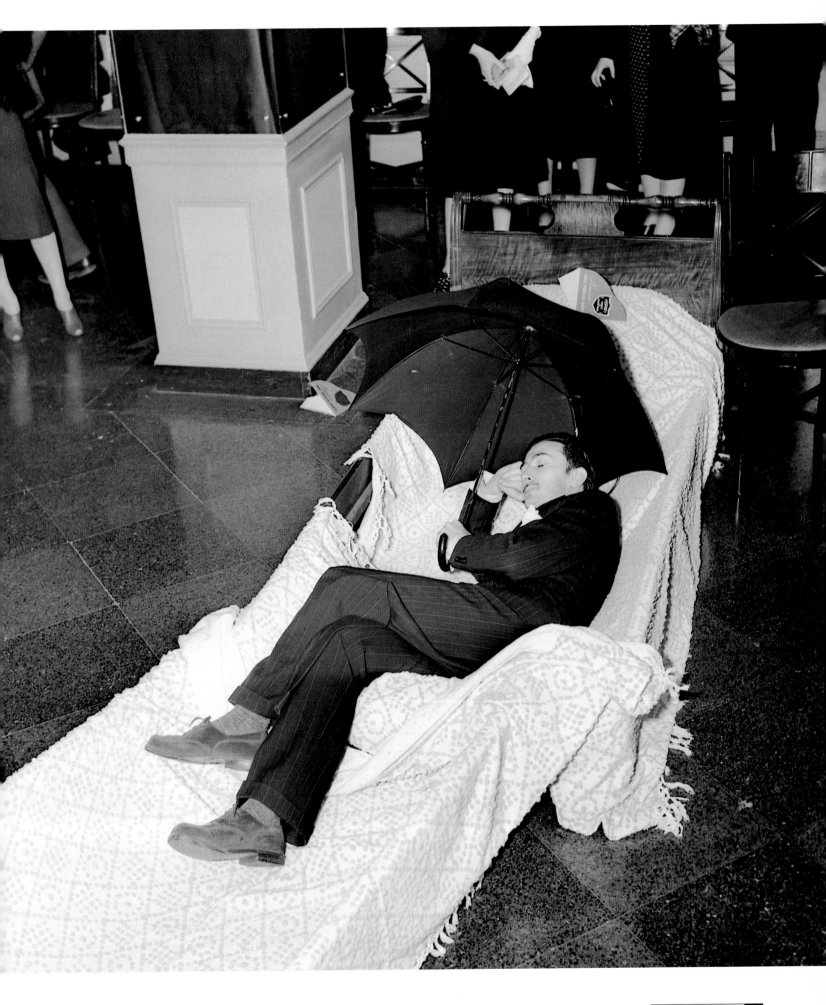

1940-1947
Dispersion

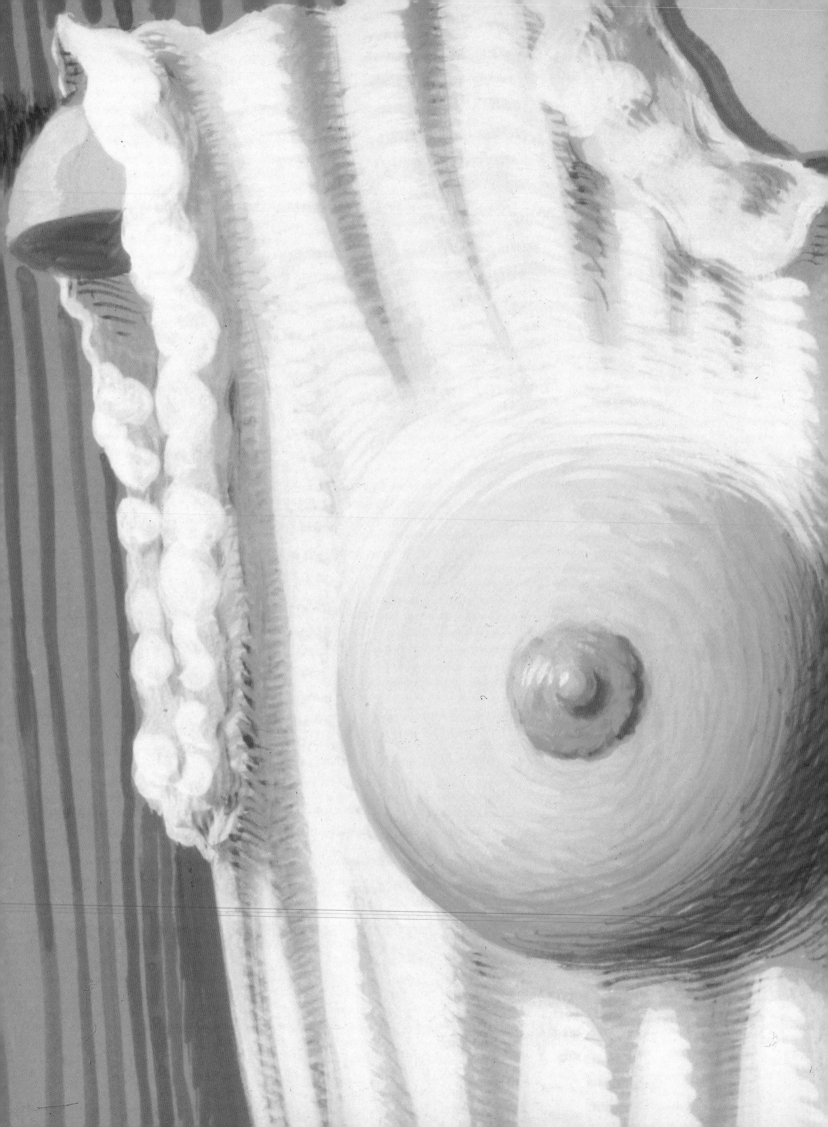

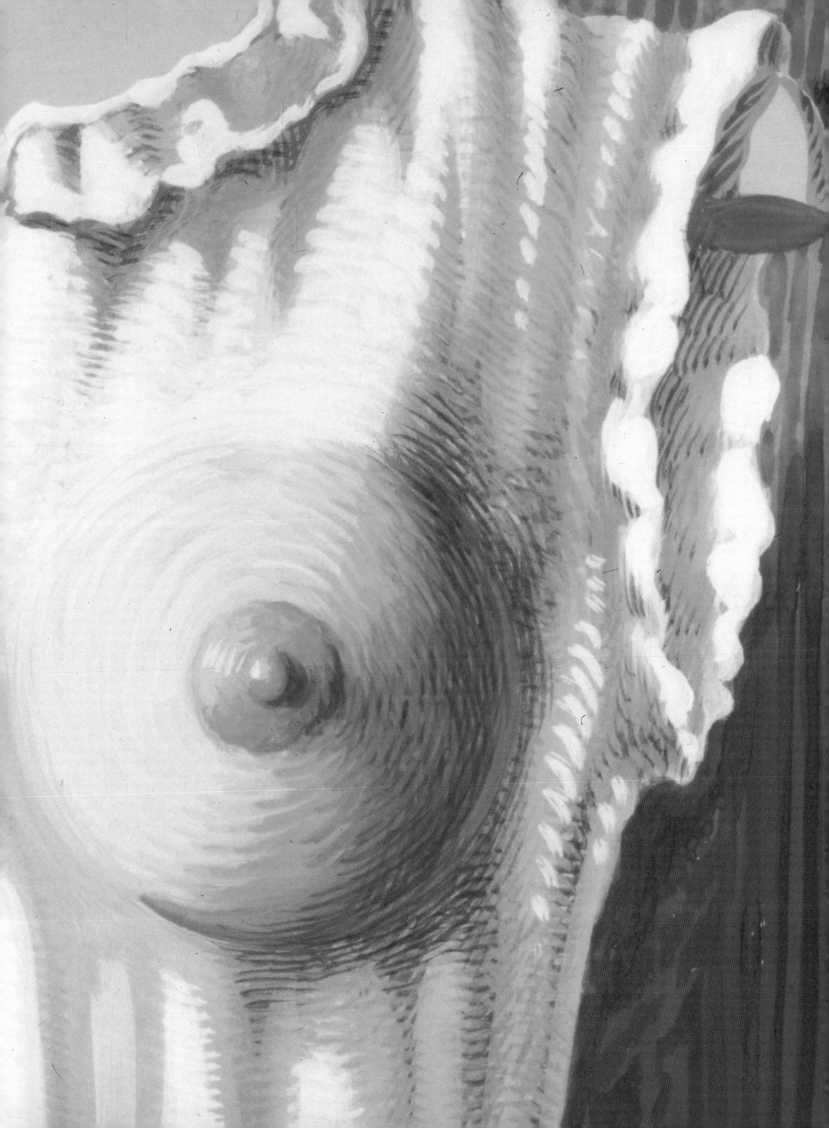

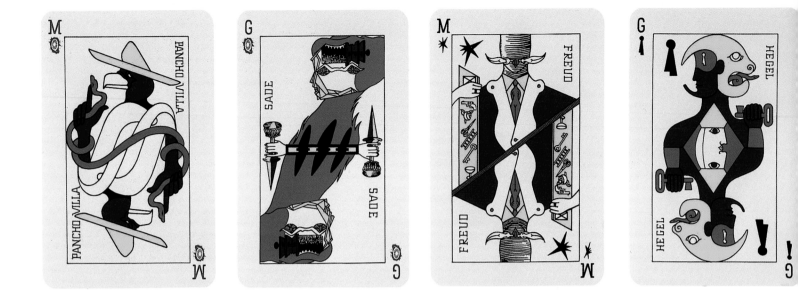

THE GAME OF MARSEILLE
1940-1941, tarot cards game.
André Breton, René Char, Oscar Dominguez,
Victor Brauner, Max Ernst, Jacques Hérold,
Wilfredo Lam, André Masson, Benjamin Péret.
Editions André Dimanche, Marseille.

Page 130 et 131
René Magritte
PHILOSOPHY IN THE BOUDOIR
Detail, 1948, gouache.
Private Collection.

In 1939 Breton was mobilized as a doctor, and attended a school for pilots in Poitiers. Péret had joined his regiment, but would soon be imprisoned in Rennes for anti-military Trotskyist propaganda within the army. Freud died in London in September 1939. Trotsky would be assassinated in 1940. At the time of the armistice, and exodus, Ernst and Bellmer being German were taken to Le Camp des Milles. The other Surrealists met at the Air-Bel residence near Marseilles (in the "Free Zone") after their discharge. They would remain housed there during the winter of 1940 41, taken care of by an American committee for aid to intellectuals, the Emergency Rescue Committee. Breton, Char, Dominguez, Brauner, Ernst, Hérold, Lam, Masson, Péret would kill time by playing cards – Tarot, "the Game of Marseille." Then thanks to Varian Fry, head of the Committee, Breton, Victor Serge, Claude Lévi-Strauss, Marcel Duchamp and Max Ernst left for Martinique in 1941.

Exile

As early as 1939, Dali, Tanguy and Matta were in the United States. Would the Surrealists re-group in America? First, in Martinique, the exiles were badly received by the Pétanist authorities. Breton went to the Dominican Republic then to New York. At the time that his *Anthologie de l'Humour Noir* (Anthology of Black

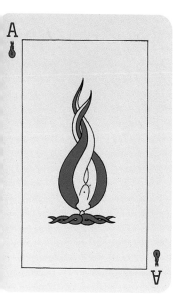
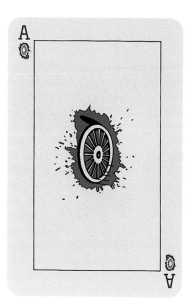
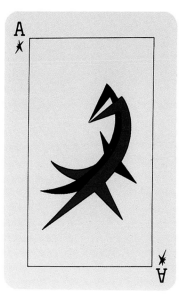
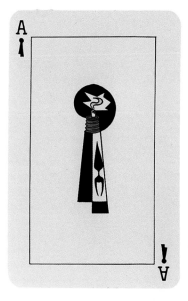

Page 134 and 135
Dora Maar,
Nush and Paul Éluard,
Jacqueline and André Breton
playing cards in 1937.

Humor) came out in bookstores in Paris, he met the great poet Aimé Césaire in Martinique. Césaire's tropical lyricism came from a Surrealist liberty, linked with a Communist commitment. The author of *Cahier d'un Retour au Pays Natal* (Notebook of the Return Home, 1939) would be the Communist Deputy-Mayor in Fort de France for years after the war. He would leave the Communist Party in 1957.

"But who takes hold of my voice? Who burns my voice? Stuffing my throat with a thousand bamboo shoots. The needles of a thousand sea urchins. It's you, dirty end of the world. Dirty little dawn. It's you dirty hatred. It's you the weight of insult and a hundred years of whippings. It is you one hundred years of patience, one hundred years of my care taking, just to stay alive … ah … oh.
We sing of poisonous flowers bursting in the furious prairies; the skies of love cut through with an embolism…"
In *Martinique Charmeuse de Serpents* (Martinique, Snake Charmer, illustrated by Masson) Breton seems to discover the luxuriance of tropical nature as an exterior echo of the inner sources of poetry. Does he not during these wandering years, begin to celebrate the *outside world*? One cannot confuse the necessity of exile with the desire to travel. The latter was never part of the Surrealist's objectives. Aside from a few epigones like Malkine, going from Cameroon to the United States by way of Oceania, the South Sea Islands, then coming to Paris to die, like Savitry, Pierre Roy, Paalen, Arshile

Gorky, Matta and, especially, the Cuban painter Wilfredo Lam – whose large forest canvas *La Jungle* (1943) had been admired by Breton – the Surrealists seemed in general seemed to share the idea formulated in *L'Immaculée Conception*: "Traveling always took me too far. The certainty of arriving has always seemed to me akin to the hundredth ring on the bell of a door that doesn't open."

In the United States, they scattered about, some in the cities, some in the country. Ernst complained of not being able to find cafés there. He established his atelier in Arizona, and began what would be quite a happy period for him. He married Peggy Guggenheim and painted the *L'Anti-pape* (Anti-Pope, 1942), *L'Oeil du Silence* (The Eye of Silence, 1944). He exhibited frequently. His canvas *Le Surréalisme et la Peinture* (Surrealism and Painting) of which we have already spoken, announced a change of tide… Masson, living in Boston said that he had discovered there "the shock of the essential" in front of Chinese paintings. His own painting drew away from the "provocative intentions of Surrealism," but continued to be nonetheless *hirsute*, shaggy. He fought with Breton, yet another time. Exile seemed to have brought on, especially among the painters, a revision of values. Dali was in Virginia at the home of Caresse Crosby, and wrote his auto-biographical *Vie Secrète*, only slightly critically-paranoiac. Breton was fed up with this "society

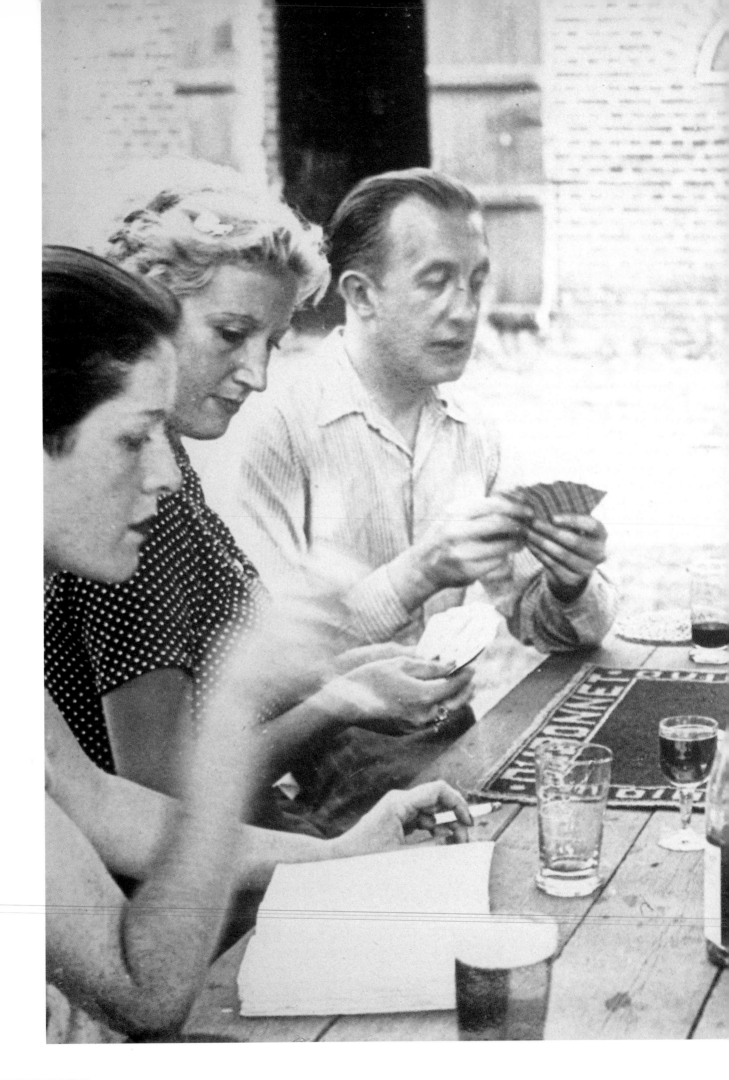

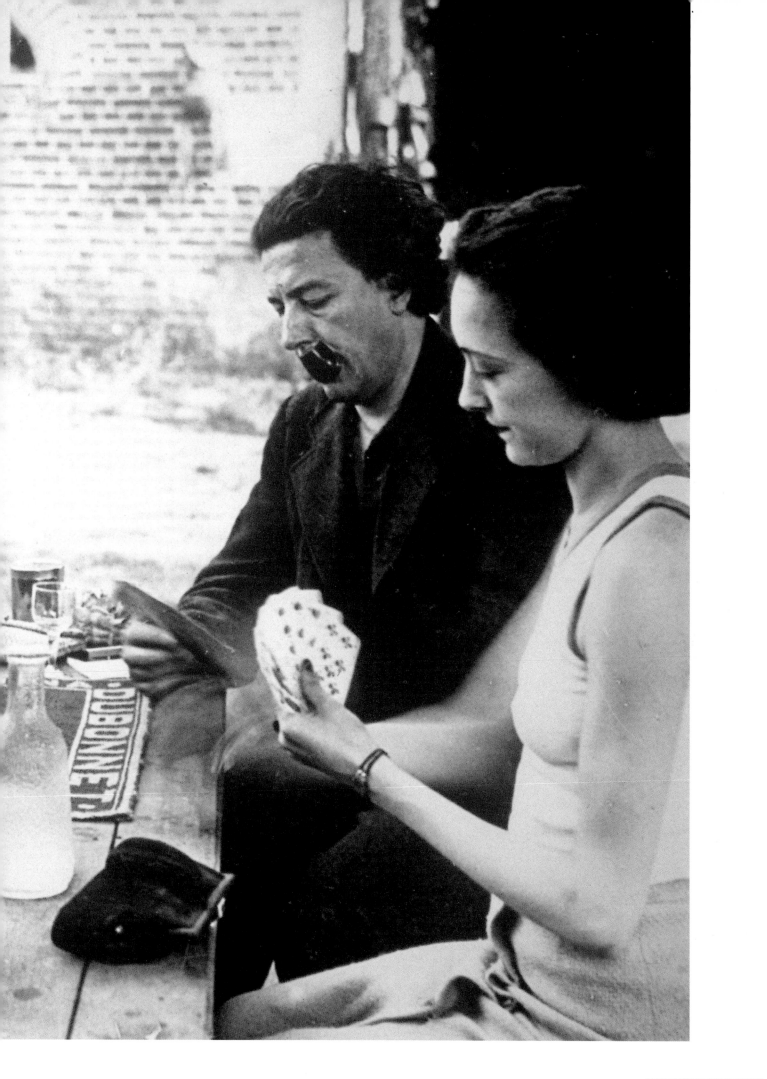

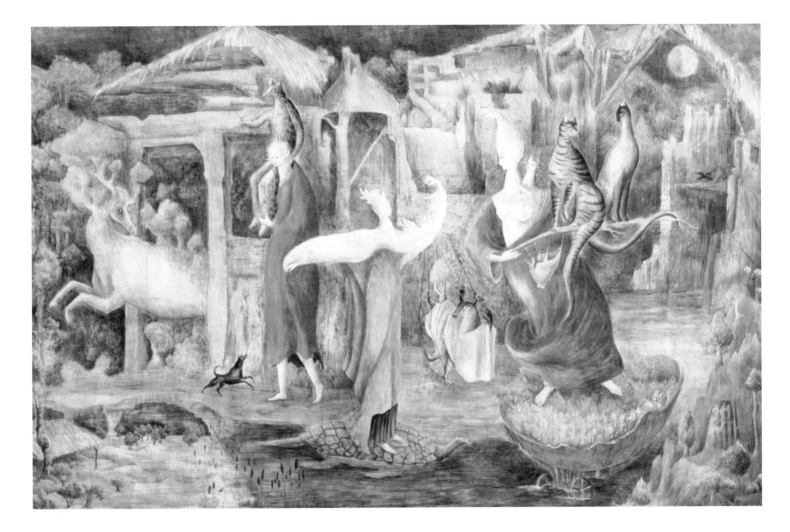

Leonora Carrington
TUESDAY
About 1917
Formerly Edward James Foundation, Sussex.

Wilfredo Lam
THE JUNGLE
1943, gouache on paper
monted on canvas
The Museum of Modern Art, Inter-American
Fund, New York

creature," and in 1941 formalized Dali's already de facto exclusion.

Dali's paintings during the war play with Catholicism whose baroque extremes enchanted him. This however did not alter his fundamental fascination with the phantasmagoric sources of mainstream Surrealism… That Jesus Christ was a "cheese," and that *Vie Secrète* ends with "I fear that I shall die without the sky," would barely indicate a religious conversion such as Claudel's. His feverish search for a substitute mother led to a state of nervous agitation that had nothing monastic about it…

When Léonora Carrington, Ernst's former lover, finally reached the States, Ernst, whom she hoped to join, had just married a famous gallery owner… She moved to Mexico. In addition to her fantastic fables and her paintings, her Surrealist creativity manifested itself in cooking recipes that were works of art.

Yves Tanguy had met Kay Sage, an American in France, in 1939. Declared unfit for service, he went to New York where he married her. They were to live in Woodbury, Connecticut as of 1941. Their paintings are not without affinities, as seen in Kay Sage's tragic and foggy Ghost Cities. Tanguy's painting develops in the tradition of dream-master pieces.

The Surrealists influenced American painters they met, such as Robert Motherwell and Arshile Gorky. On the other hand, Wolfgang Paalen distanced himself. He first came to America in 1939. In 1940 he organized a major Surrealist exhibition in Mexico City, and between 1942 and 44 published six numbers of the review DYN. In the first issue he wrote that he "no longer believed that Surrealism would determine the position of the artist in the modern world, nor formulate objectively the *raison d'être* of art." A connoisseur of Indian art, his painting

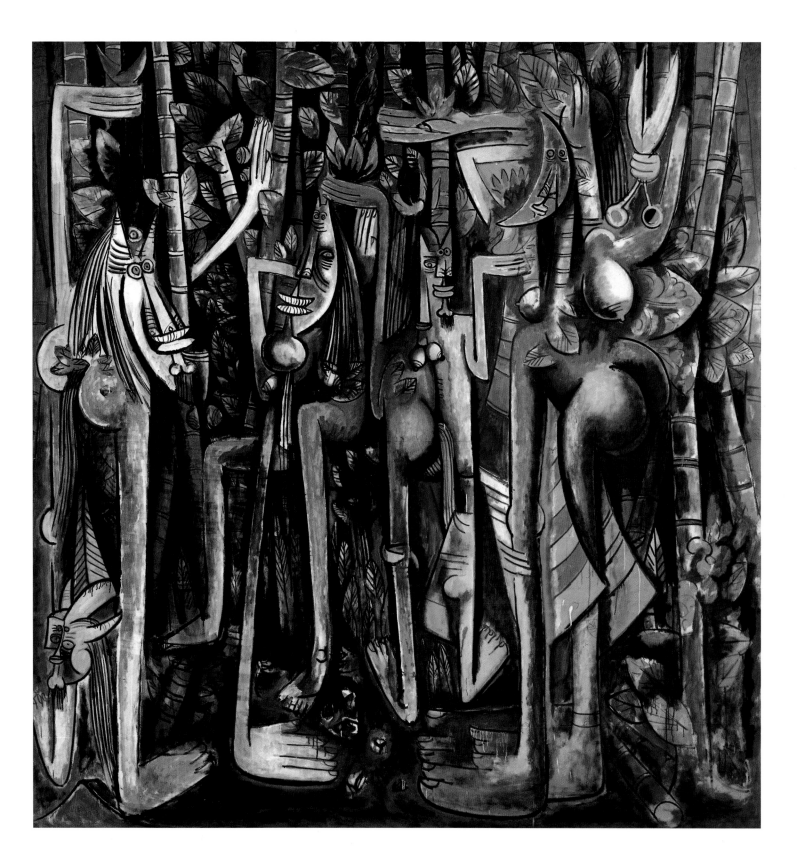

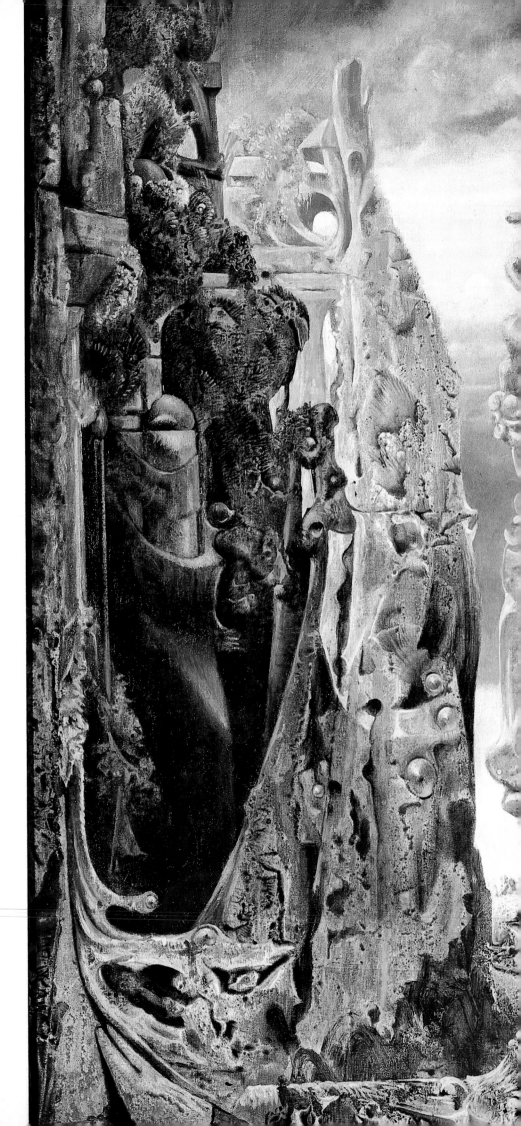

Max Ernst
THE EYE OF SILENCE
1943-1944, oil on canvas.
Washington Gallery of Art,
Saint-Louis.

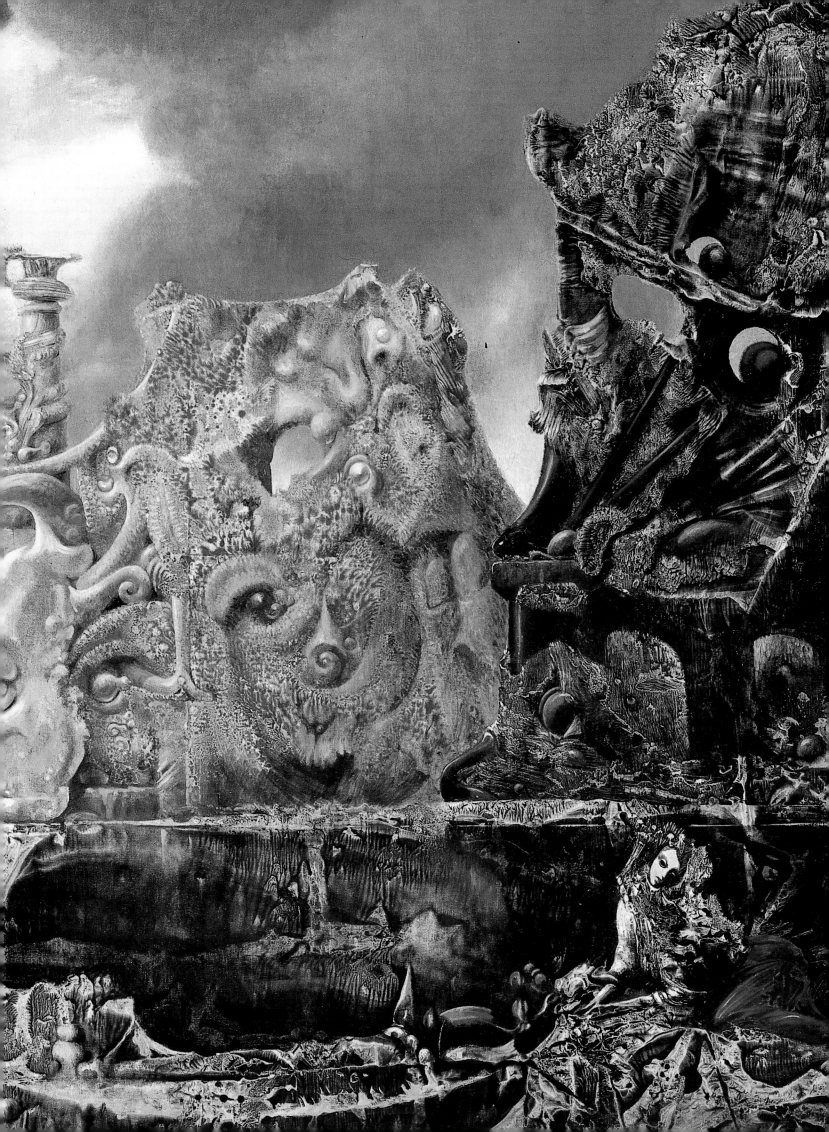

Arshile Gorky
LIVER IS A COCK'S COMB
1944, oil on canvas.
Albright Art Gallery, Buffalo.

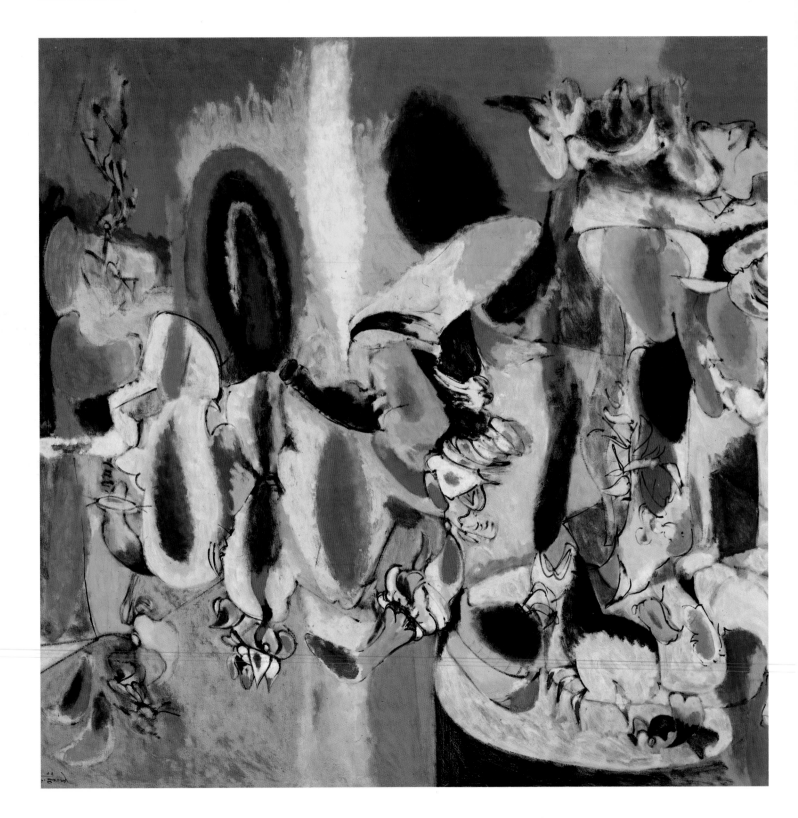

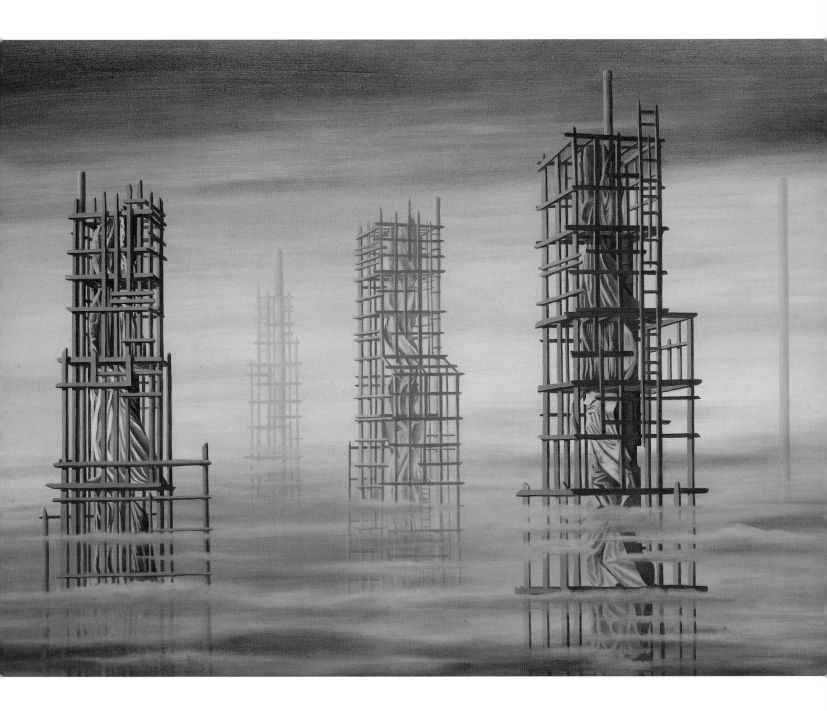

Kay Sage
TOMORROW IS NEVER
1955, oil on canvas.
The Metropolitan Museum of Art, New York

Page 142
Yves Tanguy
CONSTRUCT AND DESTROY
1941, oil on canvas.
Museo d'Arte Moderno di Ca Pesaro, Venice

Page 143
Yves Tanguy
INDEFINED DIVISIBILITY
1942, oil on canvas.
Albright Knox Art Gallery, Buffalo, New York

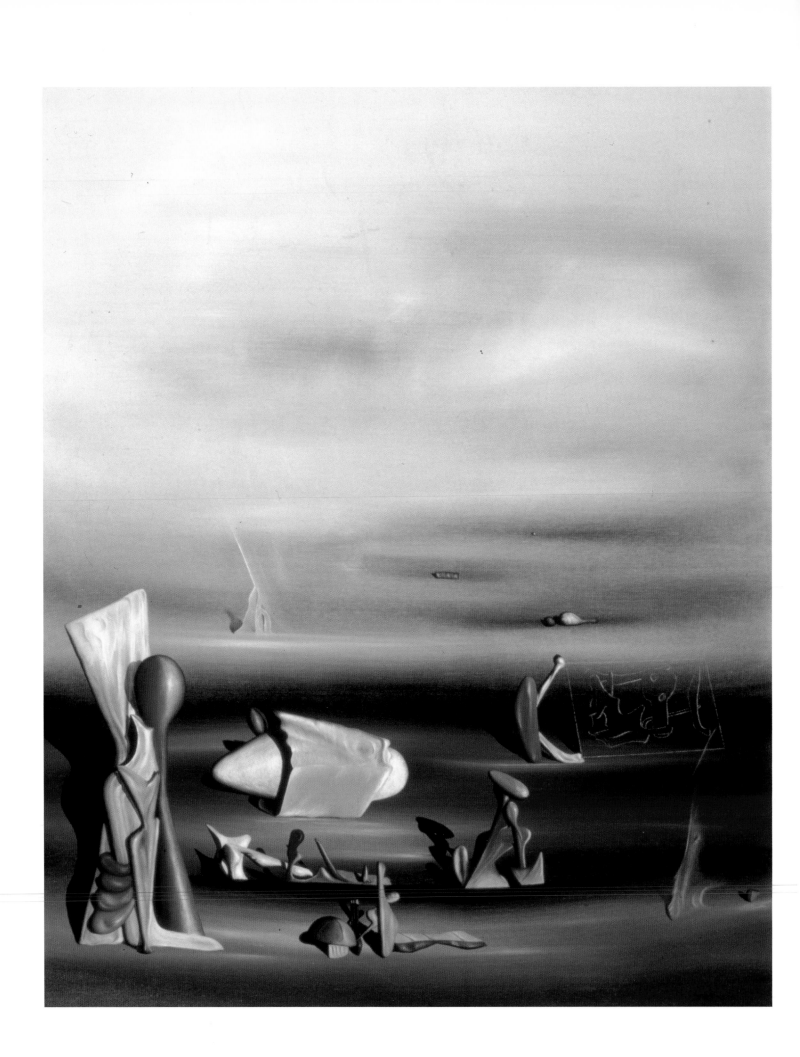

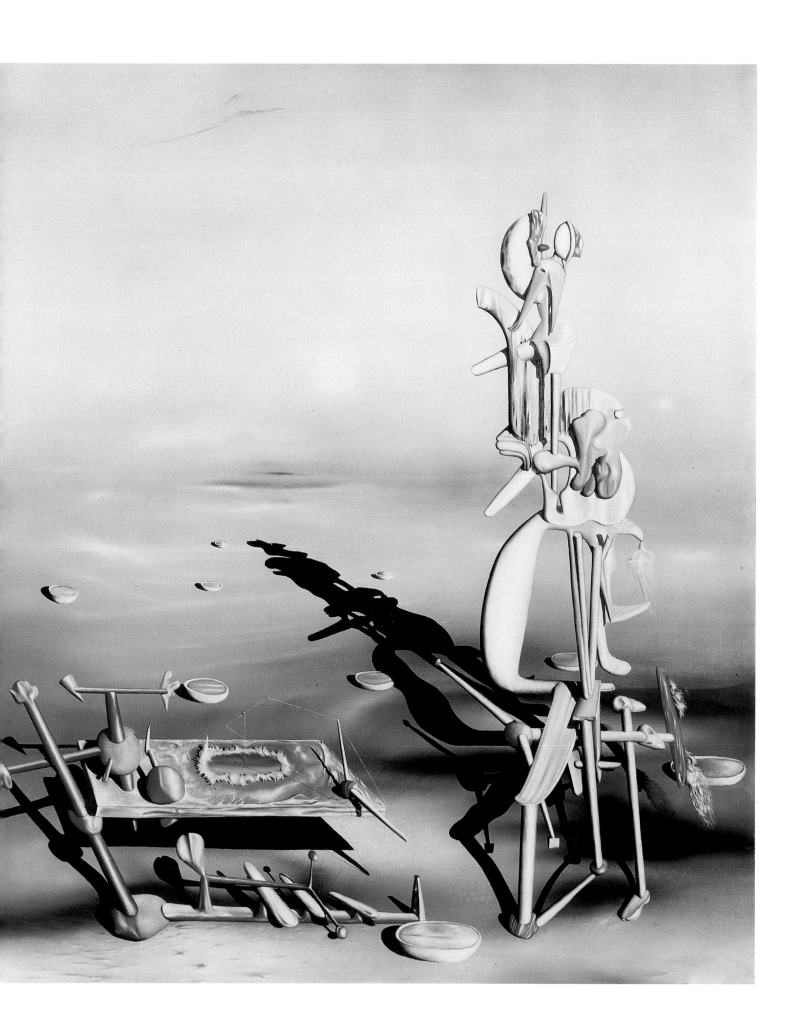

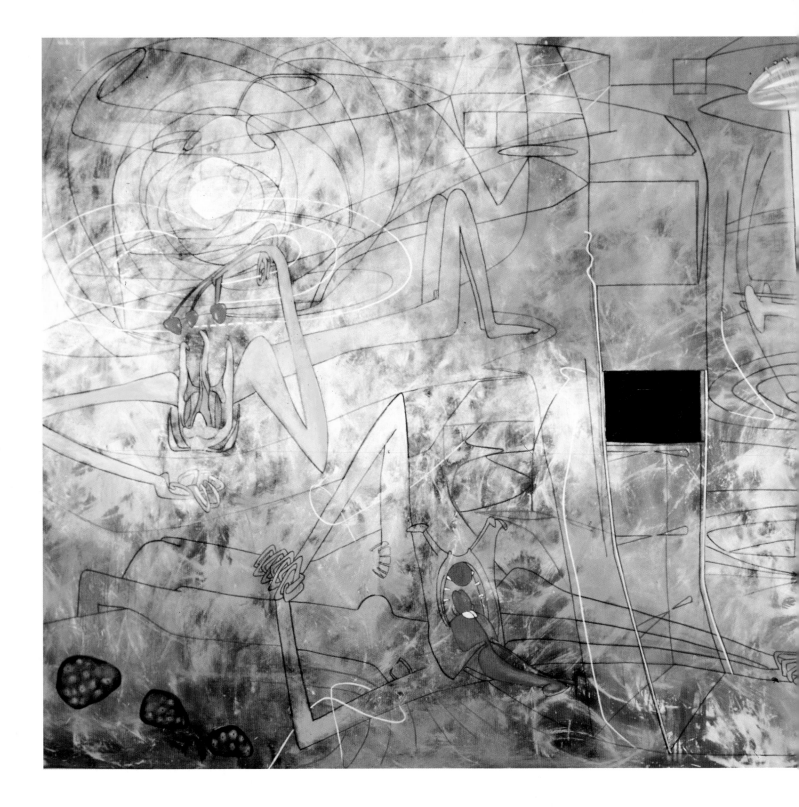

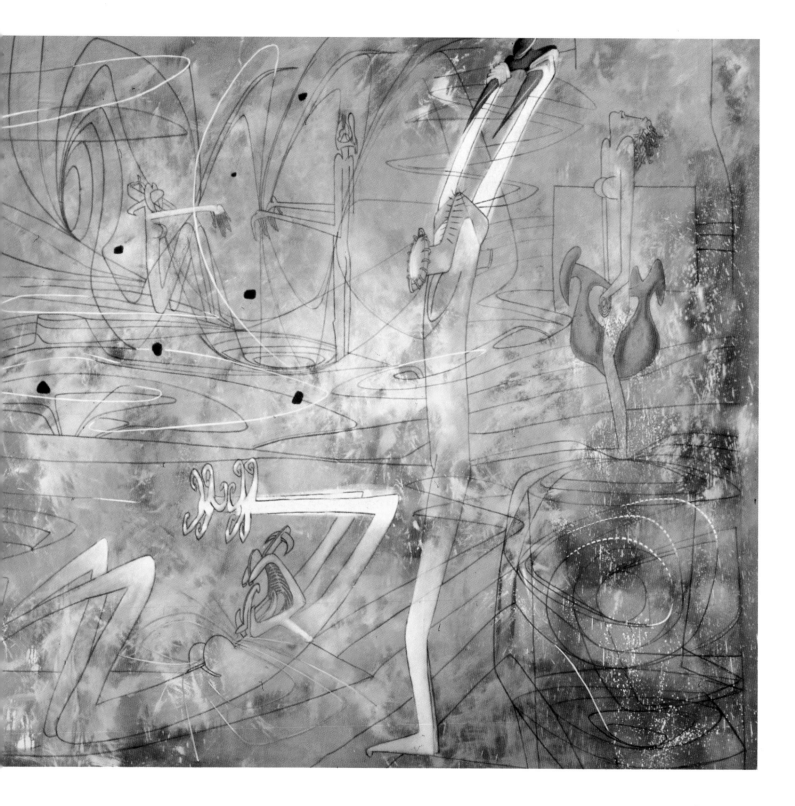

Roberto Matta
XPACE AND THE EGO
1945, oil on canvas
Centre Pompidou-MNAM-CCI, Paris

would lean towards a sort of abstract impressionism. Breton wrote in *Prolégomènes à Un Troisième Manifeste du Surréalisme ou Non* (Prolegomena to a *Third Manifesto of Surrealism* or Not, 1942): "Even after twenty years, I still feel the obligation, as in my youth, to speak out against all kinds of conformity, and in doing so, aim at a certain Surrealist conformity as well." We should observe that in his 1941 text, *Genèse et Perspective Artistiques du Surréalisme*, Breton rightly presents Surrealism as "artistic" according to the esthetic criteria imposed by *Minotaure*. This work, intended as a pedagogical study of the history of art in the 20th century, treats current innovations such as Pollack's drippings and the beginnings of lyrical abstraction with polite indifference.

It was in *Prolégomènes* that Breton wrote: "Not only must man's exploitation of man cease, but also man's exploitation by the supposed 'God' of absurd and provocative memory." Is it with the myth of "Grands transparents" (that Breton presents at the end of this text) that one can maintain faith that humanity, in spite of the archaic tearing-apart of Europe, will at last find its way out of this irrationality? For the moment, the social and political myths that operate behind these battles where the "great Aryan blond" dreams of ruling the world, are those of a "free world." We can't blame Breton for contributing to the role of the radio as a means of expressing concern over this myth. While Péret, in his pamphlet *Le Déshonneur des Poètes* (The Dishonor of Poets, Mexico City, 1945), insulted the "poètes de la résistance" that surrounded Eluard. Breton, speaker on the Voice of America radio broadcasts, and belligerent supporter of America allied with Stalin in the soon-to-be atomic war, brutally attacked the past errors of hard core Surrealism. Breton added his bit to the war against fascism of which he stated in a speech to students at Yale in 1942, that even the "virus" that produced it had to be eradicated. Beginning in 1942 the review *VVV* continued the work of *Minotaure*, mixing art and anthropology. In the same year a major *Surrealist Exhibition* was presented by Duchamp along with its catalogue, *First Papers of Surrealism*. The review *View* became interested in the American version of the fantastic. A translation of the *Hebdomeros* by De Chirico appeared in January 1943, and the March 1945 issue was dedicated to Duchamp, who's personnel role along with his notoriety in America were at there highest. It was said that Matta's painting was a cross between Duchamp and Tanguy – effectively, the young Chilian's allusions to science fiction in the vague space of his canvases, seemed to be knocking on Surrealism's door. So, life goes on.

Breton met his third wife in 1943, the Chilean, Elisa Bindhoff, for whom he would write *Arcane 17* (New York, 1944). The book, written in Gaspésie (Canada) confirmed Breton's attentiveness to the colors of nature, in the perspective of a correspondence with inner unifying flux of true love.

He was criticized for the pages concerning the "femme-enfant," but let us not forget that for the Surrealists, childhood is the state of being closest to clairvoyance, the dawn of the spirit. It was certainly not a coincidence that Breton called his only daughter, Aube (dawn). She was the daughter of Jacqueline Lamba. *Arcane 17* brings the tragedy of *Nadja* to the level of a visionary happiness.

"We Are Here to Stay"

All this time, what was happening in France? All of the "historical Surrealists" hadn't left, and beginning in 1939, young people joined in an initially neo-Dada action, that would become clearly Surrealist beginning in 1941. It was the group *Réverbères*, then *La Main à Plume*, whose tract in 1941 clearly stated, "We are here to stay" (C.F. José Pierre, *Tracts*, vol. II, p. 5). The review *Réverbères* (the title was taken from Tzara) would publish five issues from April 1938 to July 1939. The public meetings in homage to Dada (May 1938) and Apollinaire were great successes. The group had created a link between the old Dadaists who vegetated at the Dôme in Montparnasse, and the young poets from the Latin Quarter. In putting on *Les Mamelles de Tyrésias*, they resuscitated theatre that Surrealism had ignored. They integrated music, notably jazz, to the spontaneous poetic action, breaking a strange taboo established by the Surrealists. Finally, Jean-François Chabrun saw the exhibition "L'Art Dégénéré" in Germany (summer 1938) and wrote a vitriolic review in *Réverbères*, N° 3.

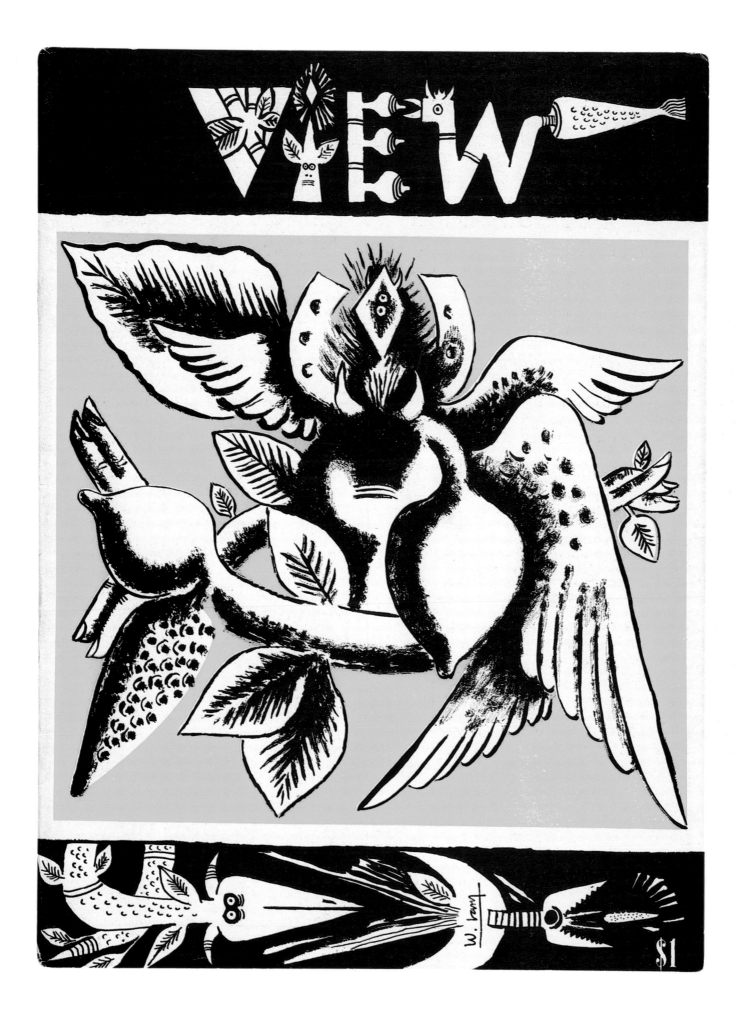

$1

LA CONQUÊTE DU MONDE
PAR L'IMAGE

Noël ARNAUD
ARP
Maurice BLANCHARD
Jacques BUREAU
J.-F. CHABRUN
Paul CHANCEL
Paul DELVAUX
Oscar DOMINGUEZ
Chr. DOTREMONT
Paul ELUARD
Maurice HENRY
Georges HUGNET

Valentine HUGO
René MAGRITTE
Léo MALET
J.-V. MANUEL
Marcel MARIEN
Marc PATIN
Pablo PICASSO
Régine RAUFAST
TITA
Raoul UBAC
G. VULLIAMY
et l'USINE à POÈMES

Objet (1942).   PICASSO.

*Il faut que la force créatrice de l'artiste fasse surgir
ces images, ces idoles demeurées dans l'organisme, dans le
souvenir, dans l'imagination; qu'elle le fasse librement sans
y mettre d'intention ni de vouloir; il faut qu'elles se déploient,
croissent, se dilatent et se contractent, afin de devenir non
plus des schèmes fugitifs, mais des objets véritables et concrets.*
GOETHE

LES ÉDITIONS DE LA MAIN A PLUME
11, Rue Dautancourt — PARIS (XVIIᵉ)

THE CONQUEST OF THE WORLD
BY THE IMAGE
24 April 1942, cover
of a copy of
La Main à la plume
Private Collection

His thoughts were identical to Breton's who, at the same moment, was in Mexico City defending the free art. Chabrun realized that this defense could only be political. The future would prove that, after *Réverbères*, the group *La Main à Plume* was alone in its defense of Surrealist orthodoxy (that of the *Second Manifesto*). During the occupation, the group would, concerning this point, take firm, semi-clandestine actions. Michel Fauré, recounts in his *Histoire du Surréalisme sous l'Occupation*, (La table Ronde, 1982) an interview with Chabrun and Breton at the Dôme, early in 1939. Chabrun having said "Something must be done," Breton was to have responded, "It is for you to do, the young must take over!" (p.32). Was it in trying to apply these melancholy thoughts that Breton left for America? The young poets of *La Main à Plume* were becoming more and more active politically and would pay dearly for this later, with deportation and death – eight deaths, out of fifteen or so members, among whom, Ménégoz, who was sixteen, and Mulotte, fifteen…

Breton having left, it was Péret, who would replace him for a while at the café, before managing, not without dif-

ficulty, to leave the country. The members of *La Main à Plume* would always have a particular affection for Péret, and for the rigorous example he set.

La Main à Plume was the publishers'logo for a series of publications, which could not appear in a regular manner due to censorship. It was also a group led by Noël Arnaud and Jean-François Chabrun. Among the members could be found the Spaniard Manuel (who had saved Péret's life during a misunderstanding with the anarchists during the Spanish Civil War – they thought he looked like a priest, and Manuel, a member of the P.O.U.M., had a terrible time getting him out of there), Christian Dotremont, Marc Patin, Raoul Ubac and the painters Schneider, Christine Boumester, Vulliamy and Tita.

These publications were spread out until 1944: *Géographie Nocturne* (Nighttime Geography, 1941), *Transfusion du Verbe* (Transfusion of the Word, 1941), with a text by Eluard and a contribution by Picasso, *La Conquête du Monde par l'Image* (Conquering of the World by Pictures, 1942) all came out with ample participation by the Surrealists who had stayed in Europe,

Arp, Delvaux, Magritte, Valentine Hugo, Maurice Henri and Georges Hugnet. The cover presented for the first time, Picasso's *Tête de Taureau* (actually pictured as a "bull's head" was bicycle saddle and handlebars). Eluard contributed "Poésie Involontaire et Poésie Intentionnelle" (Involuntary Poetry and Intentional Poetry). But having teemed up once again with Aragon who had just founded secretly *Les Lettres Françaises*, he was excluded along with Hugnet. The Surrealists gathered themselves together in *Le Surréalisme Encore et Toujours* (1943). In addition to these deliveries, *Pages Libres* published numerous individual little plaques: *Les*

Malheurs du Dollar by Péret, *Pleine Marge* by Breton, and most of all, the opus *Poésie et Vérité 42* by Eluard, containing his poem *Liberté*, printed for the first time in 5000 copies and distributed in the streets. The violence of the young generation loyal to Péret's spirit, also was expressed in numerous leaflets… The last publication of *La Main à Plume, l'Objet* (1944) which was never released, gave the floor to young poets such as Edouard Jaguer, Marco Menegoz and Jean-Pierre Mulotte. In an unpublished notebook Mulotte writes about the "Surrealizing of music," by dipping records into soup or orange soda…

Pablo Picasso
BULL'S HEAD
Spring 1942, bicycleseat and handlebars.
Musée Picasso, Paris.

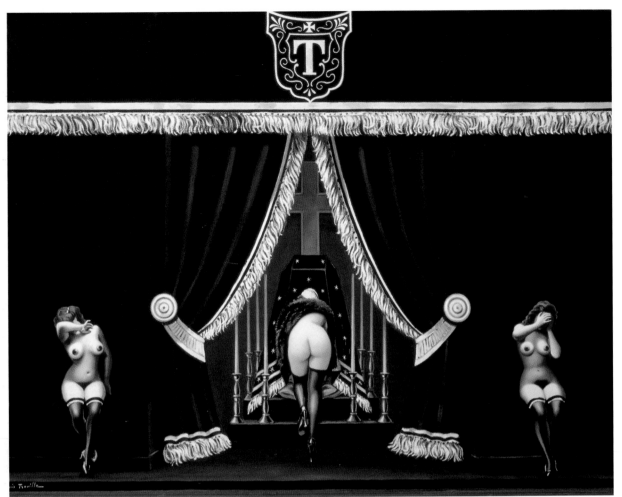

Clovis Trouille
MY FUNERAL
1947, oil on canvas.
Private Collection.

René Magritte
PHILOSOPHY IN THE BOUDOIR
1948, gouache.
Private Collection.

Jean-Pierre Mulotte was shot on the Austerlitz Bridge by a German that he had just insulted. Marco Menegoz, Robert Rius and Jean Simonpoli went underground in the Fontainebleau Forest and were executed with the others in a place called "Le Charnier" near Arbonne. Jean-Claude Diamant-Berger, a former member of *Réverbères*, would be killed in combat near Caen on 18 July 1944…

At the time of the Allies'landing, the group had suffered tensions between those favorable to drawing nearer to the Communist Party, (Arnaud, Chabrun, Simonpoli, Boquet, André Stil, who would later become the senior editor of *L'Humanité*, member of the Central Committee, and recipient of the Stalin Award…) and the Surrealists adhering to Breton's individualistic positions (de Sède, Danial Nat, Dalmas). This tension could not be overcome and the members of *La Main à Plume* dispersed. Some of them, notably Arnaud and Dotremonnt would be seen again, in 1947, in *Le Surréalisme Révolutionnaire.*

Before telling of the circumstances surrounding Breton's return to Paris in 1946, let us remember what life had been like for the friends who remained in Europe during the war, Picasso, Toyen, Magritte, Delvaux, Bellmer, Miró Dominguez, Brauner, plus a few epigones like Felix Labisse or Clovis Trouille.

A word about Aragon. First, a clandestine Communist militant, his poems were primarily concerned with Elsa's eyes. We find him after the Liberation, having become an apostle of Zhdanovism. Eluard was not as involved as Aragon, and the pamphlet by Brunius and Mesens *Idolatry and Confusion* (London, 1944) spared the author of *Liberté,* of which a translation would be published in London. This was the first attack launched by the orthodox Surrealists against the poets of the resistance (Péret's only came out in 1945). Eluard lived in Vézelay with Nusch and we know that the last word of the poem, *Liberté,* was at first, Nusch's name. One can safely say that the word *liberty* would remain the key word throughout Eluard's life until his death in 1952. He was in fact closer to Jean Lescure's review *Messages,* than to *Lettres Françaises.* Proof of this lies in his text on Bellmer's doll (1943), and those about Dubuffet and Picasso.

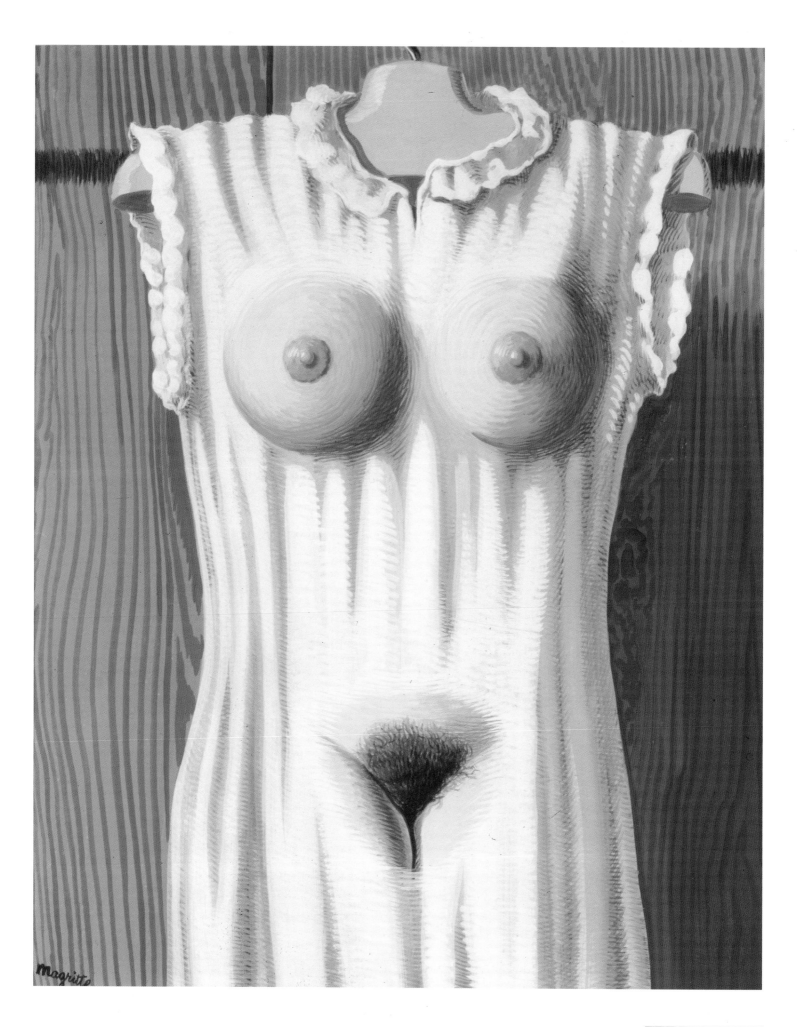

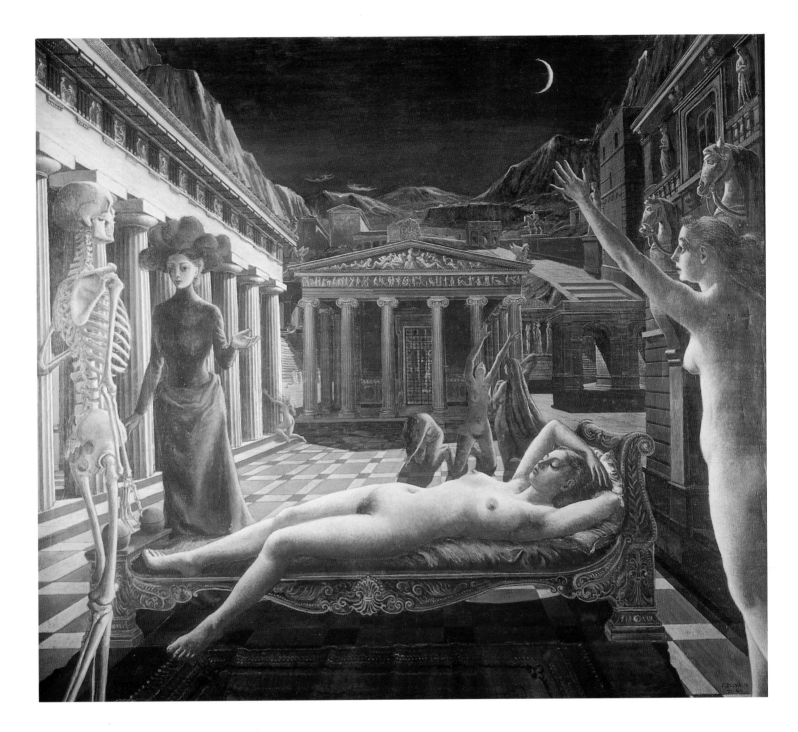

Paul Delvaux
VENUS ASLEEP
1944, oil on canvas.
Tate Gallery, London.

Hans Bellmer
NUDE FROM THE BACK
WITH SPIKE HEADS
1961, charcoal, red pencil, white
gouache highlights on paper
glued to cardboard.
Centre Pompidou-MNAM-CCI, Paris.

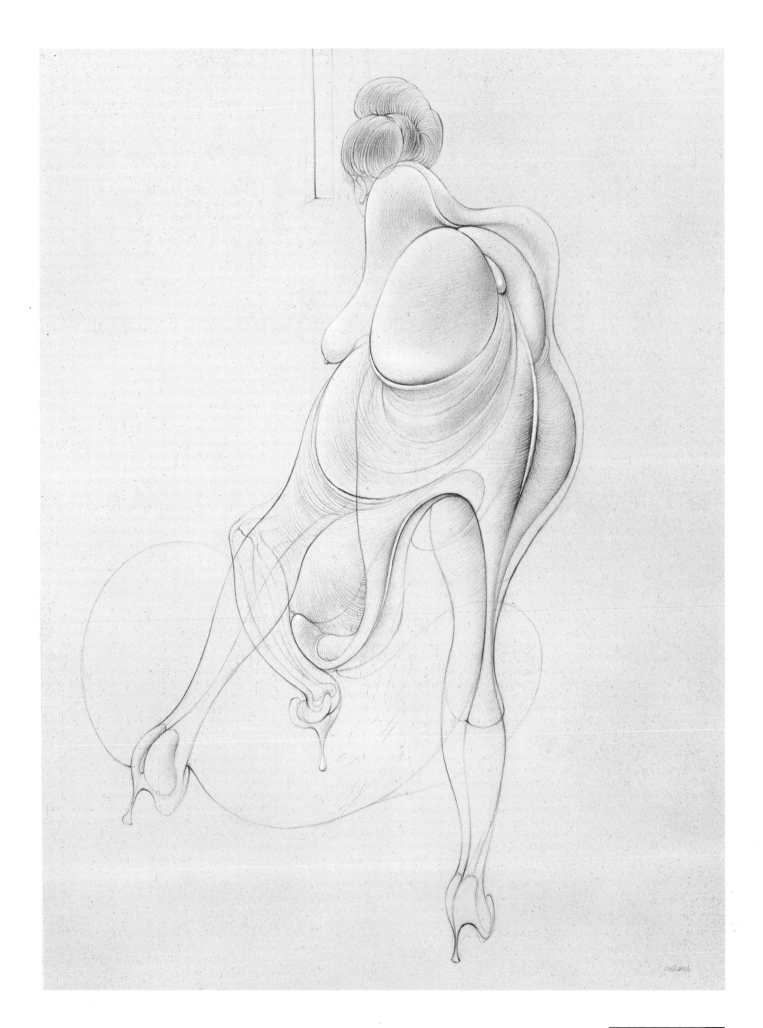

Picasso, hence a member of the Communist Party (to Breton's consternation), made an exhibition in 1944 that would remain in the annals of the Salon d'Automne. His freedom would later be a thorn in the side of his hard core Stalinist friends. And the others? Toyen made drawings that reflected the tragedy of the era, *Le Tir* (The Shooting, 1940), and *Cache-Toi Guerre* (War, Hide Yourself, 1944). Her sado-masochist paintings are summarized in canvases such as *Au Chateau Lacoste.* Magritte stayed in Belgium and joined the Belgium Communist Party en 1945. Linked with the *Surréalistes Révolutionnaires,* he broke off with Breton once again. Paul Delvaux painted calmly during the entire period and had a retrospective in 1944 at the Palais des Beaux Arts in Brussels. The women that he painted, Eluard would write, are "left to their destiny of knowing nothing of themselves." So it was with this artist. Felix Labisse, whose female nudes are often cruel, began to paint in 1938 and Desnos dedicated an homage to him in 1945. As for Clovis Trouille, the representative of a "popular Surrealism," he painted a great deal during the occupation: *Dialogue au Carmel* (Dialogue at Mount Carmel, 1944), *Mes Funerailles* (My Funeral, 1945), *Le Baiser du Confesseur* (The Confessor's Kiss, 1947), where one recognizes André Breton…

Bellmer, released from the Camp des Milles in 1940 threw his German passport in a gutter in 1941. A refugee in Toulouse, he remarried. He *illustrated L'Histoire de l'Oeil* (The Story of the Eye), by Bataille, and his sharp engravings of the sensuous intertwining of feverish anatomies, would make him famous. In 1946, separated from his wife, he met the young philosopher Nora Mitrani… Joan Miró left Varengeville and sought safety in Barcelona, his place of birth. His acrylic *Constellations* (1940-41) made their way to André Breton in America. Victor Brauner, at the time, a refugee in Gap (France) came out of his *Chimères* (Chimera, 1939) period and entered his period of flat wax surfaces: *Première Solitude* (First Solitude, 1943). Hans Arp, who had emigrated to Switzerland, was shocked by the accidental death of Sophie Tauber in 1943. He too would be scarred by the trials of solitude. On the other hand, Desnos, having escaped Surrealism long ago, was deported as a Communist resistant and died of exhaustion and sickness upon his release from the Térézine concentration camp, 8 June 1945. René Char, under the name of Captain Alexandre, directed an underground resistance group in the Vercors. He was to publish *Feuillet d'Hypnos* (Hypnosis Page) in 1946; in 1948 *Seuls Demeurent* (The Only Left), and in 1953, *Lettera Amorosa* (Love Letter, later used in *La Parole en Archipel* [The Word as an Archipelago, 1962] with an epigraph taken from the *Lettera Amorosa* by Monteverdi).

The most important poet of the young generation of Surrealists, René Char, who's *Le Marteau Sans Maître* (The Hammer without a Master, 1934 and 1935) served as the text for Pierre Boulez's music, had written in 1932 (*SASDLR*, N°4, p.12): "Poetry incorporates itself in time and absorbs it. Where the white night ceases, the white night continues. But that the clairvoyant exterminates the believer and the Surreal suddenly appears, moves in, imposes itself. A world of passion from which we can't escape, that we no longer desire to escape." After the war, he lived in seclusion in L'Isle sur Sorgue. Until his death in 1988, he continued to produce a body of mysterious and violent works:

"Time as a sub-work, years of affliction… Natural right! In spite of themselves they will once again give life to the Work of all admired times.

I cherish you. Soon he will be without the ambitious one who stays unbelieving in the woman like the hornet battling with cleverness less and less spacious. Yet I cherish you who can turn away the heavy bait of death.

This was, blessed world, a changed month of Eros, that she illuminated, built from my being, the conch of her belly: I've mingled them forever. And it was at such a second of my apprehension that she changed the blurry and abhorrent path of my destiny into a path of for the furtive happiness of the land of lovers." (Lettera Amorosa, in La Parole en Archipel, 1962, Dédicace).

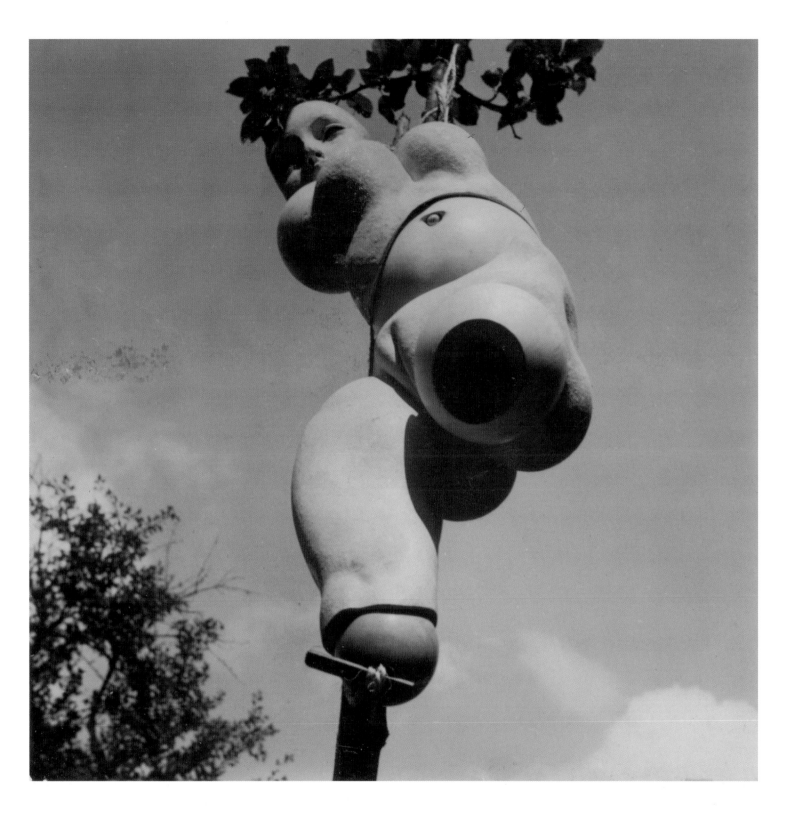

Hans Bellmer
DOLL
Page 20 of the sketch
1935-1938, gelatin silver art-
work colored with aniline,
cardboard backed
Centre Pompidou-MNAM-CCI, Paris

Victor Brauner
CUP OF DOUBT
1946, wax on cardboard
Museu de Arte, Sao Paulo

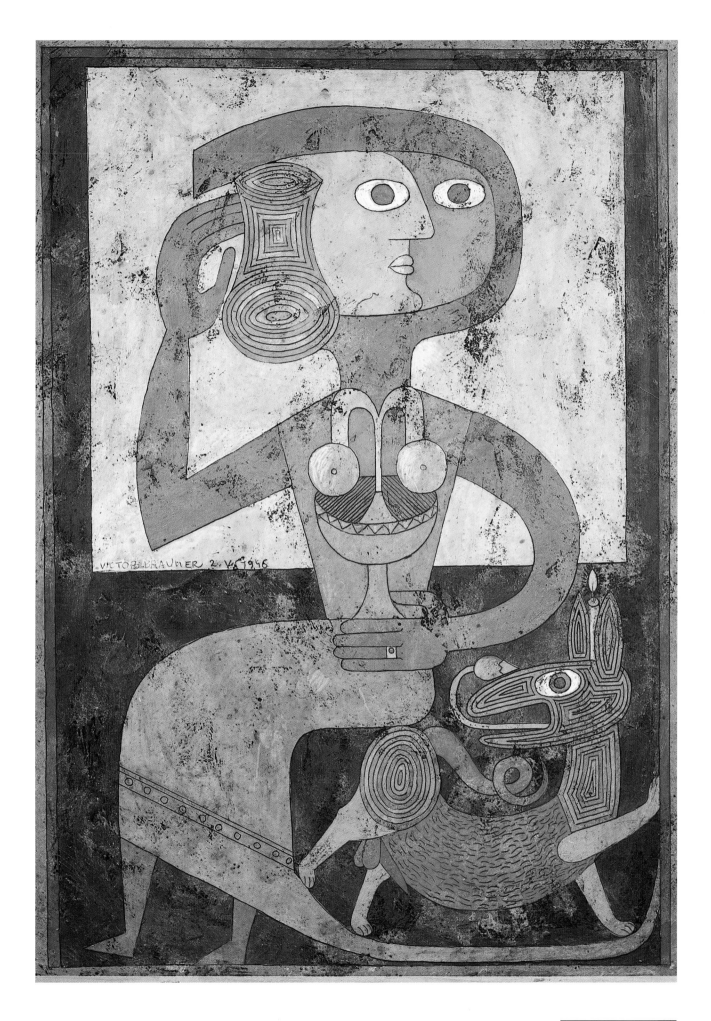

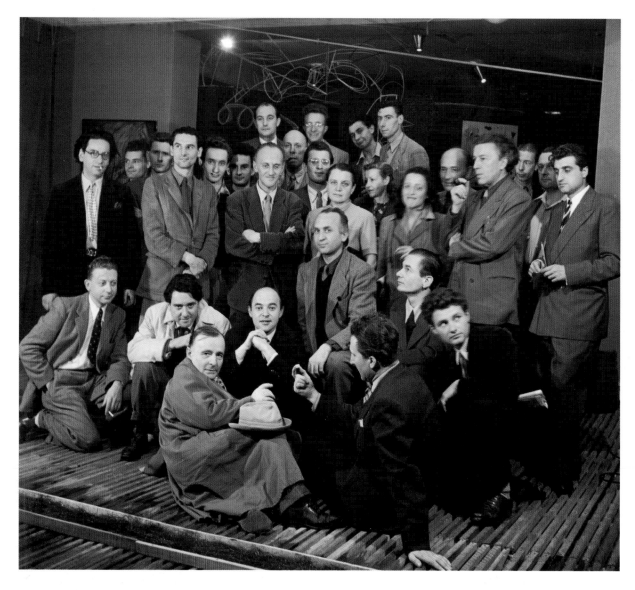

Denise Bellon
*The Surréalist Group
at the 1947 exhibition
at the galerie Maeght.*
Galerie Claude Oterelo, Paris.

1947 Exhibition at the
Galerie Maeght :
A Totem of Religions
by Frederick Kiesler

The Return of Breton

So, Breton is back. Upon arrival, he found those
Surrealists who had stayed in France scattered and scarred by the ordeal. His perspicacity had led him to write
in *Arcane 17*: "We came to quick conclusions trying to
build a bridge between the Paris of early 1940 and the
Paris of 1944, but only an idiot could maintain the illusion that they are the same city." Too much blood had
flowed under this bridge and "L'Affiche Rouge" of the
Manouchian group (those of the French Communist
Party who had been shot) had no place in Breton's
memory. He too had changed. More anti-Communist
than ever, he came to a country where de Gaulle inclu-

ded Communists in his government. He gave his first
Parisian interview in *Figaro Littéraire.* This was considered unpardonable by the young poets that had just barely left *La Main à Plume,* for Yves Bonnefoy's *La
Révolution la Nuit,* or for *Les Deux Sœurs,* by
Dotremont, and by other smaller groups in mourning
equally scarred by the war. The spectacle of the depor-
tees walking the streets of Paris in their prison uniforms,
the photographs of the Shoah's death camps provoked
an emotional shock… The Communists proclaimed
themselves "the party of those shot." It was the bombast
and pomposity of the Liberation. It was the obscene

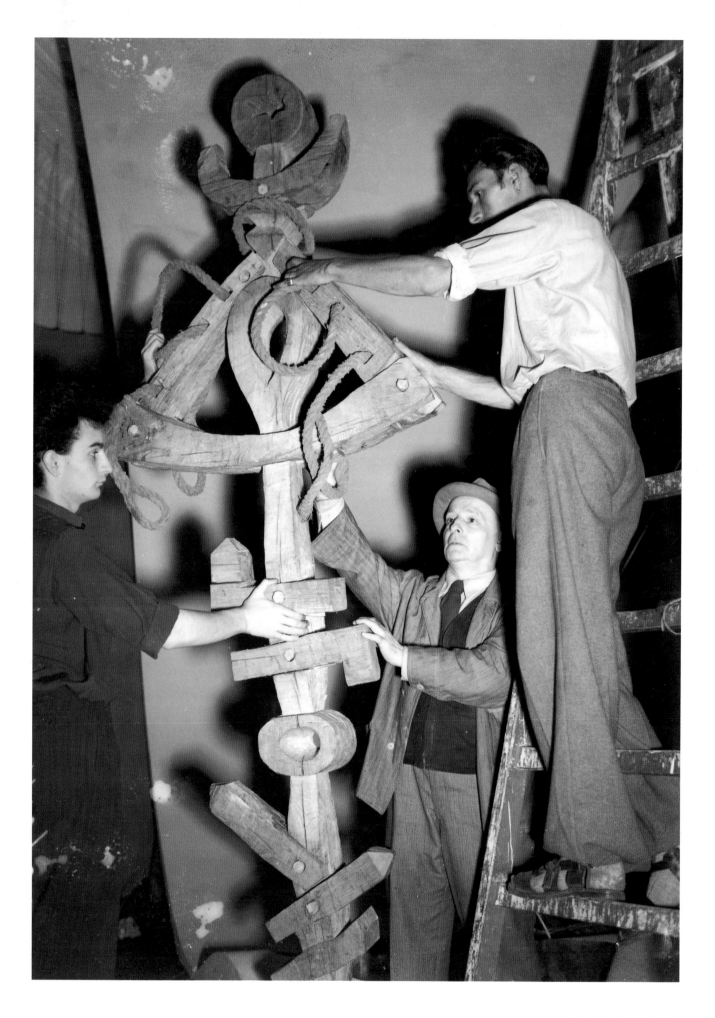

ritual of shaving the heads of women who had slept with the Germans, against which Eluard spoke out:

Comprenne qui voudra moi
Moi mon remords ce fut
La malheureuse qui resta
Sur le pavé
La victime raisonnable
A la robe déchirée
Au regard d'enfant perdue
Découronnée défigurée
Celleqaui ressemble aux morts
Qui sont morts pour être aimés…

Understand he who would like
My shame was that
Of the poor girl left
On the street
The simple victim
With the torn dress
With the gaze of a lost child
Dethroned, disfigured
She who resembles the dead
That are dead for having been loved…

Yes Paris had changed and it was a problem for Breton to have to gather together all those scattered members, while the youth no longer seemed to have need of him. What happened to the Liberation? Three important facts shed light on these turbulent times, a sort of aborted May '68, lost in the reconstruction Republican Order. Three important facts concerning Surrealism: 1. Artaud's presence; 2. the 1947 exhibition at the Galerie Maeght; 3. *Surréalisme Révolutionnaire*, shattered by the return of the French Communist Party to *Zhdanovism*, and the beginning of the cold war.
Artaud's presence. For the Surrealist movement of the post-war period, Artaud's presence was more important than Breton's return. The tragedy of the death camp survivors seemed to find an echo in the tortured voice of the Rodez survivor. Artaud entered this disgusting asylum in 1943. He became the prey of Dr. Frederic, a well-meaning man who held the poet in "terrified esteem" and subjected him to multiple electric shock treatments, a therapeutic practice in style at the time. The only effect would be the ruin of Artaud's health. Adamov and Marthe Robert went to see him and were horrified. They decided to try to get him out of this misery. Adamov managed to organize an auction with the help of members of Parisian elite. This was intended to reassure the Administration who refused to release a penniless mental patient. Jean Paulhan managed to have him freed and on 28 May 1946, he arrived in Paris. Dr. Delmas had accepted to take him on in Ivry, where he could freely come and go. On 7 June an evening in honor of Artaud was organized at the Théâtre Sarah Bernhardt. Celebrities of the theater world read his works, while he wandered about the theater outside. He had not been allowed in. Colette Thomas brought the audience to tears with her reading in the dark, during an electrical blackout. Another evening was organized at the Vieux Colombier in 1947 so that Artaud could express himself in person. Alone on stage, he had great difficulty presenting his incantation before a room full of well-to-do and inquisitive people. It was a flop…
It was in Ivry that Artaud put the final touches on *Artaud le Momo* (1947) and wrote *Van Gogh, le Suicidé de la Société*.

Le corps sous la peau est une usine surchauffée
et dehors
le malade brille,
il luit,
de tous ses pores,
eclatés,
Ainsi un paysage
de Van Gogh
à midi.

Under the skin, the body is an overheated factory
and outside
the patient shines,
he glows,
from every pore,
split open,
So is a landscape
by Van Gogh
at noon.

He also wrote his famous radio piece *Pour en Finir avec le Jugement de Dieu* (To Get the Judgement of God Over With), which was rejected in February 1948 in spite of massive protests. On 4 March, Artaud died in Ivry. He was found in the morning, on the floor at the foot of his bed.

Antonin Artaud
SELF-PORTRAIT
11 May 1946,
pencil on paper
Centre Pompidou-MNAM-CCI, Paris

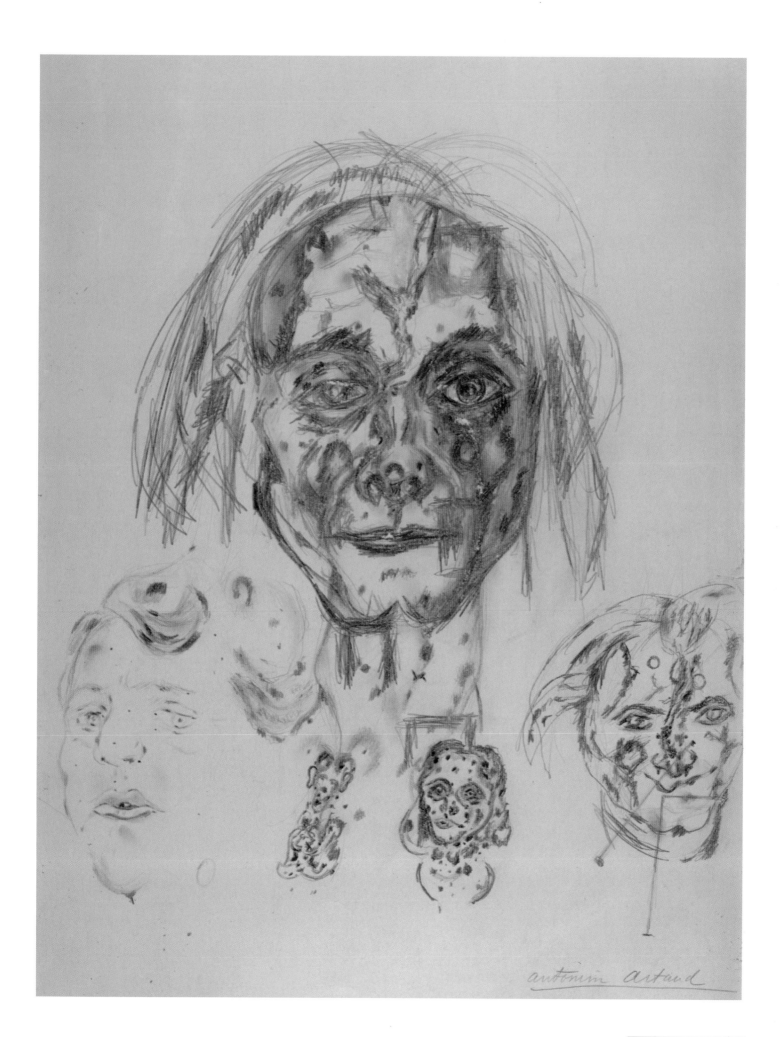

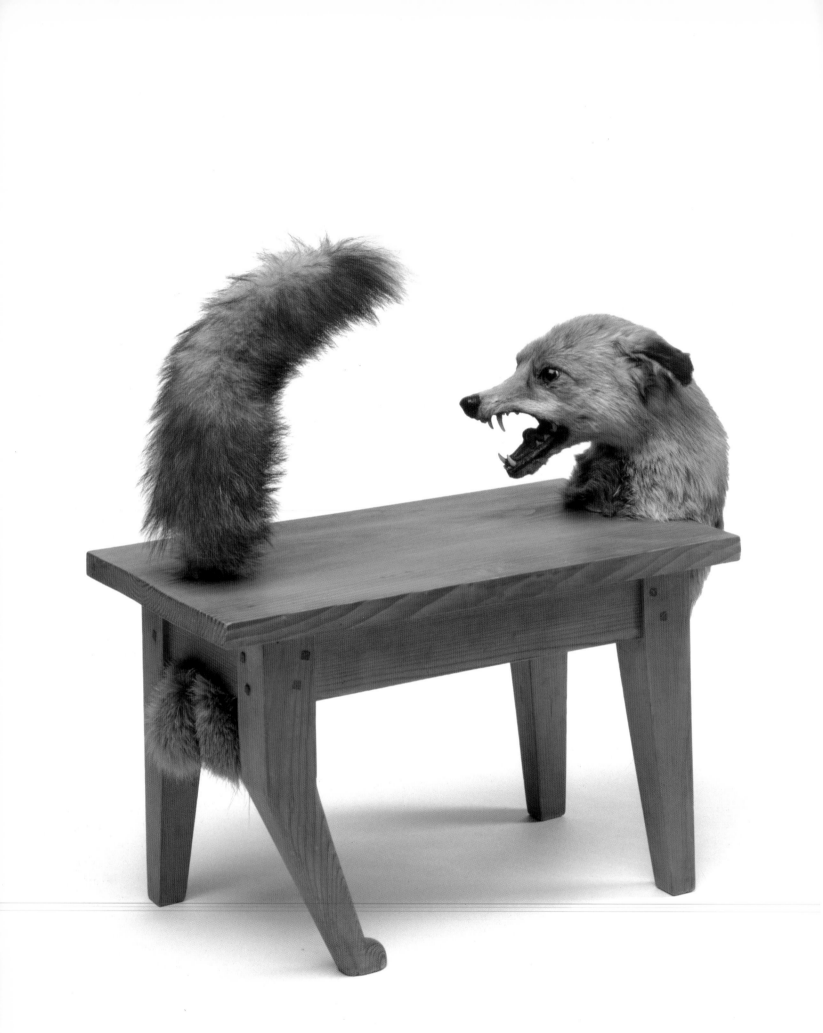

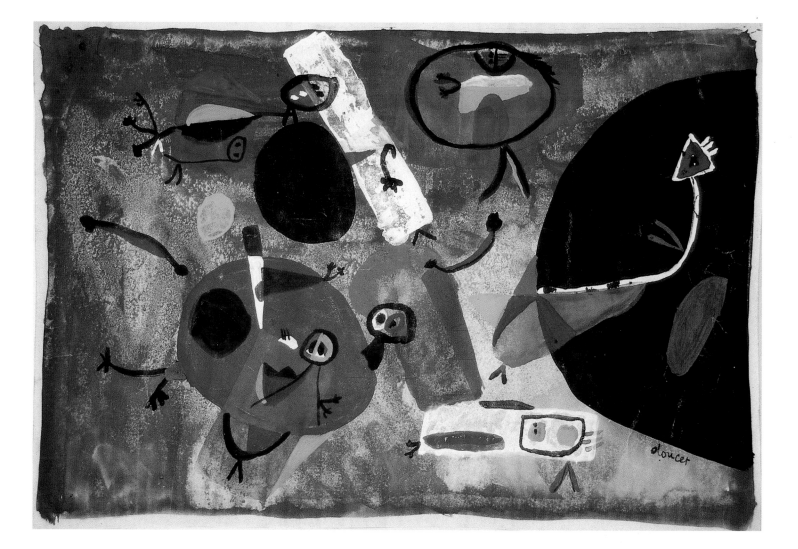

Victor Brauner
THE WOLF-TABLE
1939-1947, wood
and stuffed fox elements.
Centre Pompidou-MNAM-CCI, Paris

Jacques Doucet
UN... DEUX... TROIS... QUATRE...
1947, gouache on paper
Private Collection

Adamov, Marthe Robert, Henri Thomas, Jacques Prevel, Henri Pichette were his last friends. And even if Adamov had joined the Communist Party along with Guillevic, Vaillant, Tzara and the Comité National des Ecrivains (C.N.E., National Committee of Writers), the fact remained that Artaud's voice kept up a form of tragic Surrealism, linking the survivors of *La Main à Plume* to the apparently optimistic, fundamentally desperate supporters of *Surréalisme Révolutionnaire*. The group had protested against Surrealism's turning towards playful superstition (*superstition ludique)* and the "new myths," symbolized at that time by a big group show in Paris at the *Galerie Maeght:*
"*Le Surréalisme en 1947*" (Surrealism in 1947). On his way back to Europe, Breton, who had stopped in Haiti at the invitation of Dr. Mabille (it was said that his lec-

tures incited riots…), was impressed by Voodoo rituals, and had brought back to Paris a form of Surrealism more esoteric than ever. This was evident in the exhibition of 1947. The spectators were required to follow an initiation path, of which the twenty-one steps represented the twenty-one mysteries of Tarot. The "Hall of Superstitions" then took one through purifying rain, towards a "Labyrinth" with niches wherein lay thirteen objects "susceptible of endowed gifted with mythical life" the *Tigre Mondain* (Fashionable Tiger) by Ferry, the *Soigneur de Gravité* (Caretaker or 'Juggler' of Gravity) by Duchamp, the *Loup-table* (Wolf-Table) by Brauner, and *Les Grands Transparents* (The Large Transparents), by Hérold, etc. The catalogue contained 87 names from 27 countries, and the deluxe copies were crowned with a foam rubber breast, marked "please touch…"

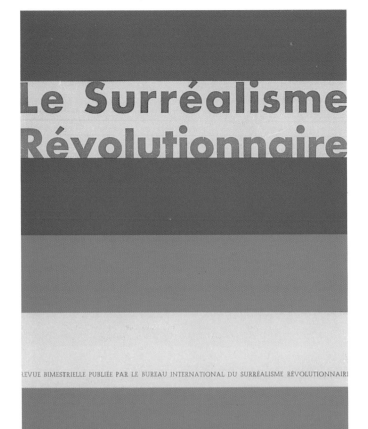

Cover of the review
« Le Surréalisme Révolutionnaire »
n° 1, March 1948.
Private Collection.

In all evidence Breton had managed to gather together a few old friends such as Duchamp, along with the younger generation whom he'd attracted – Ferry, Bédouin, Legrand, Dax, Duprey, José Pierre… We will find them again in 1952 in the review *Medium*. Many were those who would have preferred overt revolutionary action rather than the "occultation," that Breton proposed beginning in 1929. This action had been repressed, and would later become explosive, with the mere word "liberation."

Surréalisme Révolutionnaire. Former member of *La Main à Plume*, Christian Dotremont founded a "revolutionary Surrealist" group in Brussels, in 1947, which was immediately taken up and expanded by Noël Arnaud in France. The Belgian group had around twenty members, among whom were Magritte, Chavée, Mariën, Nougé, Louis Scuttenaire. The French group added the 18 signatories to the *Manifeste du Surréalisme Révolutionnaire*, among them, Suzanne Allen, Yves Battistini, Pierre Desgraupes, Pierre Dumayet, Edouard Jaguer, Hubert Juin, Jean Laude, and René Passeron… Let us

look at the attempts of the "historical Surrealists" of 1930 – to reconcile the two central concerns: responsible political action and free artistic creation – who thought they could profit from the euphoria of the Liberation to accomplish this task. The exhibition *Prise de Terre* was held at the home of Breteau in 1948, extremely open, from Labisse to Hartung, not to mention Atlan. *Le Surréalisme Révolutionnaire* review (N°1, Mars 1948) presented an broad table of contents, in which one noticed, in addition to the Belgians already mentioned, Tibor Tardos (Hungry), Zdenec Lorenc (Czechoslovakia), Raymond Queneau, Tristan Tzara, Aimé Césaire and numerous artists such as Goetz, Bucaille, Asger Jorn, Mortensen and the sculptor, Robert Jacobsen (Denmark), Atlan, Doucet, Francis Bott… The review didn't make it to the second issue. However, a *Bulletin International du Surréalisme Révolutionnaire* played the role of a bridge. At the presentation of the *Malheurs d'E*, by Jean Laude, a pianist played Webern's *Variations op. 27*, and so-called abstract paintings widened Surrealism's horizons. A memorable series of lectures, mostly Dadaist, took place in the Salle de Géographie in Saint-Germain-des-Près. The subjects discussed were eroticism and freedom, film and music. The rowdy audience got to see fist fights between Breton's Surrealists and the *Lettristes*, then quite the thing. Success was obvious…

In tracts such as *La Cause est Entendu* (The Cause is Heard), *Surréalisme Révolutionnaire* was heavily insulted by followers of Breton. In the same manner, on the other side, by the Stalinists. The "Party intellectuals" (Casanova, Garaudy, Aragon and his entourage), were overwhelmed, furious. Their dogmatic seriousness would, as early as 1948, return to Zhdanov's theory of art as a political weapon. They couldn't accept those who claimed to be French Communist Party members without its approval. Motivated by Arnaud, the French group decided to disband. The "cold war" began. Each went off to pursue his own life – Arnaud to the *Collège de Pataphysique*, Jean Dubuffet and Boris Vian, and others such as Edouard Jaguer, would found the review *Phases*, etc.

Dotremont, however, managed at the end of 1948 to bring together, *a parte*, representatives from COpenhagen, BRussels, and Amsterdam, founding the *Cobra* movement, dedicated essentially to the joy of artistic creation, in much the same way that *Minotaure* had followed *SASDLR*…

Names of collaborators
of the review
Le Surréalisme révolutionnaire
n° 1, March 1948.
Private Collection.

Collaborent à la Revue
" LE SURRÉALISME-RÉVOLUTIONNAIRE " :

Suzan Allen - Else Alfelt - Noël Arnaud - J.M. Atlan
Raymonde Aynard - Yves Battistini - Ejler Bille - Francis Bott
Kujahn Blask - Paul Bourgoignie - Marcel Broodthaers
Max Bucaille - Aimé Césaire - Achille Chavée - Bob Claessens
Paul Colinet - Paulette Daussy - Raymond Daussy
Pierre Desgraupes - Oscar Dominguez - Christian Dotremont
Jacques Doucet - Pierre Dumayet - Louis Dumouchel
Paul Frank - Henri Goetz - Benjamin Goriély - Hamel Guita
Jacques Halpern - Irène Hamoir - Marcel Havrenne
Henry Heerup - Walter Hoeber - Michel Holyman
Josef Istler - Ejill Jacobsen - Robert Jacobsen - Edouard Jaguer
Johannes Jensen - Asger Jorn - Lucien Justet - Jacques Kober
Milos Korecek - Ludvick Kundera - Félix Labisse
Bohdan Lacina - Jean Laude - Jules Lefranc - Marcel Lefrancq
André Lorant - Zdenek Lorenc - Albert Ludé - René Magritte
Marcel Mariën - Rouben Mélik - Tage Mellerup - Franz Moreau
Richard Mortensen - Georges Mounin - Jorgen Nash
Jean Noiret - Paul Nougé - Erik Ortvad - René Passeron
Armand Permantier - Carl Henning Petersen - Gabriel Picqueray
Raymond Queneau - Vilém Reichmann - Léonce Rigot
Viggo Rohde - Madeleine Rousseau - Salzedo
Jens-August Schade - Louis Scutenaire - Armand Simon
René de Solier - Pierre Soulages - Roger Steinhart
Boguslaw Szwacz - Tibor Tardos - Erik Thommesen
Vaclav Tikal - Tristan Tzara - François Van der Drift
Louis Van de Spiegele - Vaclav Zykmund

1948-1966
Persistence

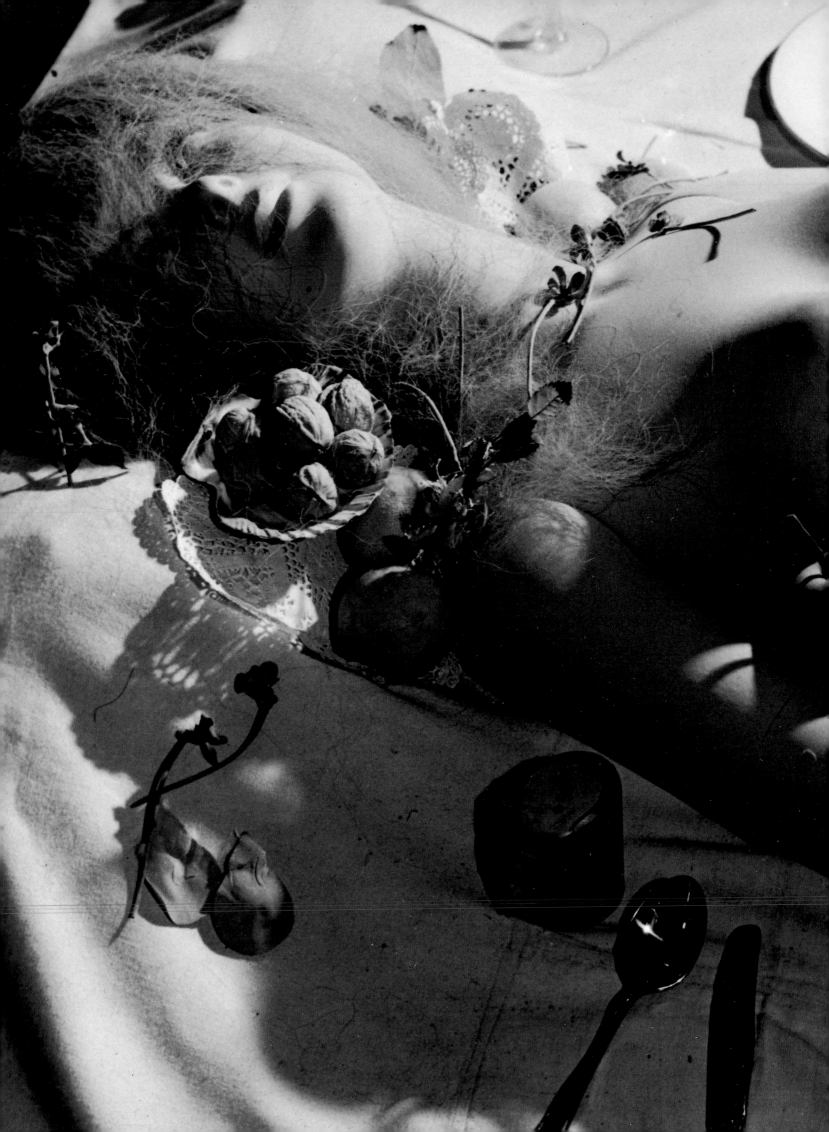

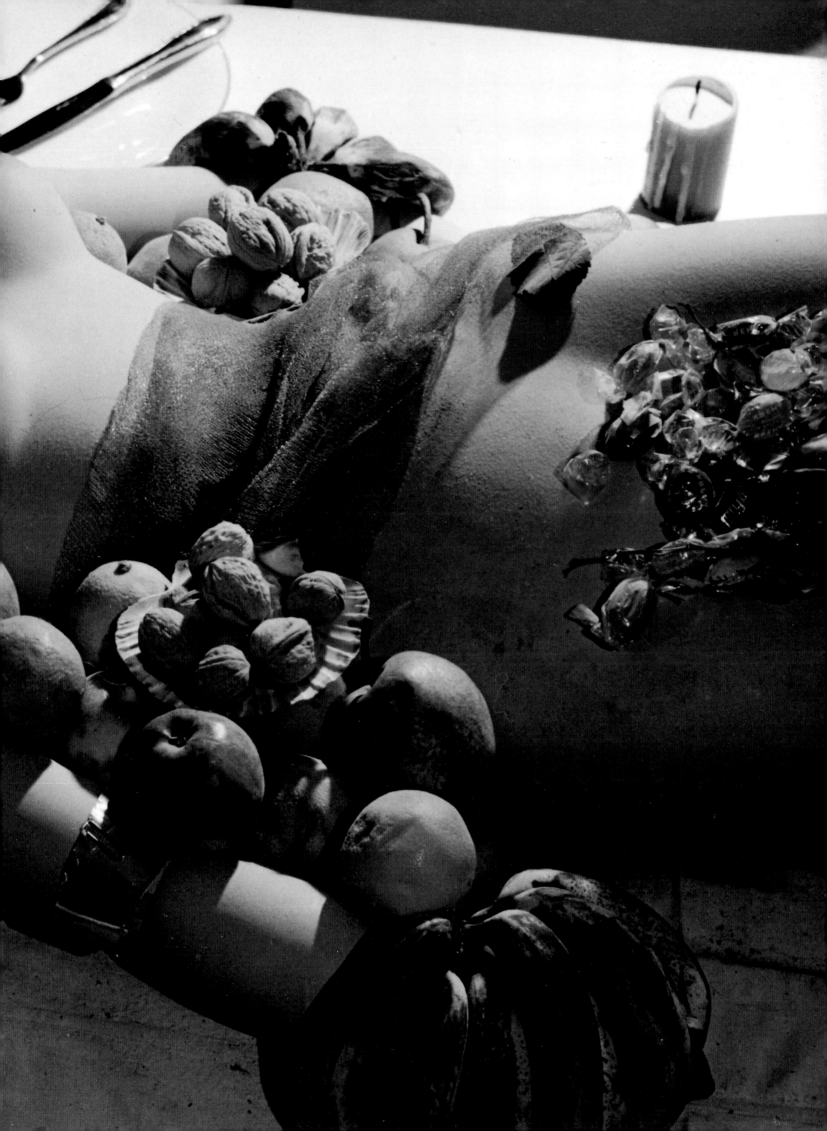

Friction and Polemics

At the end of the occupation, the major intellectual influence was not Surrealism but Existentialism. And this, in spite of the publication of Maurice Nadeau's *L'Histoire du Surréalisme,* (Nadeau had been accused by the orthodoxy of having buried Surrealism), in spite of literary reviews such as *Fontaine* (Max-Pol Fouchet) or *Les Cahiers du Sud.* Sartre had published *L'être et le Néant* in 1943. He founded the review *Les Temps Modernes,* where one could find Masson and Leiris. The success of the review, heavily involved with current politics and philosophy, may explain in part the marginalization of Surrealism. Breton soon be speaking of the theme of occultation. The word can be understood in two ways: Surrealism's rapport with the world of "occult sciences," or the relegating of Surrealism to an obscure part of society where it slowly loses its bearings. The 1947 exhibition at the Galerie Maeght corresponds to the first use of the word. Surrealism's plunge into an erotic culture, which would culminate in the exhibition EROS at the Galerie Cordier in 1960, corresponds to the second. It is remarkable, in fact, that one must wait until 1956, thus ten years, for the review *Le Surréalisme, Même* to come back to a full publication of the movement's positions. In 1948, *Néon* was only a photocopied newspaper filled with drawings that pushed the texts off into the margins. One could find one of Breton's important works (in N° 1, 1948) later used in La *Clé des Champs* (1963): "Signe Ascendant" (Rising Sign):

The most beautiful light shed upon the general, obligatory meaning that an image worthy of its name should take, is given to us by this Zen apology: "Out of Buddhist goodness, one day Basho ingeniously modified a cruel Haikai, composed by his disciple, Kikakou, full of humor. He had said: 'Pull off the wings of a red dragonfly/a chilli-pepper.' Basho put in its place: 'A chilli-pepper/give it wings/a red dragonfly.'

Néon ceased to exist in 1949. Breton and Péret were surrounded, among others, by Sarane Alexandrian, Heisler, Bédouin, along with Brauner, Toyen, Hérold and Lam as illustrators.

A certain Garry Davis interrupted a meeting of the General Assembly of the United Nations which was gathering in Paris (November 1948), in order to proclaim himself a citizen of the world. Numerous intellectuals, the Surrealists among them, supported him. An unfortunate adventure which would be short-lived – a generous utopia incarnated by a fragile herald. Breton himself put an end to it in October 1949, much to the dismay of his anarchist friends. Another strange affair made headlines and put the critics of the newspaper *Combat,* Maurice Nadeau, Pascal Pia, Maurice Saillet in a difficult position. The manuscript of *La Chasse Spirituelle* (The Spiritual Pursuit) by Rimbaud had supposedly been found; in the end it turned out to be a fake. Breton (let us note the quality of his judgement) had immediately realized through "*critique interne*" (gut feeling) that the text could never have been written by Rimbaud. *Flagrant Délit* recounts this unfortunate story.

Between the apolitical who gathered around Brauner and those who persisted, with Breton, to pretend to be in phase with the dark events of the time (massacre in Madagascar, the beginning of the Vietnam war, uprisings in Algeria) the tension was thickening. The split happened on the day that the group pronounced Matta's exclusion "for moral ignominy" (it was a sentimental affair linked with Gorky's suicide). Brauner and Jouffroy left with Matta.

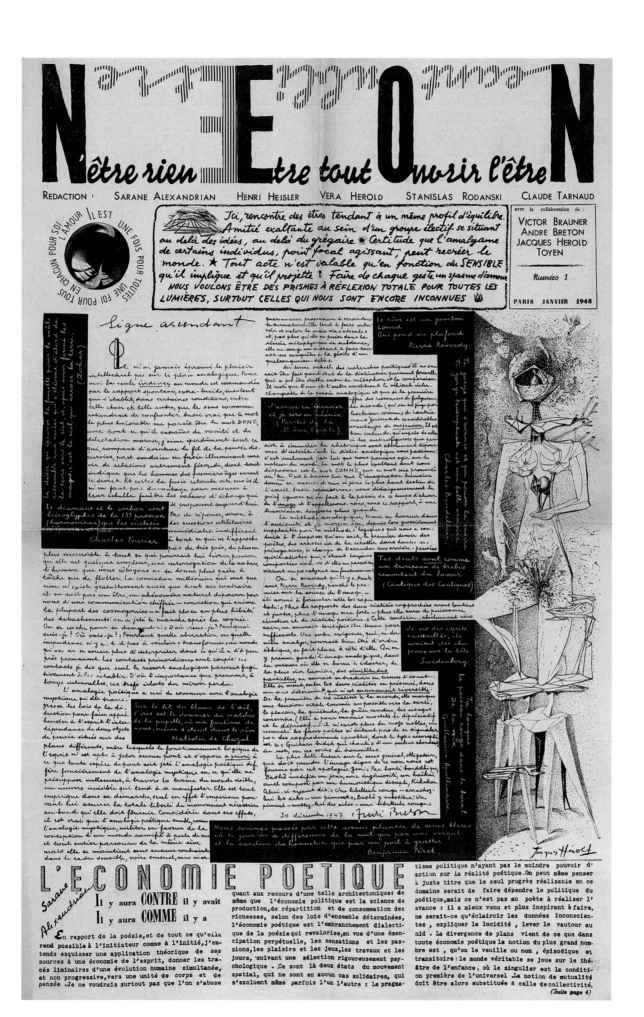

NÉON

N'être rien — Être tout — Ouvrir l'être — N

REDACTION : SARANE ALEXANDRIAN · HENRI HEISLER · VERA HEROLD · STANISLAS RODANSKI · CLAUDE TARNAUD

avec la collaboration de :
VICTOR BRAUNER
ANDRE BRETON
JACQUES HEROLD
TOYEN

Numéro 1

PARIS JANVIER 1948

L'AMOUR IL EST UNE FOIS POUR TOUTES UNE FOI POUR CHACUN POUR SOI

Ici, rencontre des êtres tendant à un même profil d'équilibre. Amitié exaltante au sein d'un groupe électif se situant au delà des idées, au delà du grégaire ★ Certitude que l'amalgame de certains individus, point focal agissant, peut recréer le monde. ★ Tout acte n'est valable qu'en fonction du SENSIBLE qu'il implique et qu'il projette ? Faire de chaque geste un spasme d'amour NOUS VOULONS ÊTRE DES PRISMES À RÉFLEXION TOTALE POUR TOUTES LES LUMIÈRES, SURTOUT CELLES QUI NOUS SONT ENCORE INCONNUES

Ligne ascendant

[texte manuscrit]

Le rêve est un jambon
Lourd
Qui pend au plafond
Pierre Reverdy

J'arrive en épervier
et je sors en phénix
(Paroles de la
3e âme, Egypte).
Charles Brunelleschi

Le diamant et le cochon sont hiéroglyphes de la 13e passion (l'harmonisme) que les civilisés...
Charles Fourier

Sur le lit du blanc de l'ail, l'iris est le sommer des maldors de la pupille, où un fantôme de nous-même s'étend dans le rêve.
Malcolm de Chazal

Tes dents sont comme un troupeau de brebis remontant du lavoir
(Cantique des Cantiques)

[signature manuscrite] André Breton

Je vis des esprits rassemblés; ils avaient des chapeaux sur la tête
Swedenborg

Nous sommes passés par cette avenue plantée de seins bleus où le jour ne se différencie de la nuit que par une virgule, et la sardine du hanneton que par un poil à gratter.
Benjamin Péret

Jacques Hérold

L'ÉCONOMIE POÉTIQUE

Sarane Alexandrian

Il y aura **CONTRE** il y avait
Il y aura **COMME** il y a

En rapport de la poésie, et de tout ce qu'elle rend possible à l'initiateur comme à l'initié, j'entends esquisser une application théorique de ses sources à une économie de l'esprit, donner les tracés liminaires d'une évolution humaine simultanée, et non progressive, vers une unité de corps et de pensée. Je ne voudrais surtout pas que l'on s'abuse quant aux recours d'une telle architectonique: de même que l'économie politique est la science de production, de répartition et de consommation des richesses, selon les lois d'ensemble déterminées, l'économie poétique est l'embranchement dialectique de la poésie qui revalorise, en vue d'une émancipation perpétuelle, les sensations et les passions, les plaisirs et les jeux, les travaux et les jours, suivant une sélection rigoureusement psychologique. Ce sont là deux états du mouvement spatial, qui ne sont en aucun cas solidaires, qui s'excluent même parfois l'un l'autre : le pragma-

tisme politique n'ayant pas le moindre pouvoir d'action sur la réalité poétique. On peut même penser à juste titre que le seul progrès réalisable en ce domaine serait de faire dépendre la politique du poétique, mais ce n'est pas au poète à réaliser d'avance : il a mieux venu et plus inspirant à faire, ne serait-ce qu'éclaircir les données inconscientes, expliquer la lucidité, lever le vautour au nid. La divergence de plans vient de ce que dans toute économie poétique la notion du plus grand nombre est, qu'on le veuille ou non, épisodique et transitoire: le monde véritable se joue sur le théâtre de l'enfance, où le singulier est la condition première de l'universel. La notion de mutualité doit être alors substituée à celle de collectivité,

(Suite page 4)

Was it in order to re-establish cohesion in the group that Patrick Waldberg and Henri Pastoureau attacked Breton, regarding a lecture by Carrouges: one would be had to believe that the Catholics were trying to recuperate Surrealism. With Jules Monnerot, *Le Surréalisme et le Sacré* (Surrealism and the Sacred, 1945), Pierre Klossovsky, *Sade Mon Prochain* (Sade My Brother, 1947), and Carrouges, *A. Breton et les Données Fondamentales du Surréalisme* (A. Breton and the Fundamental Facts of Surrealism, 1950), an attempt was made to apply a lawyer's argument to the demonstration that to be an atheist was to serve God, that to insult God was, in fact, to love him… In short, the Surrealists brought back their anti-religion theme in the tract, *A la Niche des Glapisseurs de Dieu* (All Yelpers of God to the Kennel, 1948). Having been involved with the group, Carrouges was excommunicated. Everything fell back into place after the publication of *Haute Fréquence*, which restated Surrealism's fundamental positions against all fideistic kneeling. The anarchists rushed to publish this important text in *Le Libertaire*, the newspaper in which the Surrealist's pamphlets were published between 1951 and the end of 1953.

The newspaper *Arts* published several interventions by the Surrealists, one against the Mexican painter D. Alfaro Siqueiros, who boasted to have participated in the assassination of Trotsky, another in favor of the poet Germain Nouveau, considered to be on equal par with Rimbaud and Lautréamont, and most of all a response to Camus's book *L'Homme Révolté*, where Surrealism is attacked head on, Rimbaud ridiculed, and Lautréamont considered "banal"… In fact, Camus stood up against "absolute revolt" yet his thinking is not precise enough to be able to distinguish in this formula, the revolt on one hand, which is vital to the critical mind, and on the other, the absolute, which could also be called fundamentalist. Thus, Camus would call for a "measured revolt." He should have commended the Surrealists for having had, with regard to action, done just that. For the verbal excesses, which carry to the extreme the cry of revolt, belong only to that emotional margin with which, Bergson had said long ago, all "moral heroes" go beyond their thoughts in order that they be lasting. Retrospectively, this polemic seem completely fallacious.

Another quarrel: a radio program presented Alfred Jarry as a "Christian poet." To consider the "La Passion du Christ Considerée comme un Course de Côte" (Christ's Passion Considered as a Hill Climb Race) quoted in the *Anthologie de l'Humour Noir*, by Breton) a liturgical work, is a result of the famous Jesuit dialectic, so scathingly rejected by Pascal. In short, the Surrealists answered with a text, *Bas les Masques! Bas les pattes!* (Down with Masks, Down with Paws), and in the review *Arts* Péret asks the question: "Is Jarry a Christian poet?" The answer of the entire Parisian intelligentsia was negative. End of discussion. With regards to the controversy over "realist" Soviet art, the underlying question was: "Why is contemporary Russian painting being hidden from us?" and after Aragon's response, Breton's last word: "Socialist Realism as a means of moral extermination."

A major exhibition was organized by James Johnson Sweeney (1952) at the Musée d'Art Moderne de Paris – Seurat, Gauguin, Cézanne, Van Gogh, Renoir, Münch, Picasso, Matisse, Kandinsky, De Chirico, Mondrian, Chagall, Derain, Balla, Juan Gris, Braque, Malevich, Dali, Ernst, Matta, Masson, Miró, Tanguy, Henri Rousseau "the *Douanier*," with five canvasses among which *Le Rêve* (The Dream). This wave of talent did, early on, sweep away a few cob webs.

Victor Brauner
THE UNHAPPY EXPERIENCE
1951, oil on canvas.
Centre Pompidou-MNAM-CCI, Paris.

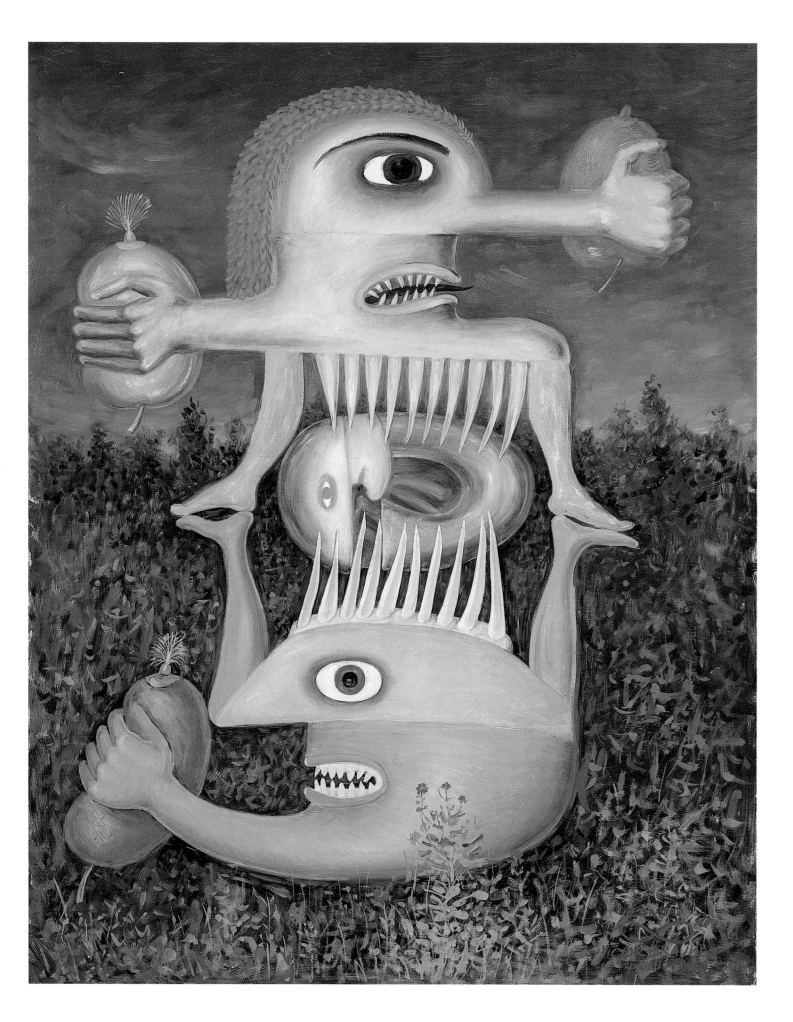

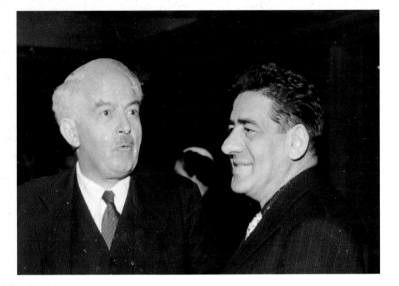

Oscar Dominguez
at the Galerie Drouant
in June 1954

Influence and Creation

We shall have understood that during these polemics, the painters went along their ways without the need for any group at all. The time for retrospectives began for the eldest: Picabia for example, in 1949. For the others, freedom in creation didn't cease developing. Brauner's individuality became high handed. He signed his paintings Victor. Joking in part, he practiced " pantheism of the self." In a Surrealist issue of the review *View* (1941), the text that he had sent to America proclaimed: "I am the birth of the object. I am the end of the object. I am the specter and the apparition. Everything starts and disappears with me, in me…" Yet in 1948 came *Totem de la Subjectivité Blessée* (Totem of Wounded Subjectivity) and the thirty seven paintings of the *Onomatomanie* series, then the "*période des rétractés*" (time of those withdrawn). Brauner did not move towards an expression of happiness as did Masson and Ernst. Solitary and dark, he died the same year as Breton, 1966.

Between 1946 and 1950 first rate works proved the persistence of pictorial Surrealism – *Le Cheval de Troie* (The Trojan Horse, Dominguez, 1947), *Agonie* (Agony, Gorky, 1947), *Umbral* (Lam 1950). Matta's work developed in the company of Gordon Onslow Ford, an Englishman. His exclusion from the group had no influence on his painting which became darker and darker because of, he said, "the horrible crisis of society." *Les Aveugles* (The Blind), or *Every Man a King* (1947), announced his later political paintings.

Max Ernst married the young painter Dorothea Tanning in 1946, in Los Angeles. The couple returned to France and settled in Touraine in 1954. Ernst's painting toned down into a sort of abstract Impressionism, close to Bazaine. Major retrospectives in Paris and New York finally give him the notoriety he had waited for so long. His Grand Prize in the 27th Venice Biennale in 1954 earned him sarcastic comments from Breton.

Masson published a collection of his articles from *Temps Modernes* under the extremely significant title of *Plaisir de Peindre* (The Pleasure of Painting). Yet, the style of *L'Homme Ivre* (The Drunkard, 1962) remains aggressive. We will see that Masson's old age, as is often the case with painters, corresponded with intense creativity. An example is the ceiling of the Odéon theatre in Paris, painted in 1964.

Miró would go the United States for the first time in 1947. His fame was becoming worldwide. He shared the prize in Venice with Arp and Ernst in 1954. It is evident that his paintings are not "windows," but in fact airy blueprints where one must follow the path of the lines, and not look for representations. For example in *Joie d'une Fillette Devant le Soleil* (Joy of a Little Girl in the Sun).

Let us add that in 1948 the Compagnie de l'Art Brut was founded, led by Jean Dubuffet, Breton, Michel Tapié de Celeyran, Paulhan, oël Arnaud. One must underline the theoretical importance of "l'Art Brut," product of a non-cultural creative activity, by autodidacts. The company included some big names: Aloïse, Gaston Chaissac, the

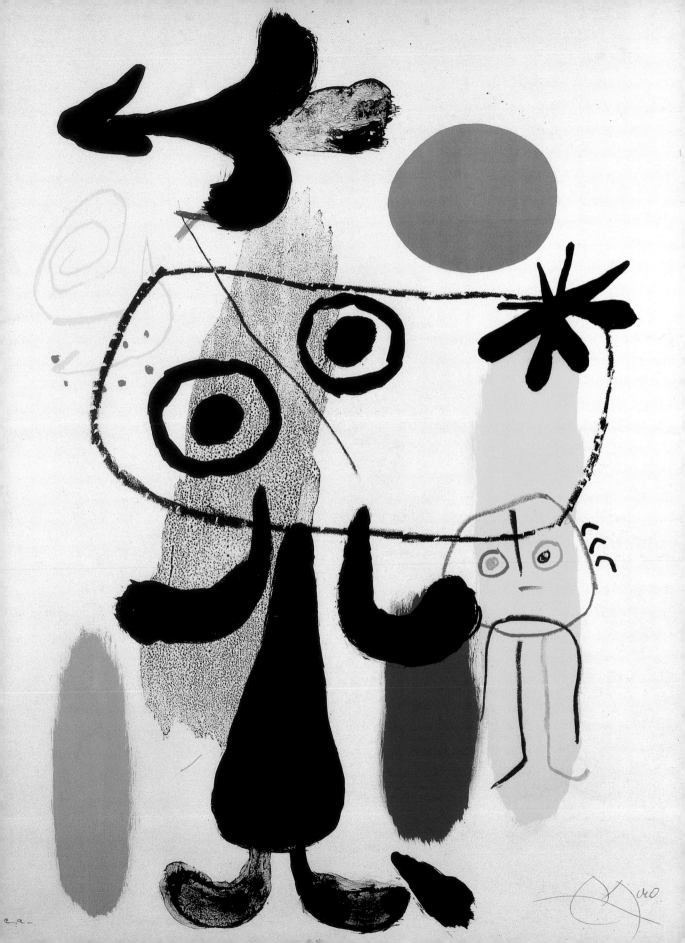

clairvoyant Joseph Crépin, André Demonchy, the mystic anarchist Miguel Hernandez, Miguel Vivancos (a former colonel in the Spanish Republican Army, hero at Teruel and Puigcerda: he painted the tender *Jardin des Oiseaux,* Garden of Birds, in 1954), "Scottie" Wilson, Adolf Wölffli – joined these "naïves" such as Benquet, Ivan Généralic, or Séraphine de Senlis, mentally ill, obsessed with virginal pregnancy, who's works today are in the Musée d'Art Moderne. In a text linked with the founding of this *Compagnie,* André Breton wrote: "I am not afraid to submit the idea, that seems paradoxical only on first hearing, that the art produced by those we put today into the category of the mentally ill, is in fact a reservoir of moral healthiness. In fact, it escapes everything that tends to blur our perception and is related to exterior influence, to calculating, to success or disappointment encountered on the social level, etc. Here, the mechanisms of artistic creation are give free reign. Because of a striking dialectic effect, the confinement, the renouncing of any profit and all other forms of vanity, in spite of what each individually presents as pathetic, guarantee the total authenticity that is missing everywhere else, and that day by day debases us." This moral prescription reminds us of Surrealism's origins and brings us to poetry where the event of the moment is the arrival in Paris of *Sens Plastique II* by Malcolm de Chazal (late 1947). An engineer in Mauritius, Chazal, a reader of Swedenborg, used short percussive formulae in his poetry – only Magloire-Saint-Aude the Haitian, was more laconic than he. He applied the principal of analogy to meditation on the identity of birth and death, that one can only know through the intimate experience of intimacy of voluptuous pleasure:

> *"Le gris est le cendrier du soleil. La volupté est un accouchement mutuel entre deux tombeaux charnels dans le cimetière désertique de l'esprit…"*

"Grey is the sun's ashtray.
Voluptuous pleasure is the mutual giving birth between two carnal tombs in the barren cemetery of the spirit…"

The Surrealists, who were slacking off a bit in Breton's *L'Ode à Charles Fourrier* (Ode to Charles Fourrier) received a veritable kick in the pants with *Sens Plastique.* In fact the young poets of the time were dominated by Henri Pichette, that friend of Artaud, who had just published his *Apoèmes* and had Roger Blin, Maria Casarès and Gérard Philippe take roles in his famous play *Les Epiphanies* (published by K, 1948): "Since the world's first heartbeat I circled around myself like an inner circumference racket has always been intolerable for me I shared a room with monotony Sounds came to me without my being able to classify them I have a blue

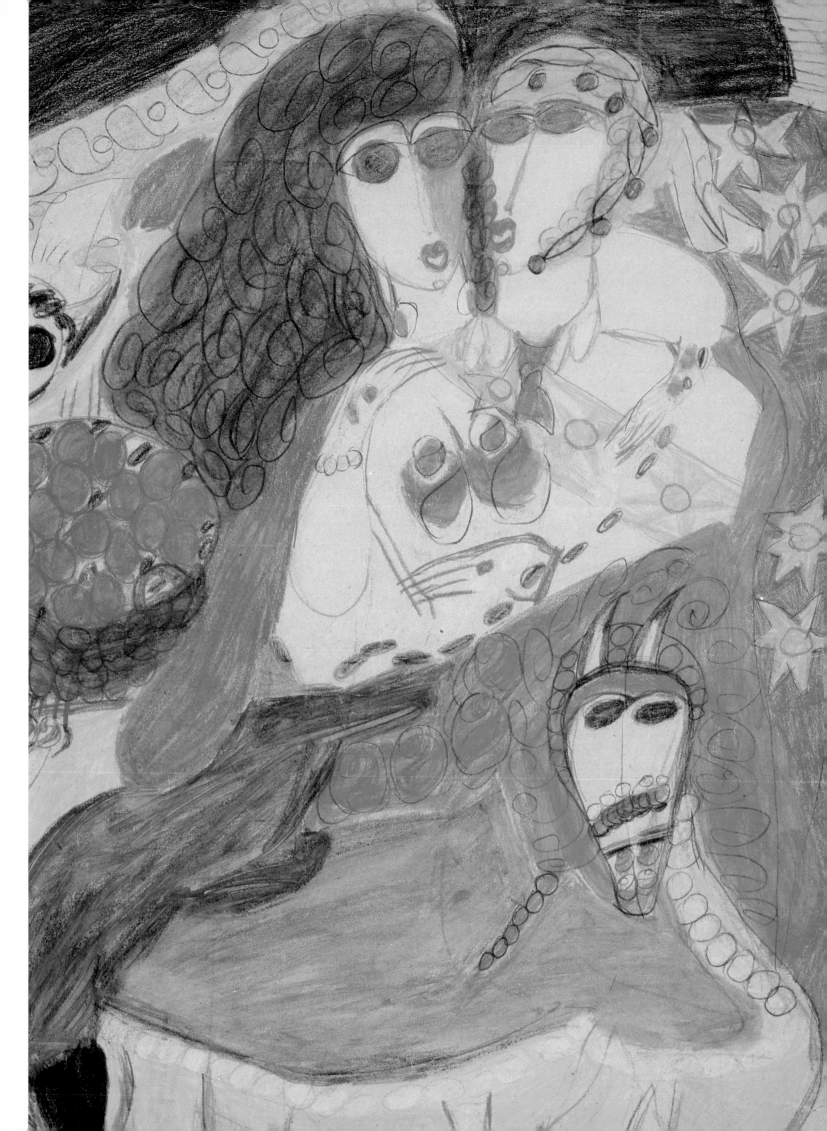

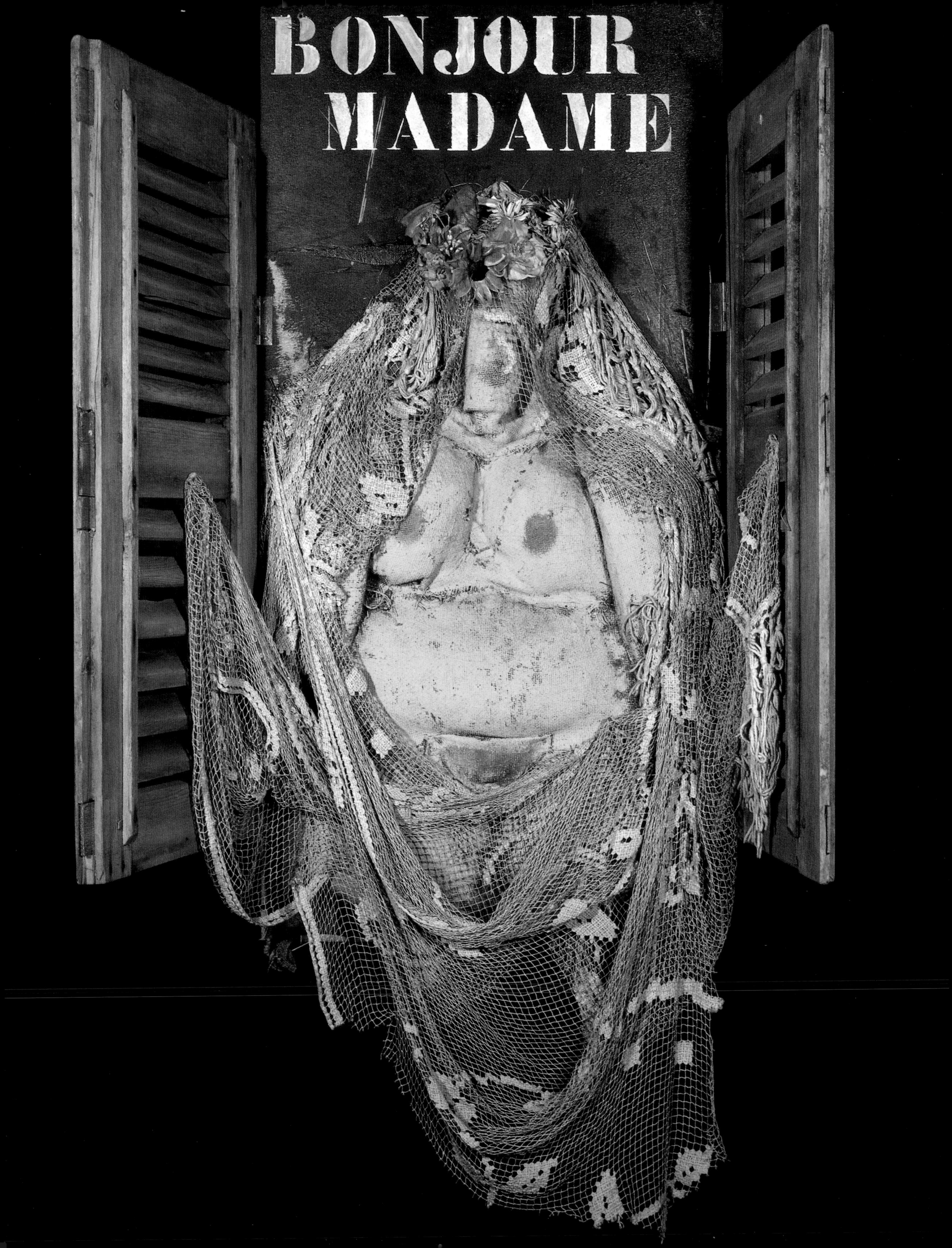
BONJOUR
MADAME

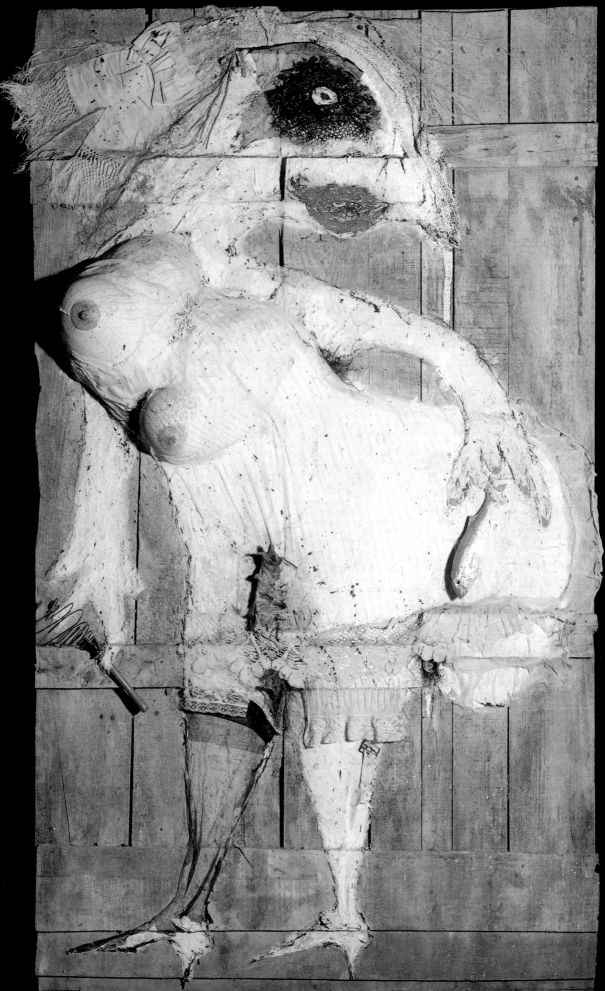

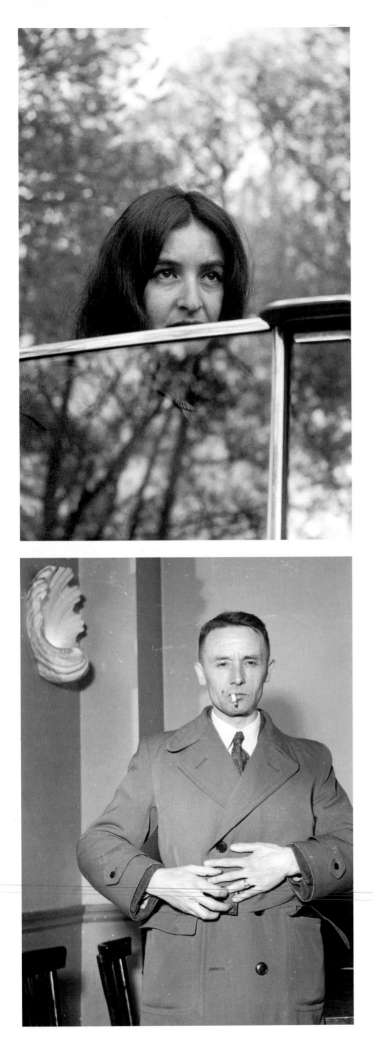

fright of space…" The magnificence of this outcry does not come from a fading form of Surrealism, but from the verbal magic of love that goes beyond tragedy.

The names of Maurice Blanchard, Aimé Césaire and Michel Leiris marked those years, when Julien Gracq was at the height of his creativity. He had come to Surrealism in 1947. Jose Corti published *Un Beau Ténébreux* (A Handsome Man of Dark, Brooding Good Looks), then *Liberté Grande* (Great Freedom, 1947). *Le Rivage des Syrtes* (The Quicksand Shore) earned him the Prix Goncourt that he haughtily declined. *Un Balcon en Forêt* (A Balcony in the Forest) recounted his war souvenirs. We should add that he adapted Kleist's *Penthesilea* and participated, with Breton, in the writing *Farouche à Quatre Feuilles* (1954).

"It is a young woman from under whose steps an abundance of images emerge. Sometimes, on April's path, she lifts a hand gentle and soft like a feather and regretfully calms the landscape's worries, –or perhaps…" ("Inabordable," in *Liberté Grande*)

Jindrich Heisler came out of the underground in Prague, arriving in Paris in 1947. Toyen's illustrator, his work as an illustrator for Néon, his research in film and his dutiful presence in the *Solution Surréaliste* office (Rue du Dragon, Paris) made him an active member of Breton's group. In 1956 he was to publish *Les Spectres du Désert* (Ghosts of the Desert). Georges Hénein, born in Cairo in 1914, founded the review *La Part du Sable* (The Share of the Sand), in Cairo in 1947 along with Ramsès Youmane. He ceased all contact with the Parisian group as of in 1950. The poetry of this representative of Surrealism in the Muslim world, made him a precursor to the Iraqi El Janaby. El Janably created the review *Le Désir Liberataire* (Libertarian Desire) in 1973 and was to violently contest the Koran: "Here is a world in which the pedantic sell the past to those who fear the future…"

A younger generation including Suzanne Allen, Edouard Jaguer, published their poems in *Le Surrélisme Révolutionnaire*: "Enough joking, what little ninny sucks her sugary fibroid tumors right up to the end in conjunctive pomposity? Let us pose the question in another manner. Have nuns rendered shame more compact? (S. Allen, "*Suite Physiologique*"). And Jaguer: "You should shred her **corsage great sun**/You should **screwthread** the squirrel by its throat/His great bell tower of brambles and oats…" (*"Roue à Miel ou l'Eau Bœuf"*).

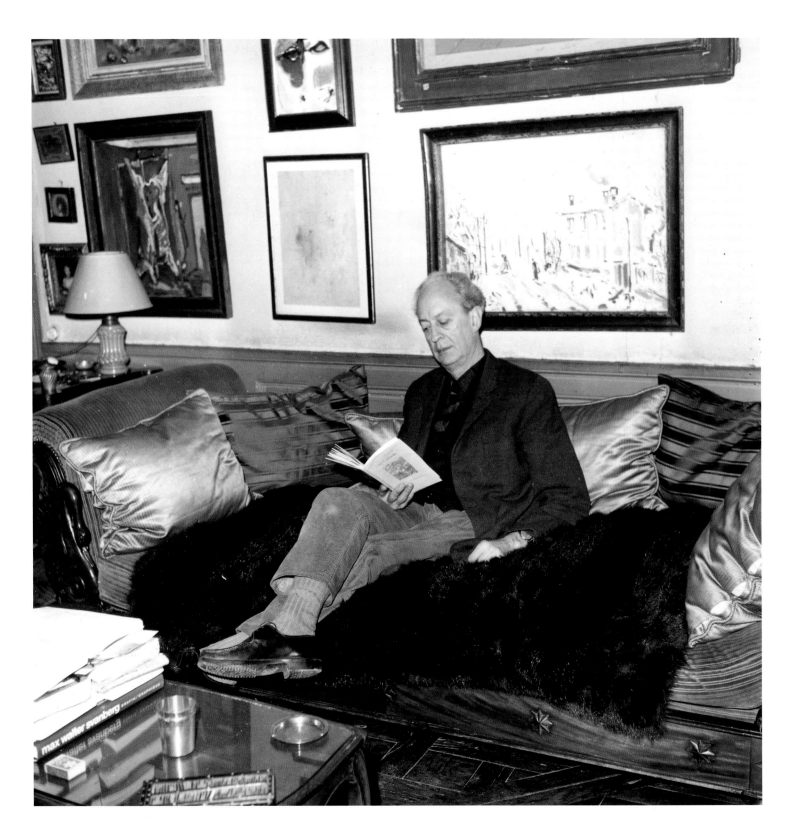

André Pieyre de Mandiargues

Left-hand page, bottom :
Julien Gracq at the time of the
Prix Goncourt 1951,
which he refused.

Gérard Legrand, who was very close to Breton since 1948, published *Des Pierres de Mouvance* (Stones **within a Sphere of Influence**) in 1953. And Jean Malrieu, *Préface à l'Amour,* the same year. *Cris,* the first collection by the Egyptian, Joyce Mansour, was published by Seghers. She published *Déchirures* (Editions de Minuit) in 1955. Her poems struck the Surrealists by a kind of freedom where sex goes hand in hand with violence ; "The *amazone* ate her last breast/The night before the final battle…" (Cris). Let us mention in addition, Jehan Mayoux, E.L.T. Mesens, who organized the 1945 exhibition, *Surrealist Diversity,* in London, André Pieyre de Mandiargues, Octovio Paz, Mariane Van Hirtum, Unica Zurn, the Peruvian, Cesare Moro, who published *Trafalgar Square* in Lima, 1954, before dying of Leukemia in 1955, the Belgian Paul Nougé, with three works between 1946 and 1956, Gisèle Prassinos, child-poet, the Egyptian Georges Schéhadé, who published nine books between 1947 and 1956. We can see that the abundance of works didn't let up; even death didn't play a role.

Eros and Thanatos

Eluard died in 1952. Since the age of thirty, this war veteran, victim of nerve gas, with the slightly haughty asymmetric face, had trembling hands… Dr. Mabille died the same year. The poet Joe Bousquet, bedridden for years, died in 1950. Death would strike heavily – 1953, Picabia and Heisler; 1954, Frida Kahlo, Diego Rivera; 1955, Tanguy; 1956, Cesare Moro, 1958, Nezval; 1959, Péret; 1961, Nora Mitrani; 1962, Gaston Bachelard; 1963, Tzara; 1964, Fraenkel; 1966, Breton, Arp Brauner; 1967, Magritte, Nougé, Brunius; 1968, Baskine; 1969, Malkine, Chavée; 1973, Picasso, Max Morise; 1974, Hugnet, Asger Jorn, Hénein; 1975, Bellmer; 1976, Queneau, Man Ray, Max Ernst, Molinier, Alexander Calder; 1977, Prévert, Bryen, Chaplin; 1978, De Chirico; 1979, Dotremont; 1987, Hérold; 1988, Char; 1989, Dali; 1991, Tinguely; 1993, Naville; 1994, Jacques Doucet; 1996, Bédouin; 1999, Lorenc; 2000, Henri Pichette… There were also the suicides: 1957, Dominguez, on New Year's eve; 1959,

Paalen and the young Jean-Pierre Duprey; 1969, Kay Sage; 1962, Seligmann; 1970, Unica Zurn; 1988, Iréna Dedicova…

Given the birth dates of the leaders of "Historic Surrealism" except for the premature death of Nora Mitroni and J.-P. Duprey's suicide – these deaths have no Surrealist particularity. And even suicides are a general tendency in the twentieth century: the right to die, an obvious return to the dignity of the stoics. But in spite of the arrival of a number of young people, it seems possible that the accumulation of these deaths – and most of all André Breton's death – might have caused a certain depression within the movement. Breton had written that he "wasn't worried about his own death." He was not however, indifferent to the deaths of his friends. Breton had been scarred by the ambiance of disaster in which he had spent his adolescence – which reached its most difficult point with Vaché's, and then Maïkovski's, suicides. His revolt against the fatality of death did not allow him to remain silent in the face of "that which doesn't depend on us." The difference between Stoicism and Surrealism is there: Surrealism thinks it honorable to protest against even the ineluctable, and that this revolt is as real and absolute in the poetic outcry of art, as in the fatality against which it rails. We can remember also that Surrealism makes the poet descend "into death" and one of the constants in Surrealist thinking is its pessimism. This pessimism would separate the movement from Aragon, in political terms, and from COBRA in painting. The fight for social revolution implies that spiritual revolt risks being diluted in obedience to orders – Surrealism thus opposed its refusal. Inversely, anarchism as a political philosophy comes up against the application of its doctrine to realities of the present, hence its failure – and a new blunt answer was no. In a conference at the Mutualité hall in 1949, Breton opposes his anarchist friends in regard to the legalization of the status of conscientious objector, which would only favor seminarists, he said… The power of priests and the police? Where can one see that the power of the intellect had softened its impact on the crowds of the great crusades, or on the persistence of police regimes? Certainly, things evolve, but only step by step.

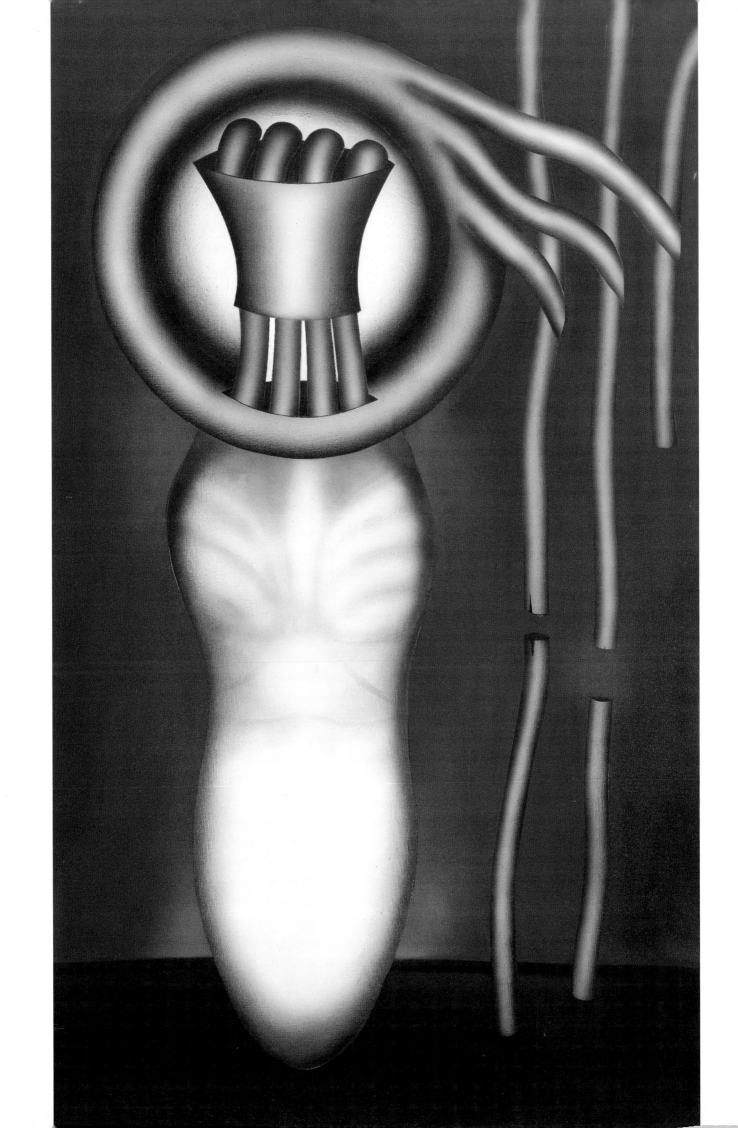

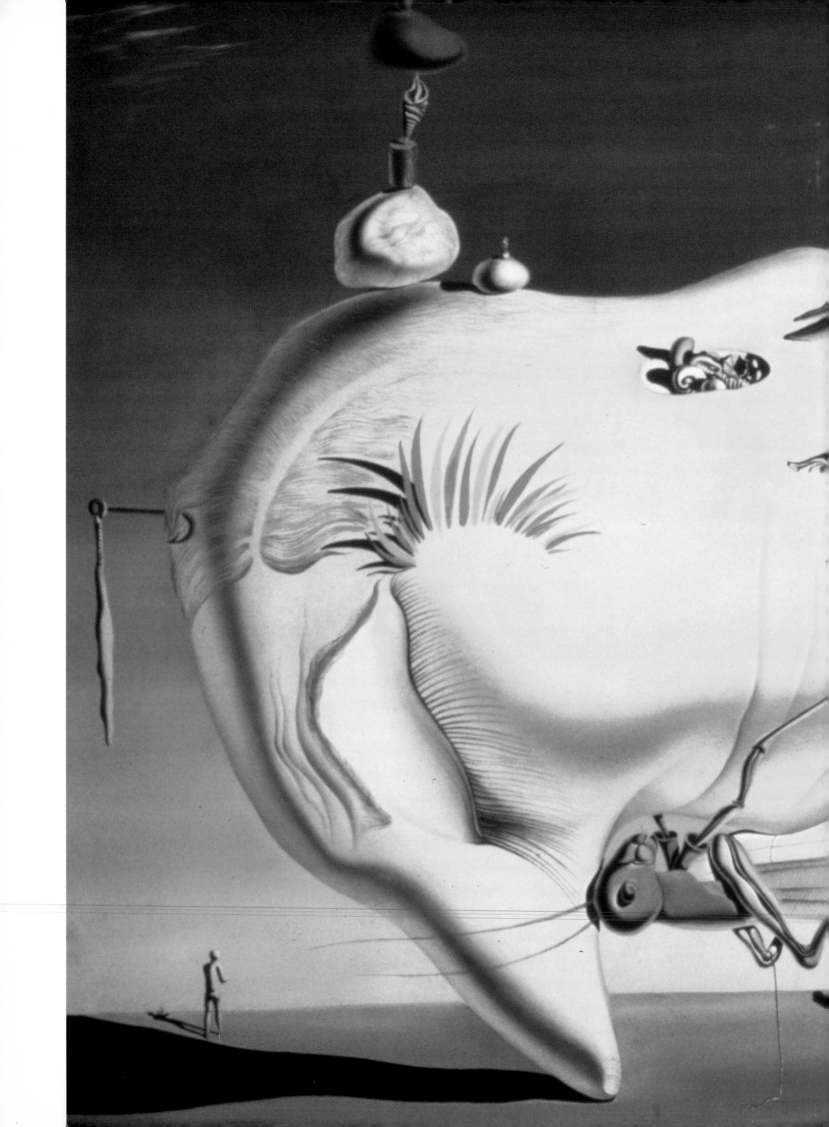

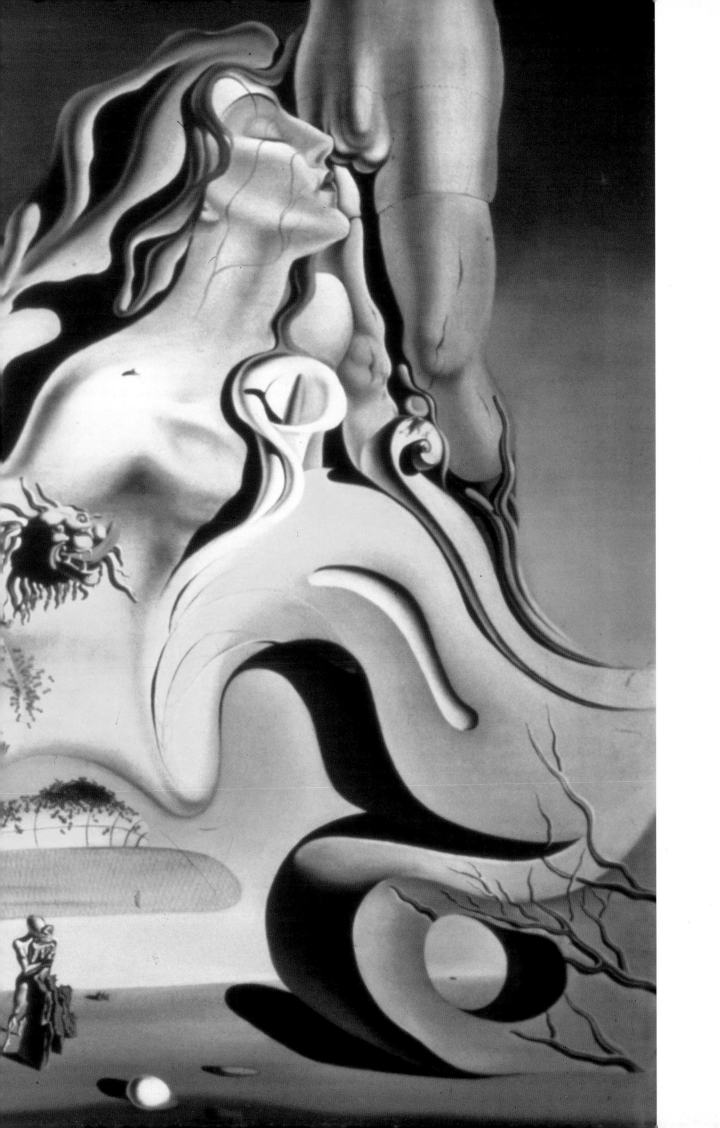

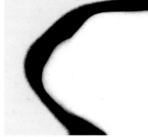

Avoue le ciel n'est pas sérieux
Ce matin n'est qu'un jeu sur ta bouche de joie
Le soleil se prend dans sa toile

Nous conduisons l'eau pure et toute perfection
Vers l'été diluvien
Sur une mer qui a la forme et la couleur de ton corps
Ravie de ses tempêtes qui lui font robe neuve
Capricieuse et chaude
Changeante comme moi

O mes raisons le loir en a plus de dormir
Que moi d'en découvrir de valables à la vie
A moins d'aimer

En passe de devenir caresses
Tes rires et tes gestes règlent mon allure
Poliraient les pavés
Et je ris avec toi et je te crois toute seule

Tout le temps d'une rue qui n'en finit pas.

A LA FIN DE L'ANNÉE, DE JOUR EN
JOUR PLUS BAS, IL ENFOUIT SA
CHALEUR COMME UNE GRAINE.

1

Nous avançons toujours
Un fleuve plus épais qu'une grasse prairie
Nous vivons d'un seul jet
Nous sommes du bon port

Le bois qui va sur l'eau l'arbre qui file droit
Tout marché de raison bâclé conclu s'oublie
Où nous arrêterons-nous
Notre poids immobile creuse notre chemin

Paul Éluard and Man Ray
Double spread from *Facile*,
1935
Musée d'art et d'histoire, Saint-Denis

Pages 186 and 187
Salvador Dali
THE BIG MASTURBATOR
1929, oil on canvas.
Private Collection.

Salvador Dali
**YOUNG VIRGIN AUTO-SODOMISED
BY HER OWN CHASTETY**
1954, oil on canvas.
Private Collection.

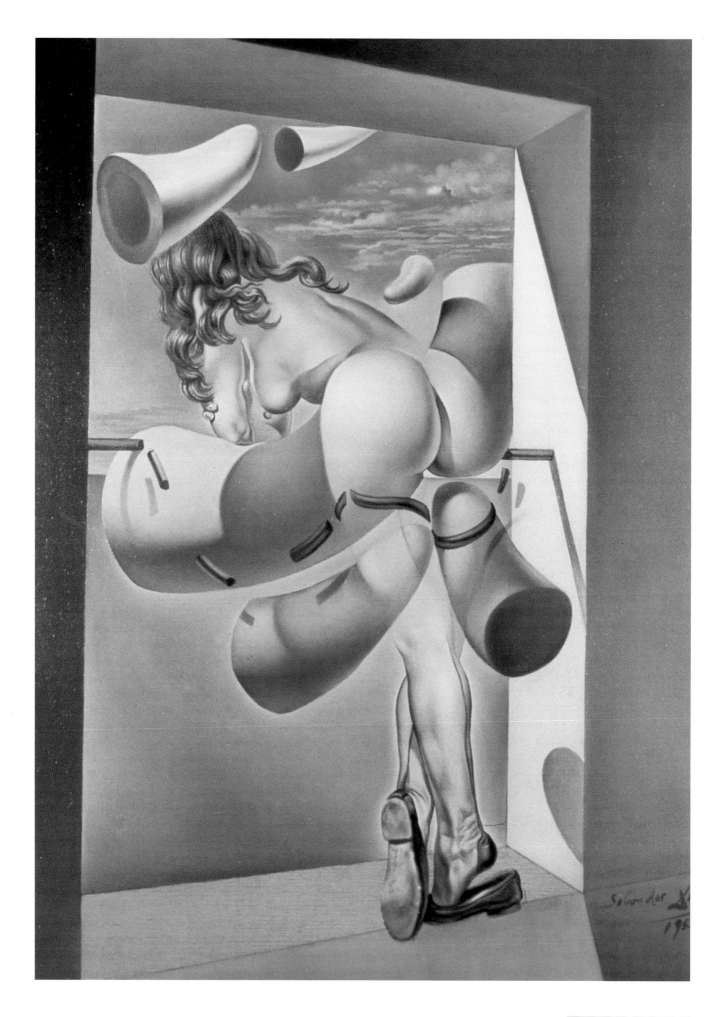

Breton's libertarian passion was never to mollify his critical capacity, anchored as it was in firm reason. This meant that his venerated precursors, such as Rimbaud or De Chirico, were spared nothing and treated harshly. It was difficult not to feel hurt by the incomprehension of those he admired. Freud – "I was tempted to consider the Surrealists complete mad men." Picasso? Breton would write in 1961 that he "would skip a step when he remembers those moments long ago, when, with his heart beating, he would climb Picasso's staircase." For Picasso, before painting his troubling portrait of Stalin, was said to have "peopled'their atomic skies with so many bloodless and fallacious doves." (*Le Surréalisme et la Peinture*, p. 118). And all those dear friends that he had to exclude – Tzara (refound in 1929, lost again as of 1934), Eluard (1938), Dali of course (1938), Mar Ernst (excluded on several occasions), Magritte, Matta, Brauner; all those refused with the *Second Manifesto*, Baron, Limbour, Masson, Prévert, Queneau, Vitrac, etc… Giacometti had chosen to follow his career as an artist. There were those who kept a certain distance – Soupault, Man Ray, Tanguy. Those he'd lost touch with – Desnos, Dominguez, Artaud himself, whom he hadn't heard from in America. Those who had loved you and than one hadn't known, or hadn't received, the young lions from *La Main à Plume*, etc…, and now, all these deaths…

The very principles of Surrealist creation got somewhat lost in the abundance of discoveries and surplus of talent among the visual artists. The history of "*l'écriture automatique* (automatic writing) was a story of continuous misfortune," Breton wrote in 1934. So what was the stage of the game in the fifties and sixties? Love? Woman? – *There* was the perfect context for revolt, brought on by the powerful magic of the unconscious, that would give the mad quest for knowledge, the beginning of a sense of accomplishment. Breton wrote: "In spite of some memorable polls, the modern sexual world in which Sade and Freud work, has not, as far as I know, stopped countering our desire to penetrate the secrets of the universe, with its unperturbable core of night."

(Introduction to *Contes d'Arnim*, 1933). The international exhibition of Surrealism (EROS) in 1959-60 at the Galerie Cordier in Paris, would emphasize (and not without a secret solemnity) the Surrealists' predilection not only for the fusion of imagination and reality, but also that of the most free eroticism tinged with odoriferous love. As Gérard Legrand well put it in *Dictionnaire Général du Surréalisme et de ses Environs*: "Knowledge without desire remains abstract, desire without knowledge becomes exhausted within its own satisfaction or becomes exasperated within its own frustration." The pre-opening of this exhibition was dedicated to *L'Exécution du Testament de Sade (Carrying Out Sade's Will and Testament)*, a performance by the Canadian poet Jean Benoit. Fascinated with Sade, the Surrealists had always allied fantastical eroticism with the general spirit of courtly love, supposedly unique, rebelling against social convention, and harbinger of supernatural, fantastic element. Hadn't Breton written that "poetry is made in bed, like love?" And Eluard, the great libertarian lover, published his 1935 poem to the glory of Nusch – "Facile" illustrating it with provocative photographs:

Ou bien rire ensemble dans les rues
Chaque pas plus léger plus rapide
Nous sommes deux à ne plus compter sur la sagesse
Avoue le ciel n'est pas sérieux
Ce matin n'est au'un jeu sur ta bouche de joie
Le soleil se prend dns sa toile

Nous conduisons l'eau pure et toute perfection
Vers l'été diluvien
Sur une mer aui a la forme et la couleur de ton corps
Ravie de ses tempêtes aui lui font robe neuve
Capricieuse et chaude
Changeante comme moi

O mes raisons le loir en a plus de dormir
Que moi d'en découvrir de valables à la vie
A moins d'aimer…

Why not laugh together in the streets
Each step lighter faster
Neither you nor I no longer count on wisdom
Admit the sky is not serious
this morning is nothing but a game on your lips of joy
The sun is caught in its own web

We lead pure water and all perfection
Towards torrential summer
On a sea with the shape and color of your body
A sea thrilled with storms donning new garbs
Capricious and warm
Changeable like me

Oh my reasons the dormouse has more for sleeping
Than I for discovering valid reasons for living
Albeit to love…

It was said that Eluard had "offered" Nusch to Picasso as a gesture of friendship. But Picasso out of friendship for Nusch, refused… Love magnifies sexuality, yet goes far beyond it.

Dali's auto-erotic texts, his ardent praise of sodomy ("Reverie"), his famous painting *Jeune Vierge Auto-Sodomisée par sa Propre Chasteté (Young Virgin Self-Buggered by Her Own Chastity,* 1944), encounter the most beautiful pages of *L'Amour Fou.* The synthesis of romantic light and night of desire was a constant in the Surrealist ethic: "Love, love alone, carnal love, I adore it. I have never stopped loving your venomous shadow, your deadly shadow. A day will come when man will acknowledge you as his sole master, and honor you, even in those mysterious perversions that you surround yourself with." (*L'Amour Fou,* p. 108).

To Breton's profession of faith, corresponds a similar affirmation made by the most erotically neurotic of Surrealist creators, Dali: "In love, I attach a great deal of importance to all that is called perversion and vice. I consider perversion and vice as the most revolutionary forms of thinking and behaving, just as I consider love as

the only standpoint in a man's life." (*La femme Visible,* 1930).

Far from hedonist sensations, and farther still from religious bans (denounced by Bertrand Poirot-Delpech in *Le Monde,* 22 May 1991, "People under fifty have no idea of the contentions, contortions and contrition to which the Church condemned its youthful flock in general between 1850 and 1950."), the Surrealists, in fact precursors of the post-May 68 "sexual revolution," had integrated their ideas of revolt, atheism, the occult, and " Surrealist games," with their concept of love. How in the world could "question and answer games" have come up with this remarkable definition of eroticism: "It is a sumptuous ceremony, held underground?…"

The EROS exhibition *was* underground and sumptuous. The ceiling of the entryway was decorated with pink satin by Duchamp. Having gone through this "vaginal partition," one passed through a labyrinth full of sighs, and entered a "fetish chamber," then a sort of saint of saints, where a "cannibal feast" was taking place. Strictly excluding form of vulgarity, this exhibition followed a certain tradition of dreamlike sado-masochism found in *Chien Andalou* and *L'Ange Exterminateur* by Buñuel. Objects by Bellmer, Duchamp, Jean Benoît punctuated this erotic space, a kind of global object where one entered as though entering the Original Cave. The catalogue "*Boîte Alerte*", included an erotic lexicon… The "right-thinking" were scandalized of course, but they wouldn't go as far as destroying everything. The mystery of Eros, so obviously sought in this exhibition, undoubtedly imposed respect…

Conclusion
"The Final Split"

The times were to provide many other examples of scandal, and the Surrealists launched their pamphlet Hongie Soleil levant. Their collective action would be somewhat revived with the 1956 publication of the review *Le Surréalisme, Même*, directed by Breton and the young Jean Schuster. They co-signed the *Manifeste des 121* in 1959, concerning the right to insubordination in the Algerian War. Their refusal would also be used against the *13 May 1958* and against the Gaullist regime in *Le 14 Juillet* (N°1 in 1958), against nuclear physicists, against cosmonauts and other paragons of technology. The crumbling of artistic tendencies, between dogmatic Surrealism and the fast-growing abstract movement, justified the existence of the review *Phases* by Edouard Jaguer, who found a position somewhere in between the two currents, thanks to his intellectual freedom and his internationalism. His break with certain Surrealists such as José Pierre, who thought they had found a Surrealist tradition in Pop Art, was indicative that his open eclecticism held strongly to the rigor of principals.

What can be said of other reviews such as *Bief-Jonction Surréaliste* (1958-1960) or of those that survived Breton's death: *Coupure* (1969-1976), *Bulletin de Liaison Surréaliste (B.L.S.,* 1970-1976), other than that the junction was no longer being made among Surrealism's disparate young adepts? Several were to be found again in the 1965 show *L'Ecart Absolu*, at the Galerie L'Oeil in Paris.

Before visiting this show, let us make a rapid inventory of the retrospectives and exhibitions around the world, that showed two obvious sociological phenomena: the efficacy of the visual artists in Surrealism's world-wide distribution, and the weakening heart of the movement when its influence stretches too far. The Parisian movement was crumbling, while a not always orthodox Surrealism flourished in New York, Chicago, Malmö (1955), Switzerland (1956 Ernst retrospective), Sao-Paulo (1965, organized by Labisse). Of course a retrospective of Ernst was held in Paris at the Musée d'Art Moderne in 1959, but the retrospective Le Surrealisme at the Galerie Charpentier (1964) was repudiated by Breton, hence the text *Les Chiens Ont Soif (The Dogs Are Thirsty),* by Ernst and Prévert. Masson, who had distanced himself, presented a retrospective at the Musée d'Art Moderne in Paris in 1965, and Picasso, at the Grand Palais (Paris) in 1966, earned great popular success.

No significant theoretical works were written by Breton and his new friends, Audoin, Schuster, José Pierre, Bédouin, Bounoure, etc. during the sixties. The catalogue of *L'Ecart Absolu* put the retrospective within the context of Charles Fourrier. This early nineteenth century utopian dreamed of a world of Harmony, obtained by taking an opposite view towards everything in our odious society, to the extent of extolling the museum as an "orgy of beauty," destined to a life which had become benevolent. This return to the origins of utopia was

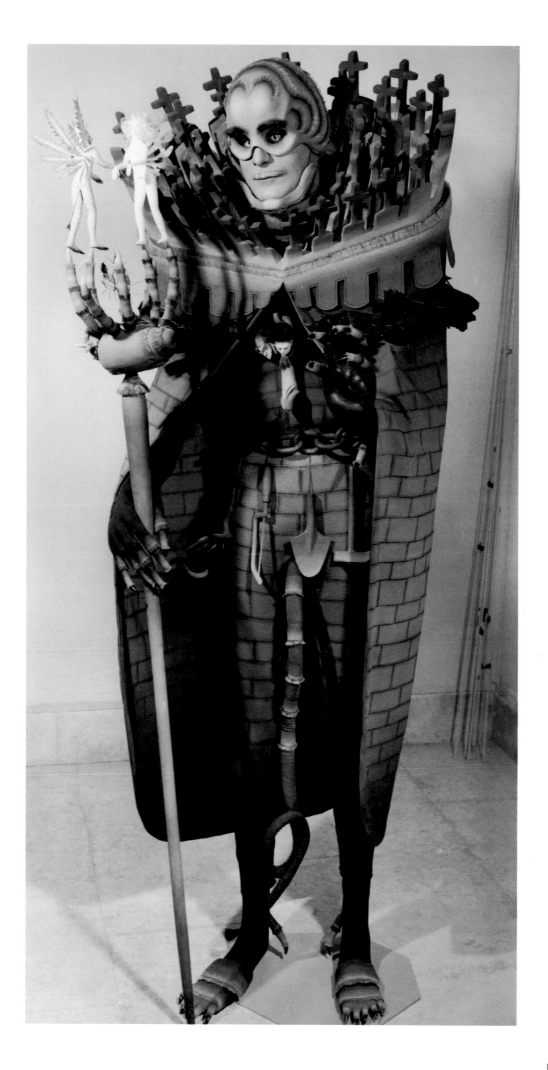

accompanied by a sort of gathering together: Münch, Füssli, De Chirico, Giacometti, Gustave Moreau, Georg Grosz, Kandinsky, Picasso and Picabia were in the same company as the formerly excluded such as Dali (believe it or not!), Brauner, Ernst, Miró, not to mention Matta or Paalen. Toyen, Arp and Lam represented old friends. The young generation was also present: Enrico Baj, Mimi Parent, Hervé Télémaque, Alechinsky, Gironella, Max Walter Svanberg (who covered a woman with sequins in order to celebrate the fantastic element), Silbermann, Camacho, Ugo Sterpini, Konrad Klapheck, Lagarde. One or two objects by lunatics, a watercolor by Charles Cros. But not a single poem! And apart from a fairly pretty playlet by José Pierre on the evolution of painting, some dense works by Breton, J.-F. Revel (against the media), Audoin (against technocrats), Legrand (against outer space programs), Raymond Borde (against the population explosion), Robert Benayoun (against automation), Audoin (again – for and against the sacred), Jean Schuster (against advertising), Jean Pierre ("Changing women"), Robert Lagarde (against sports), Georges Sebbag (against debilitating work)… All these "againsts," aren't particularly gay, nor innovative, and not really specific to Surrealism. The impression that this exhibition gave, going back to the traditional gallery show, was that Surrealism was suffering from a split, if not complete, perhaps historical, within itself.

This attempt at reunification, even repentance, had marked in the same way the conference Surréalisme held in Cerisy in July 1966, directed by Ferdinand Alquié. Former members of Surréalisme Révolutionnaire, such as the dissidents from *Phases*, were invited. A few incidents relating to essential matters (such as references to Nietszche and the attack against the Trotskyists) animated the debates.

Breton died several months later. I heard of his death on the television news, where the anchorman wasn't afraid to interrupt his desolate speech: a major poet died today, but somewhere or other France has made a touchdown…

In truth, Surrealism's values will survive its extinction in history, not watered down in mythical heavens, but as applied little by little to the history of morals. Two years after Breton's death came the events of May 68, where these values held up by the insurrection of the young were shouted in the streets before their slow integration in essential reforms: abolition of the death penalty, contraception and the legalization of abortion, de-colonization, the right to intervene… Of course Surrealism, as it happened, had encountered critical rationalism, the philosophers and the jurists who had clarified the nature of evil – non-respect of an individual's rights. Mr. Badinter can hardly be considered a Surrealist, except in his "absolute revolt" against the capital punishment, a revolt he was able to integrate into a legal tactic. Later, the May students, contrary to what is sometimes

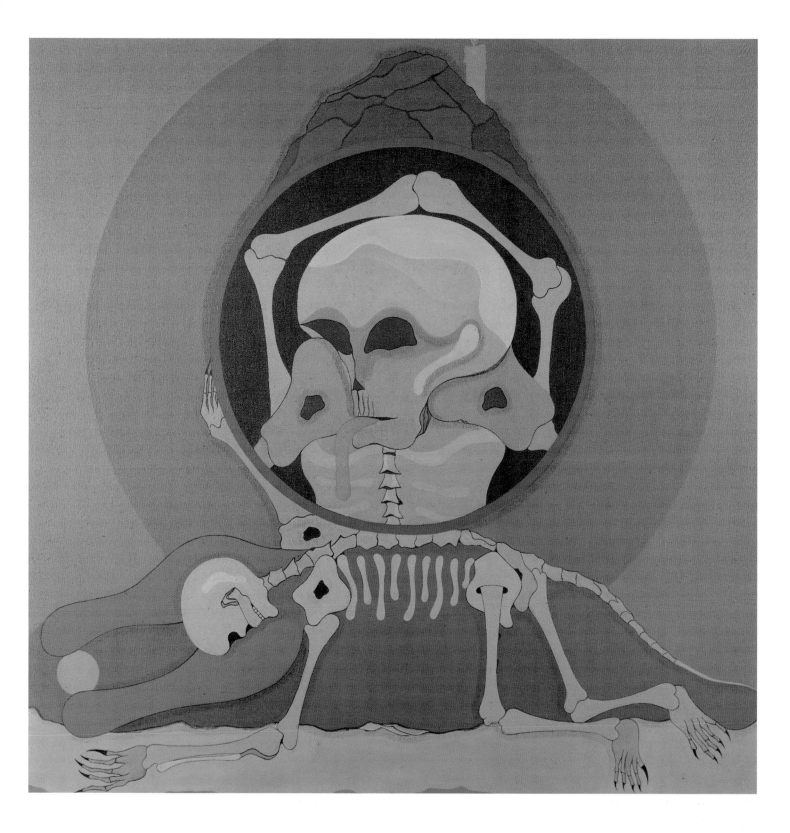

Jorge Camacho
DANCE OF DEATH
1976, oil on canvas.
Musée d'art moderne de la ville de Paris.

said, did not renounce the values of their youth – they brought them into everyday life, with the "open rationalism" that Bachelard, sensitive to the Surrealist lesson, had taught them. The retreat from ecclesiastical influence – that "mounting paganism" which the French priesthood complained of recently – and which is nothing other than the rise of women in our society, the new freedom of young men and women regarding love, the just idea that one's family, work and country are not values in and of themselves, but institutionswith their own history, leading to the best and the worst, and even falling out of fashion… Today, now that blind military obedience is no longer absolute – look at Army regulations – how can one not notice that Surrealism's "absolute" protest followed the flow of history, and that it is the absoluteness of the revolt that gave spiritual power to a poetic and moral action enlightened by the contemporary development of supra-rationalist philosophy. We see more and more, that art, science, law and political thought open into one another. Was the disappearance of the word *Revolution* from the titles of Surrealist reviews as of 1933 seen as a sign of weakening? Rather in this case, as in many others, it would be a premonition. Who still uses this lyrical word anymore, following the historic failure of the Soviet Union? In the domain of poetry and art, the changes brought by Surrealism are such that we no longer even notice them. That he held art to be a serious thing, in that it could go beyond knowledge (Breton) and towards the expression of that which is tragic in life (Artaud), is a lesson that many of today's artists hear, or should hear. Anti-psychiatry, criticism of the notion of tradition, the demand for inner authenticity, the rejection of feelings, of futile playthings, and of social rattles, the call for creative spontaneity in all fields and for individual freedom, enlivened by the fantastic element of love, remain, more than ever, pertinent in our technically fast-moving societies. Julien Gracq, in his article in *Le Monde* (16 February 1996), proposed "Going back to Breton…

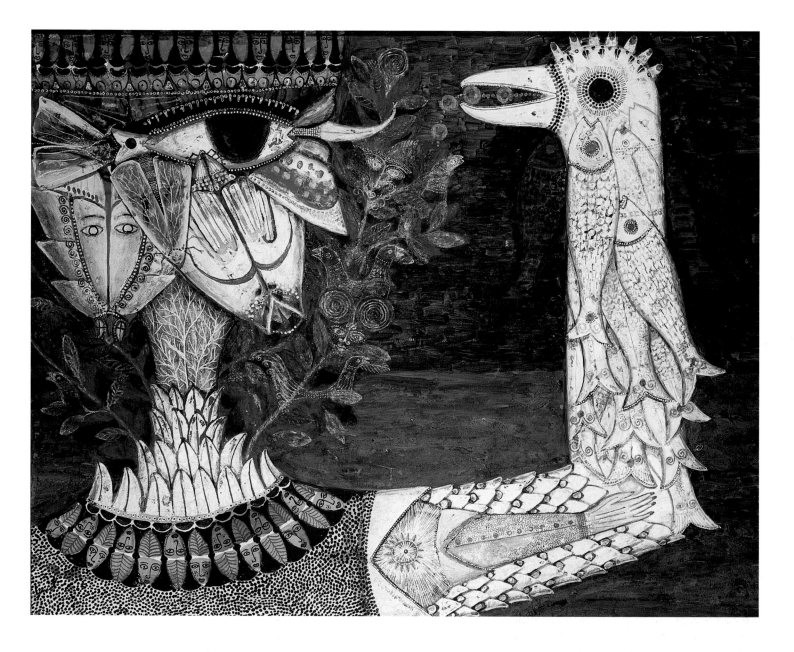

Max Walter Svanberg
**THE STRING OF PEARLS OF THE
IMAGINATIVE CONVERSATION**
1953, watercolor
and pastel on paper.
Sture Ohlsson Collection, Simlangsdalen.

Bibliography

F. Alquié, *Philosophie du surréalisme*, Paris, Flammarion, 1955.

L. Aragon, *Une vague de rêves*, Paris, Commerce, 1924.

L. Aragon, *Traité du style*, Paris, Gallimard, 1928, reprint 1980.

L. Aragon, *Écrits sur l'art moderne*, Paris, Flammarion, 1981.

A. Artaud, *Œuvres complètes*, Paris, Gallimard, 20 volums, since 1956.

J.L. Bédouin, *Vingt ans de surréalisme*, Paris, Denoël, 1961.

J.L. Bédouin, *La Poésie surréaliste* (anthology), Paris, Seghers, 1964.

H. Béhar and M. Carassou, *Dada, histoire d'une subversion*, Paris, Fayard, 1990.

R. Benayoun, *Érotique du surréalisme*, Paris, Pauvert, reprint 1978.

M. Bonnet, *A. Breton, naissance de l'aventure surréaliste*, Paris, Corti 1978.

V. Bounoure, and alli, *La Civilisation surréaliste*, Paris, Payot, 1978.

A. Breton, *Œuvres complètes*, Paris, Gallimard, Pléiade, 3 vol. (B).

A. Breton, *La Clé des champs*, Paris, U.G.E. 10/18 coll. n° 750.

A. Breton, *Le Surréalisme et la Peinture*, Paris, Gallimard, 1965.

A. Breton, *Entretiens*, Paris, Gallimard, 1952.

A. Breton and J. Legrand, *L'Art magique*, Paris, A. Biro-Phébus, 1991.

R. Char, *Œuvres complètes*, Paris, Gallimard, Pléiade.

S. Dali, *La Vie secrète de S. Dali*, Paris, La Table ronde, 1952.

Y. Duplessis, *Le Surréalisme*, Paris, P.U.F., Que sais-je, 1958.

G. Durozoi, *Histoire du mouvement surréaliste*, Paris, Hazan 1997.

P. Éluard, *Œuvres complètes*, Paris Gallimard, Pléiade, 2 vol.

M. Fauré, *Histoire du surréalisme sous l'Occupation*, Paris, La Table ronde, 1982.

M. Jean and A. Mezei, *Histoire de la peinture surréaliste*, Paris, Le Seuil, 1959, reprint 1967.

N. Nadeau, *Histoire du surréalisme*, Paris, Le Seuil, 1945.

R. Passeron, *Histoire de la peinture surréaliste*, L.G.F., Le livre de poche, 1968, reprint 1991.

R. Passeron, *Encyclopédie du surréalisme*, Paris, Somogy, 1975, reprint 1978.

G. Picon, *Journal du surréalisme*, Geneva, Skira, 1976.

J. Pierre, *L'Univers surréaliste*, Paris, Somogy, 1983.

J. Pierre, *A. Breton et la peinture*, Lausanne, L'Âge d'homme, 1987.

F. Picabia, *Écrits*, Paris, Belfond, 2 vol. 1978.

M. Polizzoti, *André Breton*, 1995 (french translation : Gallimard, Paris, 1999).

Man Ray, *Autoportrait*, (french translation : Laffont, Paris, 1964).

H. Read, *Surrealism*, London, Faber and Faber, 1936.

G. Ribemont-Dessaignes, *Déjà-Jadis*, Paris, Julliard 1958.

M. Sanouillet, *Dada à Paris*, Paris, Pauvert, 1965.

M. Sanouillet, *Marchand de sel*, (writings by Marcel Duchamp), Paris, Le Terrain vague, 1958 enlared edition *Duchamp du signe*, Paris, Flammarion, 1975.

Ph. Soupault, *Vingt Mille et Un Jours*, Paris, Belfond, 1980.

Le Surréalisme, colloque de Cerisy, Paris-La Haye, Mouton, 1968.

T. Tzara, *Œuvres complètes*, Paris, Flammarion, since 1975.

A. and O. Virmaux, *Le Surréalisme au cinéma*, Paris, Seghers, 1976.

J. Vovelle, *Le Surréalisme en Belgique*, Brusells, De Rache, 1972.

P. Waldberg, *Les Demeures d'Hypnos*, Paris, La Différence, 1976.

PAINTER'S MONOGRAPHIES
Several collections of monographies well-illustrated :

« La Septième Face du dé », Paris, Filipacchi (Bellmer, Dali, Delvaux, Dominguez, Ernst, Magritte, Man Ray, Tanguy, Clovis Trouille).

« Les classiques de l'art » (Tout l'œuvre peint de), Paris, Flammarion (Chagall, Ernst, Kandinsky, Klee, Klimt, Magritte, Miró, Gustave Moreau, Odilon Redon, H. Rousseau).

« Découvrons l'art du XXᵉ siècle », Paris, Cercle d'Art (Chagall, Dali, Duchamp, Magritte, Miró, Picasso, De Chirico, Brauner).

J.M. Campagne, *Clovis Trouille*, Paris, Pauvert, 1965.

J. Dupin, *Joan Miró*, Paris, Flammarion, 1961.

R. Passeron, *Dali*, Barcelone-Paris, Ars Mundi, 1990.

R. Passeron, *A. Masson et les puissances du signe*, Paris, Denoël, 1975.

A. Pieyre de Mandiargues, *Le Trésor cruel de Hans Bellmer*, Paris, Le Sphinx, 1979.

DOCUMENTS
Documents Dada, Geneva, Weber, 1974.

Recherches sur la sexualité (Archives du Surréalisme, n°4), Paris, Gallimard, 1990.

Tracts surréalistes et déclarations collectives, pres. by José Pierre, 2 vol., Paris, Losfeld, 1982.

Explosante-fixe, photographie et surréalisme, catalogue of the exhibition at the Centre Georges Pompidou, 1985, Paris, Centre Pompidou-Hazan, 1985.

REVIEWS REISSUED IN FACSIMILE.
Littérature, 2 vol., Paris,
J.M. Place, 1978.
La Révolution surréaliste, Paris,
J.M. Place, 1975.
*Le Surréalisme au service de la
révolution*, J.M. Place, 1976.
Minotaure, 3 vol., Geneva, Skira, s.d.
Le Surréalisme révolutionnaire, Paris,
J.M. Place, en préparation.
Bulletin de liaison surréaliste (B.L.S.),
1970-1976, Paris, Savelli.

CURRENT REVIEWS
Arsenal, Chicago, Black Swan Press.
Mélusine (Cahier du Centre de
recherche sur le surréalisme),
Lausanne, L'Âge d'homme.
Phases, Paris, Édouard Jaguer, Cf.
below *INFOSURR*.
Recherches poïétiques, n°6,
summer 1997, « Le surréalisme
au service de la création », Presses
universitaires de Valenciennes,
ae 2c g édit.
*INFOSURR, actualités du surréalisme et
de ses alentours*, B.P. 367 – 75526,
Paris cedex 11, email : infosurr @
argyronet. com
Http :/www.argyro.net/~revsur

RENÉ PASSERON'S
LAST PUBLICATIONS
Poèmes laconiques, Brax, Cahiers
de l'Atelier, 1994.
*La Naissance d'Icare, éléments
de poïétique générale*, Fourqueux
78112, ae2cg éditions, 1996.
*ASTARIM, trois poèmes
d'anti-naissance*, Tunis,
L'Or du temps, 1997.

PHOTOGRAPHIC CREDITS :

Acknowledgements

The Éditions Pierre Terrail and the author wish to thank

Claude Oterelo, madame Jacques Doucet,

Marcel and David Fleiss from the gallery 1900-2000.

We would like to thank Jean-Loup Charmet who left us last month.